The Community Engagement Professional's Guidebook

Campus Compact is a national coalition of colleges and universities committed to the public purposes of higher education. Campus Compact publications focus on practical strategies for campuses to put civic education and community engagement into action. Please visit http://compact.org for more information.

Campus Compact

The Community Engagement Professional's Guidebook

A Companion to *The Community Engagement Professional in Higher Education*

LINA D. DOSTILIO AND
MARSHALL WELCH

Campus Compact

BOSTON, MASSACHUSETTS
Distributed by Stylus Publishing, LLC.

Published by Campus Compact
45 Temple Place
Boston, MA 02111

Library of Congress Cataloging-in-Publication Data
Names: Dostilio, Lina D., author. | Welch, Marshall, author. | Supplement to (work): Dostilio, Lina D. Community engagement professional in higher education.
Title: The community engagement professional's guidebook : a companion to 'The community engagement professional in higher education' / Lina D. Dostilio and Marshall Welch.
Description: First edition. | Boston, MA : Campus Compact, 2018. | Includes bibliographical references and index.
Identifiers: LCCN 2018012562 (print) | LCCN 2018050315 (ebook) | ISBN 9781945459191 (uPDF) | ISBN 9781945459207 (ePub, mobi) | ISBN 9781945459177 | ISBN 9781945459177(cloth ;alk. paper) | ISBN 9781945459184(pbk. ; alk. paper) | ISBN 9781945459191(library networkable e-edition) | ISBN 9781945459207(consumer e-edition)
Subjects: LCSH: Community and college–United States. | Universities and colleges–United States–Public services. | Universities and colleges–Public relations–United States. | Service learning–United States.
Classification: LCC LC238 (ebook) | LCC LC238.D67 2018 (print) | DDC 378.1/03–dc23
LC record available at https://lccn.loc.gov/2018012562

13-digit ISBN: 978-1-945459-17-7 (cloth)
13-digit ISBN: 978-1-945459-18-4 (paperback)
13-digit ISBN: 978-1-945459-19-1 (library networkable e-edition)
13-digit ISBN: 978-1-945459-20-7 (consumer e-edition)

Printed in the United States of America

All first editions printed on acid-free paper
that meets the American National Standards Institute

Z39-48 Standard.

First Edition, 2019

Our work as community engagement professionals has been heavily mentored by senior leaders in the field, competent and compassionate peers, and partners who are community anchors for us and generations of others. Much of the guidance we pass along in this book is the result of a sort of mentoring lineage. Our approach to community engagement, and the guidance we offer you, is steeped in the wisdom of our mentors. There is power in naming those who form the lineage of this practice, and it is with the deepest gratitude and respect for these peers and partners that we dedicate this book to:

Terri Baltimore, Hill House Association, Hill District Neighborhood of Pittsburgh
Bill Crim, United Way - Salt Lake City, Utah
Luci-Jo DiMaggio, Duquesne University
Irene Fisher, Lowell Bennion Community Service Center - University of Utah
Char Gray-Sorensen, Campus Compact of New York and Pennsylvania
Linda Hilton, Crossroads Urban Center - Salt Lake City, Utah
Barbara Holland, Portland, Oregon
Emily Janke, University of North Carolina, Greensboro
Will Perreault, Rebuilding Hope In New Orleans
John Saltmarsh, University of Massachusetts-Boston
Sandra Scherer, Monument Crisis Center - Concord, California
Tim Smith, Center of Life, Hazelwood Neighborhood of Pittsburgh
Tracy Soska, University of Pittsburgh
John Wilds, University of Pittsburgh

CONTENTS

Chapter One

THE PATHWAY

Over every mountain there is a path, although it may not be seen from the valley.

—Theodore Roethke

Both of us (Lina D. Dostilio and Marshall Welch) frequently field questions about the work of supporting community engagement, and we have mentored those new to the field. Sometimes the questions are from someone brand new in his or her role who is asking how to start a program or unit. Other times the questions are from a soon-to-graduate higher education leadership or student affairs student who seeks input on the quality of a potential job opportunity. We are beginning to more frequently receive questions about which graduate programs prepare people for this work. Perhaps the people most commonly asking the questions are those who are trying to navigate the political environment on their campuses to expand and deepen their unit's reach.

We think there is a hunger for the answers to these questions, which will continue to grow as more and more administrative and staff positions are created to support community engagement on campuses across the country. In response, we offer this guidebook, which we hope offers some direction to those whose formal administrative responsibilities are to support community engagement at postsecondary institutions, otherwise known as community engagement professionals (CEPs; Dostilio & McReynolds, 2015; Dostilio & Perry, 2017; Jacoby & Mutascio, 2010).

Lay of the Land

The scope of community engagement practice addressed in this book is intended to describe the breadth of activity that the staff of community engagement centers, programs, and initiatives currently support. In their study of engagement centers at institutions that carry the Carnegie Foundation's Community Engagement Classification, Welch and Saltmarsh (2013) determined that community engagement units have moved past work initially focused on volunteerism and service-learning to more comprehensive profiles of community engagement, described as second-generation engagement, including but not limited to strategic partnership development, place-based efforts, community-engaged research activity, and so on. This expanded landscape is fraught with peaks and valleys that mean navigating bumps and detours along the way. Each CEP who reads this text will have a different work profile; each institution he or she represents will have a different instantiation of community engagement. What we offer cannot address each context and reality but instead seeks to represent a general notion of practice and to build the reader's competence across an array of multiple contexts, demands, and challenges.

Trailhead

The starting point, or trailhead, for this guidebook is based on the competency model developed by a team of 15 research fellows working under Campus Compact's project on CEPs (Dostilio, 2017a).[1] We expand on that model to include additional elements of practice we feel are essential based on our experience in the field and prevailing thinking drawn from relevant literature (Welch, 2016; Welch & Saltmarsh, 2013).

Bridging the Art and Science of Our Work

For some, the notion of breaking down a CEP's work into a schematic of distinct areas of skills, knowledge, and disposition hobbles the artful practice of community engagement. Moreover, even referring to the personnel who foster community engagement as professionals might signal a loss of soul, raising the specter of a technocratic administrator. We think that supporting community engagement in higher education requires an approach that is artful as well as honors a professional standard of practice that reflects decades of lessons learned through the evolution of engagement initiatives. By examining the evolution of centers of engagement (Welch, 2016; Welch & Saltmarsh, 2013) we can trace a path, or lineage, that begins with the autonomous, innovative work of committed and perhaps maverick individuals who had to "'make it up as they went' due to the limited empirical best practice and evidence on impact available in an emerging field" (Welch & Saltmarsh, 2013, p. 25). We think it's fair to say this of the faculty who sought to integrate their political activism into their academic work, the provocative student activists who called their institutions to their civic purposes, and the extension officers who began infusing their programs with participatory and democratic processes. Their efforts were passionate, avant-garde, and deeply responsive to the local context. As these practitioners honed their successful and impactful work, the broader postsecondary education field took note, and their initiatives were replicated.

The replication of their practice might also be called a diffusion of innovation (Rogers, 2003) that is concerned with not only replicating of programs but also progressive mainstreaming of an engagement culture, awakening of the civic dimensions of student development, recognizing the scholarship of application and engagement, and embracing the institution-as-neighbor paradigm. This led to a wider adoption of practice and along with it a proliferation of engagement centers and national and global associations to support this work (Dostilio, 2017c; Welch, 2016). According to the 1986 Campus Compact annual member survey (Ventresca, Waring, Wahl Halleck, Baker, & Auchard, 1986), 22 of the responding institutions indicated having a paid staff person whose job in whole or in part was concerned with supporting engagement. In 2014 nearly 100% of respondents (423 institutions) reported having an office or center with paid staff (Dostilio & McReynolds, 2015) averaging 21 staff per campus supporting student curricular and cocurricular engagement; this number increases when we include staff who support other areas of community engagement.

The path that began with a committed few who saw an opportunity to disrupt traditional higher education has led to voluminous numbers of centers and personnel dedicated to implementing community engagement on campuses across the country. We have argued elsewhere (Dostilio, 2017c; Dostilio & McReynolds, 2015) that these individuals, whom we choose to call CEPs, are key influencers on their campuses and shape the methods and values being promoted as well as the goals being pursued. The formation of these CEPs, which often comes from professional association membership, also orients the ways they shape campus practice. Although some of the national and global associations prioritize the civic purposes of higher education, the emancipatory potential of community-campus engagement, and participatory paradigms of engagement, it is not consistent across all associations (Dostilio, 2017c). Although some CEPs bring with them a rich experience in community organizing, community development, or democratic practice, others do not. This reality is reflective of a concern expressed by the pioneers of service-learning who feared that institutionalization, which includes a rapid expansion of the numbers of professional staff, would also be accompanied by a loss of its developmental power (Stanton, Giles, & Cruz, 1999). We honor and appreciate that legacy, which was perhaps situated in a more soulful time that fostered soulful work. Our worlds are now more complex in regard to the internal and external politics that affect our campuses. For example, the litigious nature of our culture and standards of accountability require different caretaking of our students. Navigating tenure and promotion policies and procedures is volatile. Campus administrators now realize they and their institutions are not dominant in public problem solving but are better positioned as collaborators among a greater number of contributors and sectors (Saltmarsh & Hartley, 2011). In a framework of full partnership, multiple, legitimate stakeholders determine how our work is done, and CEPs need to be ready to honor coconstruction and accountability in the same role. There is currently no common set of practice expectations that could be used to retain the art and soul of the work we hold so dear. This project and the constituent steps that have led to this book (Dostilio, 2017a, 2017b, 2017c; Dostilio & McReynolds, 2015; Welch 2016; Welch & Saltmarsh, 2013) seek to do just that: establish paths for CEPs to acquire the ability to replicate sound community engagement practice while developing an artful approach to what is highly relational, contextual, and political work. We offer a way to bridge and balance the science (the technical implementation of sound engagement practice) with the art (the integrative and critical expression of our commitments) of our practice. Recalling the epigraph at the beginning of this chapter, although a path over the mountain may be unforeseeable from the valley, it exists and is waiting to be uncovered and discovered.

We think it is possible to describe a commonly accepted body of practice, point to shared characteristics of a community of practitioners, and discuss a set of shared ethical commitments among CEPs. These are the bricks that cobble our path and launch an emerging profession. We know the word *profession* can connote narrow, highly technocratic practice. Our project rejects that framing and instead offers a "highly reflective, hybridized, purpose-driven, and ethically principled" (Dostilio & Perry, 2017, p. 9) idea of a CEP akin to Keith's (2015) characterization of democratic civic professionals. Scanlon (2011) endorses this notion, describing the postmodern conception of profession as socially constructed with an ever deepening commitment through iterative development. Moreover, an array of knowledge, skills, disposition, and critical commitments has been identified that inform CEPs who support second-generation engagement (Dostilio et al., 2017; Welch & Saltmarsh, 2013). This work, developed by CEPs through an extensive review of our field's practice literature, led to a framework of competencies that were reciprocally validated by more than 400 CEPs operating across a diversity of contexts and with various profiles of engagement responsibilities (Welch, Miller, & Davies, 2005).

Similar to the concerns about the concept of profession, concerns exist about the concept of competency. For some, competency smacks of an overly rationalist approach that falsely fragments the aspects of one's work and intones a neoliberal orientation. In comparison, Rychen and Salganik (2001) framed competencies as

> complex action systems that encompass not only knowledge and skills, but also strategies and routines for appropriately applying these knowledge and skills, as well as appropriate emotions and attitudes and the effective self-regulation of these competencies. (p. 8)

Our model of competence is illustrative of the latter construction, which is holistic and integrative. More about the research design used to coconstruct the competency model along with a thorough consideration of the limitations of framing our work as a profession and a critical examination of using competency to name the body of practice can be found in *The Community Engagement Professional in Higher Education: A Competency Model for an Emerging Field* (Dostilio, 2017b).

As part of that research, a number of critical commitments also surfaced, which describe principles adopted by CEPs who prioritize transformation of institutions toward more just and emancipatory environments, attend to issues of power, and cultivate authenticity in their relationships (Hernandez & Pasquesi, 2017). It would be wrong to categorize these priorities as competencies; they are commitments honed through deeply reflective and critical practice. They are threaded across our praxis, interwoven with the daily expectations of work in higher education, and tested repeatedly. Even though they are not competencies, these critical commitments are an important part of the CEP model and make visible the political nature of the work. As a result, in the preliminary competency model (Dostilio et al., 2017) and in the chapters of this book, critical commitments are presented alongside competencies but are mentioned separately to illustrate their importance and distinction. The chapters introduce areas of competence to readers and provide opportunities to reflect on these areas. Each chapter concludes with questions meant to help readers deepen their critical sensibilities and commitments.

Identifying the knowledge, skills, and dispositions necessary for CEPs to foster second-generation engagement makes the tools of our work visible and claims that a threshold of knowledge is necessary to do this work adequately. Reflecting on how one becomes a craftsperson, Crawford (2009) described how we have lost facility with the tools of the trades, and in many cases, actively seek to hide away the inner workings of the machinery on which we rely. His writing is about the literal use of tools in manual work. We invoke his ideas to illustrate a similar idea: Without articulating the basic building blocks of our practice and requesting CEPs have proficiency with its tools, we unwittingly offer various misconceptions of our practice. We may construct an image of the CEP as a charismatic thought leader with little need to attend to the intricacies and technical aspects of practice such as risk management, staff development, or meeting facilitation.

Alternatively, we may construct an image of supporting community engagement as unskilled work that can be done by just about anyone (with a small stipend and a course release). Given the decades of experience and the mountain of scholarship that has been written since the earliest innovators took up community engagement, there is no reason for new CEPs to move forward blindly. And yet, job descriptions continue to be developed by people who are unfamiliar with this area of work and positions are filled by people with very little preparation. It is difficult to have confidence in the work of these peers, certainly at the outset, and yet some of them who find good mentors, seek support to attend professional development experiences, and are curious learners can evolve into strong colleagues and change agents in their institutions. Yet their growth depends on the nature of the content and experiences of the mentor, professional development programs, and the information consulted. Moreover, it is dependent on the willingness of these people's supervisor and institution to support and provide resources for their development.

The issue of having confidence in our peers is an important one. The Latin roots of the words *competence*, *cognizance*, and *responsibility* (Rychen & Salganik, 2001) suggest an expectation for peers of a profession to recognize and feel responsible for a high standard of practice. We offer this book as a structured way for people in our field to find a path toward competence using a coconstructed, reciprocally validated model that emerged from our colleagues in the field. We hope to enhance the confidence we have in our unknown peers, which is essential in this new environment in which most colleges and universities have engagement units. These personnel are beginning to move about, relocating geographically to seek new professional opportunities as frequently as in other areas of academia. Without a common practice framework, it is difficult to determine whether their notion of engagement practice and their skill set are commensurate with an institution's agenda and practice of community engagement.

In addition to presenting the skills and tools inherent in our work, the effort to articulate a competency model for an emerging profession is a direct response to the potential loss of art and soul in community engagement administration. Without a strong professionalizing effort that prioritizes artful practice and critical commitments, the explosive growth in the number of centers and personnel will lead, and in some cases already has led, to some degree of soulless practice.

Preparing for the Journey

The competency model (Dostilio, 2017b) is a road map that charts the course for CEPs. This book is the travel guide for the journey. Using the competency model, we hope to help CEPs develop greater levels of ability and confidence in their work. Toward the beginning of each chapter, we offer a table listing the competencies explored in that chapter. The rest of the chapter is then organized by areas of competence under their corresponding headings. Competence is gained through didactic education, socialization, experiential learning, practice, mentorship, and knowledge of ethical standards, or in this case critical commitments (Bowman, West, Berman, & van Wart, 2016). A minimal integration of competency occurs when we automate our practice through repetition. A moderate integration occurs when we couple reflection with practice. Intense integration, or *transformative integration*, occurs when we employ critical self-reflection and cultivate an openness to change (Baartman & de Bruijn, 2011). We endeavor to offer a transformative integration of competency by emphasizing the technical and artful practice of community engagement support. Consider, for example, a carpenter, who can have technical knowledge of how to build a house and have the necessary tools, but it does not mean the house will be finely crafted. Glover (2010) described craftsmanship as

> the quality that comes from creating with passion, care, and attention to detail. It is a quality that is honed, refined, and practiced over the course of a career. . . . Craftsmanship, obviously, isn't something that just happens. It requires a great deal of time, patience and effort. . . . Craftsmanshp is the difference between good design and great design. (para. 6)

We feel these characteristics are applicable to the work of CEPs.

The Purpose of This Guide

This guidebook is intended to provide a description of highly effective practices used among those who have administrative and leadership responsibilities for supporting community engagement in institutions of higher education and to offer a road map on how to deepen and enrich one's practice. Although this work is labeled administration, it requires exercising leadership, which can take many different forms. Like the word competency, the term *leadership* has various understandings. For us, leadership takes the following forms: (a) stewarding, which is being responsible for what is entrusted to us; (b) facilitating, which is crafting processes and spaces that allow collaborators to call forth a shared vision; and (c) shepherding, which does not mean leading from the front but includes being right in the middle, in the thick of things, working alongside others, even taking up the rear, and nudging people along the path.

The audiences for the book are CEPs at various stages of their careers, those who aspire to become CEPs such as graduate students, and those responsible for hiring, supervising, and mentoring CEPs. Professionals currently practicing will use this book in a variety of ways. For some, the content complements their existing professional development activities (e.g., attending conferences and mentoring) and promotes more regular reflective practice and clarity about changes to their practice. For others who do not have access to institutionally supported professional development or who find themselves working alone, this book may be their primary source of professional development guidance. In addition to individual readers, the book is also suited to groups of CEPs who seek a resource to support their peer learning communities, professional development workshops, institutes, or retreats.

We use a conversational tone throughout this book because we feel this is a conversation among colleagues. Imagine us riding with you along the journey. As we were writing this book, we reflected on how we have introduced this information to our mentees, what our mentors have said to us, or the facilitation methods we've seen and delivered in workshops that were really outstanding. We consulted colleagues, asking for their guidance. What began as a movement 25 years ago has evolved into a robust field (Welch, 2016). Simply, we are writing from the field to the field, having a conversation. Because we are not with you to have this conversation in person, we've interspersed opportunities to stop, pause, and reflect throughout the narrative to engage with us in these pages, which is what Baartman and de Bruijn (2011) call the practice of critical self-reflection.

Following this introductory chapter, the remaining nine chapters are organized around different functional areas typical of community engagement practice, based on research on the competencies of CEPs (Dostilio, 2017b), and engagement infrastructure (Welch & Saltmarsh, 2013). Chapter 2 concerns adopting and promoting the public purposes of higher education; chapter 3, leading change in higher education; chapter 4, institutionalizing community engagement; chapter 5, knowing about the administration of community engagement programs and units; chapter 6, doing the administration of community engagement programs and units; chapter 7, facilitating students' civic learning and development; chapter 8, facilitating faculty development; chapter 9, cultivating high-quality community-campus partnerships; and chapter 10, implementing anchor institution programs.

The images of journey, path, road, trail, and guide are important to us. In our humble opinion, most people misunderstand roadtripping. The kind of journey we're taking here doesn't involve getting on the highway and sailing on through, no stops, no distractions. It's not linear. As the saying goes, it's the journey, not the destination that matters. The journey we're offering aligns with Scanlon's (2011) view of professionals developing deeper and deeper levels of expertise iteratively and through socialization and mentorship among their colleagues. Roadtripping, when done well, is filled with adventures of discovery. We drive for a while, then stop, and encounter something new or something we've heard about but haven't yet experienced. We talk with people about their lives and escapades. We chat with our fellow roadtrippers about the journey. Despite having a planned route, we detour easily, accepting that the unexpected is where the payoff lies and knowing that we will have bumps along the way. Once home, we revisit the mementos we collected, finding new meaning when reflecting in different seasons of our lives on the journey we've had and the moments along the way. We revisit places, particularly those we didn't exhaustively explore, and we take new friends with us.

The imagery we use is also concerned with pathmaking (Brook et al., 2010). Learning is often concerned with following a predetermined path of content and instruction. Pathmaking involves setting out on "a collaborative quest for learning that encompasses exploration of the unknown, discovering new understandings" to facilitate the "richly textured, relational and passionate process through which creative possibilities emerge" (Brook et al., 2010, p. 657). Each chapter in this book contains an explanation of the competencies associated with the particular chapter (a path of knowledge), interspersed with a variety of tools such as practice case studies, activities in boxes titled "Compass Point," and questions to deepen

BOX 1.1

Compass Point: The Pathway

1. The word *competency* conveys a range of notions and meaning. What does the word *competence* mean to you?
2. As professionals, we develop, use, and rely on tools to help us do our work. We can build a shed or we can build a mansion with the same tools. The difference is the development and application of being a craftsperson. What makes one a craftsperson or artist versus a technician?
3. Reflect on how you've been prepared up to this point for the challenges of CEP work. What was it that you saw or experienced about this work that made you want to pursue it professionally?
4. People's preconceived notions and assumptions of leadership may not match the artful performance of a CEP. What are the typical notions of leadership? What do others (e.g., administrators, community partners, etc.) perceive to be the role of a CEP, and what do they assume about his or her work?
5. Is it reasonable to expect to be an artisan in every aspect of the practice presented here? Briefly review the competencies listed at the start of each chapter. Critically reflect on your current skill level or lack of it. Which of these areas are you most drawn to? Are you seeking to amplify your strengths or remediate your weaknesses?

our critical commitments, which we hope readers will discuss with others as a means to develop their own group of supportive travelers who engage with them in pathmaking.

We invite you to begin this journey by pausing and reflecting on your own personal trailhead and starting point by responding to the prompts in Box 1.1.

Deepening Our Critical Commitments: Questions to Ask

The remaining chapters of this book concludes with dedicated prompts to help you consider the critical commitments associated with each area of the competency model. As discussed previously, critical commitments drive the CEP to attend to issues of power, privilege, and equity. We begin this reflective process by asking the following questions:

1. In what ways has consideration of power and privilege been incorporated into your work as a CEP? Do these issues create discomfort? With whom and why?
2. What does equity-centered community engagement practice look like?
3. Because certain terms and concepts resonate better than others at different institutions, what is the key vocabulary and characterization of critically informed engagement used at your institution? What are the semantic land mines to avoid on your campus?

If the language of critical perspective is new to you, we suggest you read Hernandez and Pasquesi (2017).

Note

1. The CEP Project developed a robust literature review to identify the areas of skill, knowledge, and disposition needed for a CEP to foster second-generation community engagement. These three areas, referred to as *competencies*, were refined and validated by more than 400 CEPs and resulted in the development of the *Preliminary Competency Model for Community Engagement Professionals* (Dostilio, 2017b).

Chapter Two

ADOPTING AND PROMOTING THE PUBLIC PURPOSES OF HIGHER EDUCATION

Increasingly, the campus is being viewed as a place where students get credentialed and faculty get tenured, while the overall work of the academy does not seem particularly relevant to the nation's most pressing civic, social, economic and moral problems. (Boyer, 1997, p. 85)

Community engagement professionals (CEPs) have a commitment to develop and support engagement programs that help people become active citizens, involve institutions of higher education in their communities in contributive and collaborative ways, and work toward social change. Without clarity about the public purposes of higher education and the frameworks that inform those purposes, a professional's work could slip into a mundane practice that is concerned with the mechanics of engagement but not its greater purposes. This chapter introduces three ideas as tools for advancing an institution's public purposes: professionalism, democratic engagement, and a critical orientation, which underpin the competency model and substance of CEP work.

Just as we begin by reviewing the major equipment needed for a journey (backpack, boots, and water bottle, or perhaps car, gasoline, and road snacks), we begin here by discussing each of these underpinning ideas that are important tools for advancing an institution's public purposes. Once we discuss these frames, we then begin to address each of the competency items from Table 2.1. Other chapters in this book move more quickly into the competency items. After completing this chapter, those working in the field of community engagement or currently working as a CEP will be able to reflect on professionalism, democratic engagement, and critical orientation as well as specific areas in which they are competent and identify areas they would like to further develop as they relate to public purposes of higher education. For those who are new to supporting community engagement or who aspire to enter the community engagement profession, they will demonstrate awareness and an emerging understanding of these underpinning ideas and areas of competence.

Professionalism

The concept of professionalism is presented here as an overarching umbrella for this chapter as well as the fundamental principles, concepts, and practice described throughout this guidebook. The term *CEP* (Dostilio, 2017a, 2017c; Dostilio & McReynolds, 2015; Jacoby & Mutascio,

TABLE 2.1
Competencies and Critical Commitments Associated With Adopting and Promoting Public Purposes of Higher Education

2.1 Knowledge of ideologies and political, social, and historical contexts underpinning higher education 2.2 Knowledge of and ability to encourage a democratic engagement orientation (participatory processes, cocreation of knowledge, coplanning, inclusivity, etc.) 2.3 Able to unveil and disrupt unequal power structures	2.4 Able to recognize one's subject position in connection to privilege and oppression 2.5 Desire to participate fully in the institution (participating in governance, serving on committees, representing ethical concerns) 2.6 Able to name injustices and power differentials 2.7 Embrace the tension between charity and social change	2.8 Committed to developing critical consciousness through meaningful praxis (reflection, dialogue, and action) 2.9 Able to challenge problematic language use (e.g., paternalistic, dehumanizing, oppressive) 2.10 Committed to dialogue with communities

2010; McReynolds & Shields, 2015) is presented here not merely as a title but as a vocation that embodies an array of identities that may include pedagogical, philosophical, and political roles and responsibilities, characterized as a border-crossing practitioner scholar who occupies a third space (Whitchurch, 2012) in higher education. Up to now, many serving as director of a community engagement center have had their role and responsibilities limited to those of an administrator overseeing staff and cocurricular and curricular programs rather than as a professional serving as an institutional leader and change agent (Dostilio & Perry, 2017).

Dingwall (2008) maintained that the concept of being a professional has a long historical foundation focused on a narrowly defined context of specialized knowledge in a discipline and on the preparation of physicians, lawyers, and clergy. Eraut (1994) argued this serves as a way of maintaining power and control over others. This model of expertise manifests itself in the academy across an array of disciplines, which in many ways makes higher education complicit, perhaps naively and unintentionally, in oppressing some groups by maintaining and incorporating a traditional expert model that typically emerges from a specific disciplinary perspective. Benson, Harkavy, and Hartley (2005) refer to this dynamic as disciplinary guildism, in which new knowledge is generated solely for the intellectual benefit of a discipline, coupled with an individual scholar's professional advancement toward tenure, doing little to advance the public purpose of higher education. Scanlon (2011) suggested that this exclusivity of knowledge based in a specific context is no longer possible in a postmodern world consisting of a web of social interactions. Dostilio and Perry (2017) proposed "socially-constructed notions of a profession that promote its relationship with the larger world" (p. 5), which embodies Keith's (2015) concept of border-crossing democratic civic professionals as well as Weerts and Sandmann's (2010) similar characterization of boundary crossing.

Border crossing is an apt description in that the next generation of CEPs must go beyond the walls and duties of a community engagement center and the role of an administrator and out into neighborhoods with community leaders and residents as well as into various units and committees on campus. A traditional role of a campus center director was liaison and matchmaker for faculty and community agency directors to establish partnerships for service-learning and community-based research. We propose, however, that even this role has evolved and expanded to include being a change agent, in which the CEP plays a meaningful part in marshaling resources from the academy while working with and not merely in the community to bring about social justice and facilitating multifaceted partnerships between communities and higher education. Likewise, the evolving role of the CEP includes collective leadership in the academy to advance institutionalization of community engagement requiring interaction and working with multiple stakeholders across campus. And finally, border crossing is manifested when CEPs combine their professional practice with their unique knowledge base of engaged pedagogy and scholarship, thus becoming practitioner-scholars. This reflects and encompasses the following quadrants of boundary spanning described by Weerts and Sandmann (2010): (a) community-focused roles, (b) institutional roles, (c) technical and practical tasks, and (d) socioemotional and leadership tasks. Sandmann, Jordan, Mull, and Valentine (2014) have even constructed a process and matrix for measuring boundary spanning behavior.

As a result, border crossing creates what Whitchurch (2012) described as a third space in which the CEP no longer fits neatly into existing niches of academic affairs or student life in the academy or of community organizer or nonprofit staff person in the community. Although the CEP is housed in the academy, much of the work is conducted in and with the community, literally constituting yet another divergent physical space. Whitchurch (2009) conceptualized this as blended space, whereby a CEP combines scholarly and public expertise and practice by straddling the academy and community boundaries Take a moment to reflect on the idea of being a third space professional by responding to the prompts in Box 2.1.

Dostilio and Perry (2017) demonstrated that CEPs' work constitutes a professional body consisting of four concepts of professionalism as described by Bowman and colleagues (2004): a distinct body of knowledge, practice, and development; practice scholar communities; professional identities; and a shared set of ethical commitments.

Body of Knowledge, Practice, and Development

The competencies presented in this guidebook represent the knowledge and practice deemed necessary to support the community engagement

BOX 2.1

Compass Point: Public Purposes–A

Reflect on ways your role and position as a CEP reflects on being a third space professional. What are some of the advantages and disadvantages of being in that space? Identify ways and examples of how you currently work or potentially could work in blended space. Identify ways and examples of how you currently or could potentially cross boundaries; what might or would you hope to accomplish in doing so?

practices advocated in the literature as well as those that more than 400 CEPs felt were important (Dostilio, 2017a). As explained in great detail in the previous chapter, the body of knowledge in this volume emerged from a robust process of reciprocal validity (Welch et al., 2005) and shared knowledge creation. Through practice, CEPs hone their craft while advancing community engagement, which promotes personal and professional development not only of the CEP but also of the field itself through advancing community engagement on and off campus.

Practice Scholar Communities

We characterize a practitioner-scholar as a knowledgeable professional who applies theoretically and empirically based practice in authentic settings and contexts. McReynolds (2015) suggested that practitioner-scholars are in a position to identify limitations to theoretical constructs and practice created within the confines of the academy that are not practically applied in authentic settings. This insight reflects what Schwartz and Baer (1991) described as social validity by testing the applicability of theory in the trenches. The dissemination and sharing of knowledge with colleagues is critiqued, revised, and adopted by colleagues who do this work, resulting in a blend of theory and practice, thus creating a community of scholars (Dostilio & Perry, 2017; Shulman, 1987; Wenger, 2010). In the past two decades, a number of scholarly venues for dissemination have emerged, including the annual conferences of Campus Compact, the Coalition of Urban and Metropolitan Universities, the Engagement Scholarship Consortium, Imagining America, and the International Association for Research on Service-learning and Community Engagement. Additionally, what might be referred to as intentional communities of practitioner-scholars have been established, including the Practitioner-Scholar Forum of the International Association for Research on Service-learning and Community Engagement, Outreach and Engagement Professionals Network of the Engagement Scholarship Consortium, and the American Democracy Project, which provides professional space for dialogue and mentoring.

Professional Identities

Professionals share and coconstruct a vocational identity with colleagues (Palonen, Boshuizen, & Lehtinen, 2014). In many respects, CEPs are socialized into a culture of engagement, which, like any culture, espouses certain values, practices, ideas, and traditions. Traditionally, the professional identity of scholars has evoked a sense of intellectual elitism. Members of the academy have historically been viewed as experts, which can and does create a type of cognitive and social caste system. However, there is a growing postmodern trend for professionals to reject scholarly superiority and to continually reflect on and reconstruct their role and identity as professionals (Scanlon, 2011). This suggests a shift from a traditional linear approach of progressing toward achieving a certain professional stature of expertise to nurturing a deeper, nuanced way of being in this work (Scanlon, 2011). In this way, the identity of CEPs is not defined by a job title but by the purpose of this work they are called to do (Dostilio & Perry, 2017). Reflect on the ways you build community with other practitioners around your shared purposes by responding to the prompts in Box 2.2.

Shared Set of Ethical Commitments

As mentioned previously, the cultural constructs of professionals typically include a shared set of values and norms that guide ethical behavior (Bowman et al., 2016; Evetts, 2006). Scanlon (2011) suggested professions have epistemological (a way of knowing) and ontological (a way of

BOX 2.2

Compass Point: Public Purposes–B

A group of directors of campus centers for community engagement at Catholic colleges on the West Coast annually convene in January for a day-and-a-half retreat designed for self-care, personal and professional renewal, and professional dialogue. Each year a different campus hosts the gathering of seven colleagues, beginning with a social dinner on a Sunday night. Prior to the gathering, the group collectively selects, organizes, and facilitates readings and activities for Monday morning designed to nurture self-care and reflection. Following lunch, the group shifts its conversation to a professional topic that has been collectively identified. The group concludes by sharing takeaways and scheduling the next gathering.

How does this case study example reflect basic principles of practitioner communities?

How might you consider establishing a similar type of practitioner community? Who would it include as well as where and when might it be convened?

What are some of the perceived benefits of such a group?

being) foundations that frame what we know and how to be in the world. Bowman and colleagues (2016) expand on this by presenting a triadic framework to understand the interrelated aspects of professional work: Technical expertise is the how, leadership is the what, and ethics are the why. Over time many administrators, faculty, students, and community partners came to view the why of our work as the effective administration of cocurricular or curricular programs. Although this is somewhat true, the deeper why of our work is a commitment to the public purpose of higher education to advance a just and democratic society, a mission that seems to have been lost. As the next section illustrates, the cornerstone of our professional foundation is the democratic and public purpose of higher education, which is the basis and driving force behind the work of a CEP (Dostilio & Perry, 2017). Take a moment now to reflect on how your ethical commitments and driving purposes are made visible by responding to the prompts in Box 2.3 and Box 2.4.

Another unique aspect or subtext of this ethos is the commitment to a socially and collaboratively constructed body of knowledge and practice, which gives voice to public scholars in the community and to those

BOX 2.3
Compass Point: Public Purposes–C

The kinds of things posted on the office door of a professional often serve as a portal to that individual's professional soul as it reveals values and attitudes displayed to others. Today that notion of a doorway to the soul can be expanded to include what you post on social media or what books you have on your shelf. Take an inventory of these portals and displays to reflect on what they reveal about your personal and professional identity to others.

In what professional organizations are you a member?
What conferences do you attend?
What do these affiliations suggest and reveal about you as a professional?

BOX 2.4
Compass Point: Public Purposes–D

If a CEP is defined by purpose rather than by a job description, how would you describe your vocation so that your description captures the public purpose of higher education to a colleague or even a family member? What is your why?

they serve. This in turn enhances and contributes to disciplinary knowledge that informs and advances this work. In this way, much of the how of our profession occurs through democratization of knowledge and a form of mutual mentorship. This includes going beyond traditional didactic approaches of *learning* the content to *practice* the content, which Schön (1984) characterized as being a reflective practitioner coupled with Freire's (1970) approach of praxis to integrate theory, reflection, and action.

We recommend two books for further exploration of practitioner-scholar communities and professional identity. A group of faculty committed to civically engaged teaching and scholarship met as a learning community to share a meal and their stories as well as seek professional support from kindred spirits. They collected their stories and experiences in a volume titled *Finding Meaning in Civically Engaged Scholarship* (Diener & Liese 2009). The project came out of a scholar practitioner community, and the book is a form of a scholar practitioner community in which the individual chapters reveal the authors' professional identity. A collection of essays titled *Publicly Engaged Scholars* by Post, Ward, Longo, and Saltmarsh (2016) reveals the professional identity and vocation of the next generation of engaged scholars. Part one of the book presents a collaborative engagement paradigm, and part two introduces the reader to the new public scholars and their stories.

Democratic Engagement

We now shift our attention to how the professional competencies of a CEP reflect and advance the public purpose of higher education as described earlier through democratic engagement in the academy and with the community.

Knowledge of Ideologies and Contexts

As noted by Welch (2016), the public purpose of U.S. higher education has taken a circuitous route over the course of its history (see Figure 2.1.), returning to its original mission in the past 30 years of serving the public. It is important for CEPs to have knowledge and an understanding of the various contexts and phases of U.S. higher education because those events and circumstances still influence our work today. Many of the cultural and systemic challenges impeding community engagement stems from these historical events and trends. At the same time, a knowledgeable CEP can justify and trace the civic mission of community engagement in higher education to its historical roots.

Figure 2.1 Cyclical pathway of purpose.

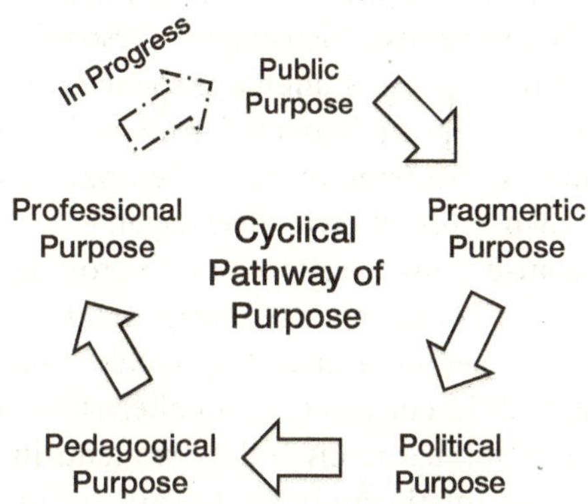

Note. From *Engaging Higher Education: Purpose, Platforms, and Programs* (p. 65), by M. Welch, 2016, Sterling, VA: Stylus. Copyright 2016 by Stylus Publishing. Reprinted with permission.

In the first phase, colleges in colonial America were religious institutions from various Protestant denominations with faith-based service at their core to promote the common good and prepare young adults to be meaningful members in a just and democratic society (Harkavy, 2006; Saltmarsh & Hartley, 2011). More than 100 years later, in an effort to rebuild the country after the Civil War, land-grant institutions born out of the Morrill Act of 1862 were established to advance education, democracy, and agricultural science in rural communities (Harkavy, 2004).

The second phase was launched during the post–Civil War reconstruction era when Johns Hopkins University adopted the German university model in 1876, thus establishing the U.S. research university. This in turn generated a narrow disciplinary specialization resulting in greater loyalty of faculty to their discipline than to the broader public purpose of higher education (Benson et al., 2005). This period represents a transition from grand, abstract intellectual idealism to generating an educational product that could be consumed by the government and business. This push toward big science during the Cold War evolved into the entrepreneurial commodification of education (Benson, Harkavy, & Puckett, 2007). Universities began to create research parks on campus to generate products leading to patents that would financially sustain the institution. Government agencies and corporate entities provided grants that influenced universities' research agendas. Although the products make significant contributions to the economy as a whole, this trend contributed to a shift from civic scholarship and the public mission of higher education.

The third phase began following the activism and political turbulence of the 1960s and 1970s, when many individuals, including college students, retreated into a political malaise, focusing on personal interest and gratification that characterized college students as the me generation. A number of national studies and reports lamented students' civic disengagement. In 1998 the National Commission on Civic Renewal characterized higher education with its own sense of civic disengagement. This key descriptor is worth noting because it may very well be the root of a movement that has come to be known as community engagement in higher education. Rimmerman (2006), however, argued that college students were indeed civically active but in different ways. As an alternative to participating in conventional partisan politics, many college students in the late 1980s and early 1990s chose a pragmatic approach toward social change by engaging in voluntary service. In this way, students were able to achieve personal satisfaction as they saw more immediate and tangible results of their efforts as opposed to waiting and watching for long-term systemic political change. The Campus Outreach Opportunity League was established by college students to promote community service and social action among their peers. Similarly, Campus Compact was established by a handful of college presidents to promote civic engagement on their campuses by sponsoring and coordinating volunteer service. College campus administrators took note of this trend and began establishing programmatic infrastructure through campus centers that could support and sustain this new surge of student volunteerism (Welch & Saltmarsh, 2013).

Faculty began combining service with instructional objectives in credit-bearing courses, creating what is known today as service-learning. Combined with other forms of engaged teaching, learning, and scholarship, this led to the fourth pedagogical phase of this movement, which was beginning to arc back toward higher education's original public purpose.

Although community engagement had arrived pedagogically, there was no formal academic discipline guiding the field. Professional associations and a new scholarly field began to emerge by the late 1980s and early 1990s, leading to and creating the fifth phase of professionalization currently in progress. Embedded in this growing professionalization was the advent of new institutional platforms for community engagement that emerged beside the early service-learning courses. Faculty and students began conducting community-based research either as part of their service-learning courses or through independent investigations. More and more attention and emphasis on long-term, sustainable partnerships focused on capacity building in the community framed by a sense of place began to emerge. This manifests itself through anchor-based community engagement, which has become a hallmark of the efforts of the Netter Center at the University of Pennsylvania. Anchor-based institutions, which are often synonymous with place-based programs, are examined in more detail in chapter 10.

Knowledge of Democratic Engagement

Boyte and Fretz (2011) acknowledged that the current engagement movement has the potential to redirect higher education to its original public purpose to address social issues and build community capacity to promote a just and democratic society. However, they also argued that the "civic movement has ghettoized activities in discrete programs or centers and, in the case of service-learning, often times isolated efforts of single faculty members within academic departments. This model is proving to be unsustainable" (p. 83). They are essentially calling for transforming the institution of higher education.

Most institutions of higher education still operate from a positivist, commodified, expert model that grew out of adopting the research university model from Germany. Saltmarsh and Hartley (2011) argued that current approaches to community engagement have been unilaterally driven by an expert model in institutions of higher education "grounded in an institutional epistemology that privileges the expertise in the university and its application externally, through activities in the community" (pp. 18–19). Thus, they characterized the current framework of civic engagement as a system in which the academy is the producer of knowledge and the community serves as knowledge consumers. To counter this, Saltmarsh and Hartley (2011) suggested that civic and community engagement should assume a form of democratic engagement that "seeks the public good *with* the public and not merely *for* the public" (p. 20; italics in original) through reciprocity that integrates academic knowledge with public knowledge. They envision a democratically engaged epistemology that integrates teaching, research, and service so that the academy is in a dynamic and collaborative "ecosystem of knowledge production" (Saltmarsh & Hartley, 2011, p. 21), where faculty, students, and community partners benefit from an ebb and flow of problem-solving and knowledge production. This approach of engaged epistemology is depicted in Figure 2.2, whereby the community is a meaningful partner, contributor, and beneficiary of the cocreation and democratically produced knowledge (Welch, 2016). In turn this minimizes perpetuating the silo of community and civic engagement emanating from isolated programs and centers.

Figure 2.2 Integrated engaged epistemology.

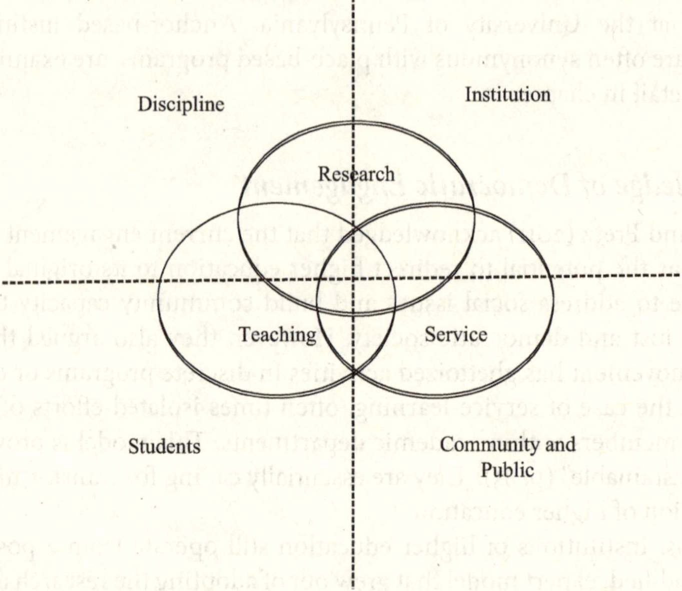

Note. From *Engaging Higher Education: Purpose, Platforms, and Programs* (p. 65), by M. Welch, 2016, Sterling, VA: Stylus. Copyright 2016 by Stylus Publishing. Reprinted with permission.

Critical Orientation

This examination of critical orientation is primarily drawn from the comprehensive review and exploration of critical perspectives and commitments by Hernandez and Pasquesi (2017), who argued for and facilitated the developmental process for articulating critical commitments in the CEP project (Dostilio, 2017b).

Able to Name Injustices and Disrupt Unequal Power Structures

Power can be thought of as a product or commodity that can be given, received, transferred, or taken away (Bloome et al., 2005). Traditionally, institutions of higher education have been viewed as bastions of intellectual and economic power because of the disciplinary and scholarly expertise of faculty. Certainly, and without question, faculty and researchers provide a wealth of knowledge and information that has led to significant contributions that benefit society at large (Levine, 2007), and no one is suggesting that we should eschew intellectual expertise. Saltmarsh and Hartley (2011) noted that community partners respect and invite expertise into partnerships. However, they also add and caution us that it requires respect and reciprocity to cocreate new knowledge that is mutually beneficial. The challenge for CEPs, therefore, is to identify and dismantle the power differential that inherently exists between the academy and community and inside the academy among institutional stakeholders with differing levels of status and authority. In this way, a CEP must become an ambassador, broker, and bridge builder in an attempt to reengineer existing and potential power structures at the institutional level that could thwart and threaten the cocreation of new knowledge. Hernandez and Pasquesi (2017) argued that CEPs must develop a nuanced consciousness of power dynamics while comprehending theoretical concepts and historical contexts that frame power struggles in community engagement.

Able to Recognize Connection to Privilege and Oppression

Unveiling unequal power structures requires CEPs' recognition of their subject position in connection to privilege and oppression (Hernandez & Pasquesi, 2017). Mitchell (2013) goes on to say that CEPs must also unveil and name injustices in an effort to reallocate power inside and outside the academy. In addition to recognizing and dismantling institutional power structures, CEPs must be aware of their own personal and professional power by virtue of being a part of the academy and its inherent power. Pitner and Sakamoto (2005) presented an effective model, originally designed and intended for service providers in the medical and mental health field, which can be used by CEPs to practice and develop their own critical consciousness and with others. They suggest that the practice of critical consciousness involves and integrates *cognitive*, *affective*, and *behavioral* dimensions at personal and structural levels (see Figure 2.3). At a personal level, critical consciousness requires continuous cognitive and affective reflection and observation of how one's own experience, identity, biases, assumptions, and cultural worldviews influence one's perception and understanding of diversity and power dynamics. This personal examination considers one's positionality and social identity that is influenced through membership in specific groups (Tajfel & Turner, 1986) and standpoints. This requires CEPs to "locate" their own positionality in terms of privilege and oppression to reveal their own power or lack of it. Take a moment to reflect on your positionality by responding to the prompts offered in Box 2.5. Standpoint theory (Swigonski, 1994) posits that members of privileged groups have worldviews that differ from

Figure 2.3 Personal and structural dynamics of practicing critical consciousness.

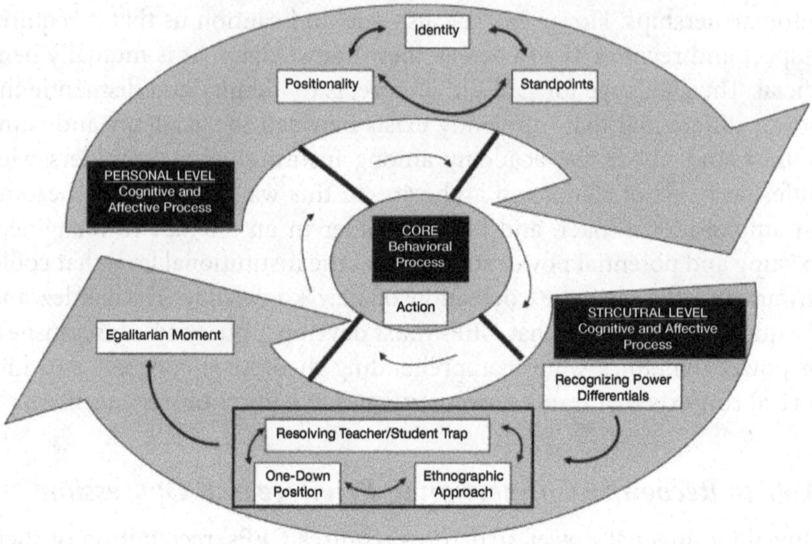

members of oppressed groups. Furthermore, standpoint theory maintains that members of privileged groups can maintain and justify the status quo when they suppress (or ignore) the worldviews of oppressed groups. Interestingly, even CEPs from marginalized groups must consider their own position of power by virtue of being part of the academy while navigating the complex and nuanced power structures within the academy that can oppress or impede their influence.

At a structural level, critical consciousness involves similar cognitive and affective dimensions that necessitate surrendering professional power to forge an authentic relationship with a partner. The behavioral component serves as a significant catalyst in integrating the cyclical personal and structural aspects of this process. This process incorporates and embodies key concepts from Freire (1970) in which the positionality of one over another (e.g., teacher and student) is replaced by an inclusive lens that incorporates an array of diverse perspectives. This, in turn, minimizes privilege and oppression by creating an egalitarian or democratic setting and context to cogenerate new ideas and methods.

Desire to Participate Fully in the Institution

As discussed in more detail in chapter 4, an institution of higher education is a complex interactive system of administrators, staff, offices, and

Box 2.5
Compass Point: Public Purposes–E

> Using Pitner and Sakamoto's (2005) model, reflect on your own power and privilege. Begin by identifying cultural, geographical, economic, and political factors that have shaped you. Next, reflect on how those factors, coupled with your own experience, identity, biases, assumptions, and cultural worldviews, influence your perception and understanding of the world as well as diversity and power dynamics. What aspects of power (if any) must or can you surrender and in what contexts or settings to promote an egalitarian approach to community engagement?

programs. The culture and dynamic of shared governance in which faculty and sometimes staff have a very significant voice in establishing policy and procedures through formal governance bodies and committees adds to this complexity. This is complicated even further if a CEP is not a faculty member. An effective CEP strategically participates in the shared governance process and committee work whenever and wherever possible. In this way, the CEP is not only aware of an array of issues, policies, and initiatives but also has an opportunity to influence those discussions and actions in ways that may promote the public purpose of the institution and advance community engagement. This is another reason why careful consideration must be given to developing the job description of a CEP that transcends traditional administrative tasks to include opportunities for this type of visibility and participation. CEPs' roles and responsibilities require them to emerge from their safe and familiar silo of engagement and expand their boundaries. Likewise, being at the table for various discussions and meetings gives you and your work a presence and a sense of legitimacy that extends beyond your colleagues' traditional expectations and assumptions of who you are and what you do. Therefore, it is incumbent on the CEP to discern the most appropriate committees to join and whether they are even eligible to serve, even in an ex officio capacity. Initial consideration might involve reviewing the list of academic committees in the faculty handbook and discussing the possibility of service on these committees with a supervisor as well as with administrative colleagues in various divisions across campus such as student life, residential life, campus ministry, external affairs, and even athletics. The strategic aspect of this level of participation is to carefully discern to what degree you can and should take on additional roles and responsibilities. Carefully weigh how

BOX 2.6

Compass Point: Public Purposes–F

Review the list of committees for your institution on its website, in the faculty handbook, or in an administrative policies document, and identify which ones you might be able to serve on even as an ex officio observer. Seek your counterparts from other institutions and inquire which, if any, committees they serve on. Discuss possible committee roles with your immediate administrative supervisor. As part of the deliberation, consider the investment of time and energy committee membership will require, which could interfere with your existing roles and responsibilities.

your active involvement on various committees and tasks will interface with and support your work. by following the instructions in Box 2.6.

Embrace Tension Between Charity and Social Change

In the critical literature, charity is juxtaposed with social change (Hernandez & Pasquesi, 2017). More than 20 years ago, Morton (1995) conceptualized service on a continuum ranging from charity to project to social change, noting that value doesn't decrease along the spectrum but that any of these activities can be done in thick, robust ways or thin, disempowering ways. Advancing social change is a significant shift from the traditional pedagogical approach of "offering a service" (Mitchell, 2008, p. 54). Social change requires a critical pedagogy with communities that empower traditionally marginalized people (Webster & Coffey, 2011). Critical practice requires CEPs to become "believers in and not . . . resisters of social change" (Wu & Dahlgren, 2011, p. 291).

Given the unique and precarious nature of CEPs operating as third-space professionals as described earlier, you may find yourself juggling multiple and conflicting commitments to your institution with the social justice aspects embedded in the public purpose of higher education. Meyerson and Scully (1995) referred to this type of individual as a tempered radical who generally falls into one of two categories: those positioned or perceived to be outsiders or insiders whose values are in conflict with those of the institution. As presented earlier in this chapter, the notion of the public purpose of higher education is generally unknown or not appreciated in the academy. Consequently, the person advancing it, namely, you, may be perceived as an outsider who simply does not know how things are done around here. Given this scenario, Meyerson and Scully (1995) suggested that the adjective *tempered* is likely to manifest itself in three ways: taking a moderate stance and approach, being honed or toughened after being repeatedly heated and cooled, and filled with temper or anger resulting from the internal conflict between personal commitment to social justice and the institution's lack of commitment.

As discussed in greater detail in chapter 3, the role of a tempered radical is to challenge the status quo and advance incremental change in an organization by taking advantage of strategic opportunities when they present themselves by creating alliances of like-minded stakeholders (Meyerson, 2004). This role once again presents an opportunity for effective CEPs to carefully implement the art and craft of this work to avoid the risk of alienating themselves from their colleagues in ways that inadvertently undermine their work and mission to advance the public purpose of the institution. Creating a craft does not occur overnight. It requires a subtle and strategic understanding of institutional culture coupled with identifying formal and informal movers and shakers on campus, which can only be accomplished through relational interactions and conversations. These respected individuals can serve as allies and champions who are likely to be heard by skeptical colleagues. This also requires an ability to deftly engage in constructive dialogue that calls into question the prevailing attitudes and practices in the academy that is viewed as evocative and thoughtful as opposed to accusatory (see Box 2.7). Using and mixing a barrage of metaphors to characterize the process, CEPs new to campus must first pay their dues and learn the ropes to get a lay of the land before making too many waves.

Developing Critical Consciousness Through Praxis

As discussed earlier in this chapter, the early and traditional role of a CEP was to oversee curricular and cocurricular programs. Many, if not most, of your colleagues are operating under that assumption and expectation. However, the emerging leadership role of committed CEPs includes advocating and practicing critical consciousness in all settings with all stakeholders through what Freire (1970) called *praxis*. But what does this grand and abstract philosophical concept look like, and how is it practiced? It requires an ability to listen carefully to all stakeholders (especially those who have traditionally had no voice), engage in authentic dialogue, and demonstrate respect through actions. It also means we shift from the predominant lens of our own social and professional identity to view a situation from the perspective of others. In this way, we are reminded that not everyone we interact with views the world from the same disciplinary, abstract, intellectual lenses or the same lived experiences. You can practice this while attending a committee meeting on campus, having a one-on-one consultation with a faculty member, mentoring a student leader, or working with a community agency and those it serves. Listening transcends the process of merely receiving auditory factual information to include hearing the story of those telling the story. This includes an awareness of the affective and emotional dynamics of the context, generating a sense of place as well as an understanding of the factual information. Through hearing, a CEP can reflect on the meaning and context of what has been said, which includes identifying where and how power is conveyed and how it is used to empower or control others. The reflection process requires us to contemplate the implications of context and settings on the actions and welfare of all participants: Is it mutually beneficial or is it perpetuating oppression? Thus, praxis requires the CEP to ask these types of critical questions across settings and stakeholders. The answers and process in turn influence what we do and how we do it. As a change agent, the CEP models the approach of collectively and collaboratively identifying mutually beneficial goals coupled with identifying and using resources to meet those goals. This is a dramatic shift from the traditional academic paradigm of imposing disciplinary expertise, even with the best of intentions, on others through *shoulding on* (i.e., "You should") rather than collaboratively cocreating a mutually beneficial approach to promote the public good while contributing to new knowledge in a field.

Able to Challenge Problematic Language

CEPs must unveil and disrupt power differentials by challenging problematic language use, discursive practice, and abstractions (Hernandez & Pasquesi, 2017). This can be accomplished by calling into question the pervasive assumption that community is composed of homogenous units devoid of multiple experiences, identities, contexts, and perspectives (Dempsey, 2010). Similarly, CEPs must address othering language that evokes paternalistic perspectives and practices by affluent or White students or faculty participating in various forms of community engagement (Seider & Hillman, 2011). Paternalism often manifests itself through deficit thinking and color-blind ideologies (Veloria, 2015) that can dehumanize others.

CEPs must also endeavor to unveil and challenge power structures that perpetuate injustice within the academy (Maurrasee, 2001). This requires dismantling hegemonic structures that impose a dominant normative paradigm, typically consisting of a White male Euro-American perspective,

BOX 2.7

Compass Point: Public Purpose–G

Read each of the following scenarios, and reflect on how you might respond and challenge some of the apparent prevailing structures of power and privilege.

A task force to explore ways to formalize the development and approval process of service-learning courses has been formed by the vice president for academic affairs. At the first meeting, you look around the table noting that the members of the group are mostly male faculty with one White female adjunct instructor.

The research committee at a large public urban research university provides seed grants of $5,000 to $10,000 to faculty, primarily new assistant professors working toward promotion and tenure. Most of these dollars are institutional funds allocated for this purpose. However, some flow-through funds come from larger grants from corporate sources such as pharmaceutical companies or government agencies like the U.S. Department of Defense. One application from a faculty member in the Department of Public Policy requested $5,000 to help conduct community-based research with two local nonprofit organizations to explore capacity building in a neighborhood located in a food desert. One member of the committee objected to the proposal saying, "This isn't research! This faculty member is being manipulated to use institutional dollars to help an organization with its own political agenda."

A committee consisting of excited and well-meaning faculty is exploring ways to expand community engagement in the form of community-based research by individual faculty members. Examine each of the statements that emerged from the ensuing conversation and consider how you might respond in ways that affirm the positive intent of what has been said while adding layers of meaning that reframe and challenge the problematic language in these remarks.

- We could really help these people solve some of the problems they are facing in their neighborhoods.
- Let's invite some directors from some of our current partner agencies to campus to tell them about our exciting initiative.
- This is really exciting. It's clearly going to provide some publishing opportunities for our junior faculty who are working toward tenure.

to establish respect, trust, and authentic relationships for traditionally underrepresented or marginalized faculty (Verjee, 2012). Likewise, CEPs may need to take the role of the institutional conscience to remind the academy of its complicit, albeit unknowing, role in perpetuating town-and-gown differences that manifest themselves in discordant relationships with nearby neighborhoods, resulting in gentrification, exploitation, and segregation (Dempsey, 2010; Sullivan et al., 2001).

Committed to Dialogue With Communities

Dialogue with partners and stakeholders in the community is key to effective community engagement and can take place in various settings and formats, depending on the purpose and goal of the conversation. Some conversations are logistical, others are deeper as they attempt to resolve issues or tensions, and others are ongoing professional discussions. It may be useful to envision an arc of dialogue and behaviors that depicts various entry points and contexts of communication. Given the historical tension between the academy and community, it is incumbent on the CEP to make gestures of outreach to the community, perhaps by going out into the neighborhoods and community settings. Personal visits to community agencies send a strong signal of interest and intentionality. It is a means of being responsive to overtures that community partners often make to higher education. A CEP should accept invitations from community partners to attend regularly scheduled meetings in the community. Above and beyond attending meetings, effective CEPs establish a presence by participating in the life of the community whenever possible, including attending neighborhood festivals and events at local churches and schools to celebrate the pride and sense of place embedded in these communities. This type and level of initial dialogue is a nuanced art that bridges yet incorporates a professional context and purpose with authentic personal conversation that leads to trust and relationships.

There are other types of dialogue beyond those that occur between you, the CEP, and community partners. Consider establishing and convening a community partner advisory committee or inviting a representative from the community to participate on a broader advisory committee consisting of faculty, alumni, and students. We offer some questions about partner advisory committees for you to consider in Box 2.8. These gatherings include hosting administrators, faculty, students, and other community organizations for dialogues, described later.

Effective CEPs recognize they must work and communicate with multiple communities, including groups on campus. Dialogue with

BOX 2.8

Compass Point: Public Purposes–H

Consider how you might develop a community partner advisory committee.

1. Who would you invite and why?
2. What is and how would you articulate its role and responsibility?
3. Where, when, and how often would you convene the group?
4. Should there be distinct advisory groups (e.g., community, faculty, student), and what are the pros and cons?

communities should include exploring ways to broker conversations on and off campus between community partners with administrators, faculty, students, and even other community partners for networking. This may include making contact with or being receptive to various student organizations, especially for traditionally marginalized groups. Such an approach was common during the Black Lives Matter movement on many campuses (see more on civic dialogue in chapter 6). Another straightforward approach is to establish a community partner advisory group that meets at least once a semester. These meetings provide a safe space for community partners to provide direct and candid feedback or input on programming. Consider alternating the venue of the meetings from on campus to one of the community sites.

Our Critical Commitments: Questions to Ask

The deeper ethos and broader commitment of a CEP to community engagement transcends being an administrator and managing programs that merely place students in community sites in what has been traditional short-term projects to developing meaningful and sustained partnerships that are mutually beneficial. The historical, ethical, political, and critical dimensions of this work are in many ways counter to the present-day realities facing higher education. Pragmatic challenges associated with student admissions and retention, funding, building and maintaining facilities, risk, and garnering a reputation coupled with the commodification and neoliberalization of higher education can often shift attention and priorities from this work. You are invited and encouraged to ponder these complex issues and the following questions with colleagues and mentors.

1. How does and how can a CEP as a tempered radical articulate the public purpose and mission of higher education in light of these competing perspectives and priorities? Can such a dialogue be enveloped into the present narrative and focus in ways that do not alienate administrators and faculty?
2. Likewise, how can a CEP embrace and advance social change and a critical consciousness in a culture that values objectivity and what some may call political neutrality? How can a CEP move the narrative and practice beyond a focus of effective pedagogy for students to explore and advance the integration of research, teaching, and service to democratize knowledge and build capacity in the community?
3. Conversely, some communities are often reluctant to work with institutions of higher education. This is the result of previous negative experiences with faculty and the institution imposing an elitist expert model. Many traditional approaches of outreach to the community exploit those we assume to serve with little or no mutual benefit. Interactions may not honor, respect, or use the public expertise and culture of the community. How then does and can a CEP and an engaged institution articulate the institution's public purpose to a justifiably cautious community partner or neighborhood?
4. These changes do not occur overnight. Enthusiastic and zealous CEPs must strategically and incrementally educate administrators, faculty, and community partners that community engagement is more than students placed in the community doing charity-based projects. What is the current climate on your campus? Is the public purpose of higher education understood? Embraced? Practiced? Why or why not?

Chapter Three

LEADING CHANGE IN HIGHER EDUCATION

When I arrived at the University of Wisconsin–Milwaukee in the summer of 1998 I knew then, and am more convinced now, that this urban campus has the potential to be a powerful force in our community and nation. But how to get there? . . . . It soon became clear to me that what UWM needed was an elevated idea—something that would get people excited for change . . . . I believe that universities are put on the face of the earth to make both an academic and social contribution. We are to model civic engagement and prepare students for active lives in our democracy. We make our contribution in terms of our teaching, the programs we offer, the lives we enable, the discovery and inquiry we conduct, and through our service. Our links to our community give legs to our mission because our partnership and connections benefit this community and that, in turn, benefits us. The Wisconsin Idea says that campus and community are intimately connected, a possibility that holds enormous potential for urban universities for the new millennium. (Zimpher as cited in Zimpher, Percy, & Brukhardt, 2008, pp. 9–11)

Frequently when we speak of leading change, or leadership, in higher education, we imagine individuals at the executive level. This is true. However, we as CEPs can occupy the roles of leader and change agent from many different locations in an institution. According to a former University of Wisconsin regent, "Changing the direction of an institution of higher education is a lot like trying to move a battleship with your bare hands. It takes strategic leadership—and a lot of people willing to help push" (Zimpher, Percy, & Brukhardt, 2008, p. 1). To realize the audacious ideas that Nancy Zimpher called on the University of Wisconsin–Milwaukee to undertake requires a unique leader, but perhaps more importantly, a cadre of innovative and talented colleagues who are willing to catalyze and steward the change agenda. CEPs who occupy middle spaces (those of us who are not chief engagement officers and may

TABLE 3.1
Competencies and Critical Commitments Associated With Leading Change in Higher Education

3.1 Knowledge of change as a process that involves cultural and structural change 3.2 Knowledge of one's own personal agency as a change maker 3.3 Able to articulate connection between institutional mission and community engagement 3.4 Knowledge of the relevance of community engagement to other campus goals 3.5 Able to integrate goals and strategies of common initiatives	3.6 Knowledge of external pressures and trends systemically facing higher education 3.7 Able to work in fluid environments 3.8 Able to use data to create a case for change 3.9 Embrace a proactive stance 3.10 Embrace innovation 3.11 Embrace perseverance 3.12 Embrace adaptability and risk taking 3.13 Embrace diversity among collaborators and promote inclusion	3.14 Desire to participate fully in the institution (participating in governance, serving on committees, representing ethical concerns) 3.15 Able to facilitate meetings and programs that are inclusive, are participatory, and promote reflective practice 3.16 Knowledge of democratic engagement and ability to enact a democratic engagement orientation (participatory processes, cocreation of knowledge, coplanning, inclusivity, etc.) 3.17 Able to strategically plan
Critical Commitments • Embrace the tension between charity and social change • Committed to developing critical consciousness through meaningful praxis (reflection, dialogue, and action) • Able to challenge problematic language use (e.g., paternalistic, dehumanizing, and oppressive) • Knowledge of ideologies and political, social, and historical contexts underpinning higher education		

not have formal, positional authority to direct change efforts) fall into that cadre.

After completing this chapter, those working in the field of community engagement or currently working as a community engagement professional will be able to reflect on the areas in which they are competent and identify areas they would like to develop further (see Table 3.1). For those who are new to supporting community engagement or who aspire to enter the community engagement profession, they will demonstrate awareness and emerging understanding of these areas of competence.

Although some suggest that higher education in the United States has been undergoing significant change over the past decade, organizational change scholars tell us that change is continuous in organizations (Kezar, 2014). This current moment in the longer evolution of higher education is marked by an acceleration in the use of online technologies, a shift in humanities and sciences degree programs to a more public orientation, pressure for institutions to be more inclusive and equitable environments, and continued public demands for access, accountability, and affordability. Frameworks of full participation, democratic knowledge generation, and public scholarship position community engagement as integral to institutional changes that respond to these times. For CEPs to effectively support, and perhaps lead, change from the middle spaces requires an awareness of self and institutional change processes. Even before change occurs, CEPs need to be able to envision the desired change (Hübler & Quan, 2017) and determine if they have the relationships necessary to support the desired change (Kezar, 2014). Once a change process has begun, the CEP needs to activate and nurture those relationships while also managing conflict so that others can take collaborative action. This chapter discusses change as being cultural and structural; calls on the concepts of the tempered radical and leading from the middle; emphasizes the importance of developing a deep understanding of the institution's mission, type, history, and purpose; and discusses how knowing how community engagement fits with the other change agendas pursued at the institution and that influence the institution. The chapter concludes by describing how data can be used to make the case for change and ways that CEPs can support and convene change processes. Suggestions for further reading about change in higher education are provided. A small number of institutional scenarios are presented in which the reader is asked to identify opportunities for community engagement (and, by association, a CEP's leadership) to be featured in institutional change strategies. Readers are assigned the task of collecting and examining documents from their institution and reflecting on a short list of questions to consider what part community engagement might play in solidifying a more promising future for their institution. Finally, a list of questions encourages readers to hone their critical understanding of change possibilities.

Knowledge of Change as a Process

CEPs are often eager to implement new structures to support engagement or alter existing ones as their primary tool of change. Although attractive, change is a process that involves cultural as well as structural change. Changing the structures of engagement in an institution might involve establishing a unit or center, implementing (or dismantling) a curricular requirement, revising faculty review and tenure policies, or creating committees or task forces. Yet if people do not think or act differently despite these changes, cultural change has not occurred, and the structural change might not take hold (Eckel, Hill, & Green, 1998). Welch (2016) wrote, "Cultural factors entail values, beliefs, traditions, and attitudes that have a powerful effect on behavior. Those cultural variables manifest themselves into policy and procedures" (p. 215). Cultural changes might include reclamation of the institution's civic purpose (as discussed in chapter 2), a widely supported agenda to align the institution's intellectual assets with the region's issues and agendas, or a reorientation of what is considered valuable faculty work.

Structural change is often prescriptive, whereas cultural change is often constructive. It enlists the hearts and minds of an organization's stakeholders. The notion of building together (from the Latin *con* meaning with and *struere* meaning build) demands that we understand how to authentically engage our organizational peers in the change endeavor we hope to undertake. One might even say that structural change comes as a result of cultural change, that we have worked together to cocreate our idea of the future and then implement structures to carry out the changes that are necessary.

Without the combination of structural and cultural change, it's difficult to imagine that any real change is possible. Yet many people who have not learned about organizational change think that creating a new structure is all that is needed to reorient a campus approach to community engagement. Kezar (2014) flags this as one of the typical problems that plagues change efforts in higher education: ignoring the change process along with being led by implicit (and often overly simple) theories of change, ignoring context, and not basing change in research. It is vital for CEPs who are involved in institutional change agendas to take the time to learn about organizational change, become familiar with a diversity of theories of change, and know the differences between first- and second-order change (Bartunek & Moch, 1987). First-order changes occur within (or correspond to) an organization's existing paradigm. Second-order changes

BOX 3.1
Compass Point: Leading Change–A

For those of you who are in the middle of a change process, make an outline of the structural changes that are happening. Now examine what cultural changes have made these structural evolutions possible and list them. Who initiated or what events spurred these cultural changes? Are they explicitly recognized as readying the ground for the structural changes? Are there any cultural practices or beliefs that haven't changed but may need to for the structural changes to take root?

For those of you who are not currently in a change process, brainstorm a change you think would enhance the quality of community engagement at your institution (e.g., increase in undergraduate community-based research opportunities, implementation of an economic partnership dashboard, realignment of community-based federal work-study positions to support key community-campus partnerships). What beliefs or cultural practices would need to change to make this happen? Who could help to facilitate changes to those beliefs and cultural practices? What would prevent such changes?

result in changes to the organization's actual paradigm (Bartunek & Moch, 1987). As this relates to the civic purposes of our work, first-order changes might result in improvements to practices (e.g., adopting service-learning pedagogy because learning experientially results in better subject matter acquisition) but not in the fundamental transformation of the campus's identity to more fully embrace its democratic and civic commitments (e.g., harnessing service-learning to academically engage students in the larger campus project to collaboratively develop knowledge with communities to address specific challenges to the region (Hartley & Saltmarsh, as cited in Plater, 2011). Having knowledge of organizational change (including theories that explain change and types of change) will help CEPs to intentionally customize a strategy to best address the cultural and second-order changes along with structural and first-order changes. Take a moment and reflect on the instances of structural and cultural change embedded within your own practice by responding to the prompts in Box 3.1. For those new to organizational change literature, an excellent place to start would be to review Kezar's (2001) synthesis of research on organizational change in higher education and then consult Kezar (2014) for an overview of change theories and frameworks of change.

Knowledge of Personal Agency

Agency refers to a group of identity-related beliefs we hold about ourselves, such as having a sense that we have some responsibility for the future, we are in control of our decisions and thus have some responsibility for their outcomes, and we are confident that we can overcome obstacles (Schwartz, Cote, & Arnett, 2005). The concept of personal agency is part of a larger psychosocial debate about whether it is the degree to which we are part of the structures (in this context, our level of formal authority, our status as either faculty or staff, our institutional location such as student affairs or academic affairs) or the personal agency we exert that influences our ability to overcome challenges.

With the exception of chief engagement officers, most CEPs are situated at midlevel in an institution's management structure, typically located in one division or unit of an institution rather than shared among all divisions, and may operate in an institutional culture where community engagement is disconnected from other change agendas such as diversity and inclusion or is one of a number of institutional priorities rather than threaded throughout. This set of structural conditions might lead people to think they have no possibility of influencing institutional change. However, if a CEP has a sense of agency as a change maker, it is possible to lead from the middle and to use processes that make the institution a better version of itself by setting a precedent (or reaffirming an existing practice) of inclusive, collective, cocreated change processes. The ideas of Meyerson and Scully (1995) and Bolman and Gallos (2011) are especially helpful when developing our sense of agency as change makers.

Tempered radical is a concept from a body of work by Debra E. Meyerson (Meyerson & Scully, 1995) in which she describes individuals who are capable of influencing organizational transformation by remaining committed to the organization and at the same time to a cause, identity, or community that is at odds with the culture of the organization. Tempered radicals represent a departure from the norm. The concept is built on the idea that tempered radicals challenge the status quo in modest, incremental ways from within the system as opposed to outside the system, and they are tempered in three ways. First, they seek moderation in their approach to transformation; second, they have become toughened by being alternately heated and cooled (challenged and affirmed); and third, they have a temper, in that they are angered by the incongruity between what they value and the values of the organization (Meyerson & Scully, 1995). For many of us, this accurately describes our experience as we remain dedicated to a particular college or university or to the enterprise of higher education while also having a steadfast commitment to the ideas of community engagement, communities that extend beyond the campus border, or to identities as public intellectuals, scholar activists, or agents of social justice. The tools of tempered radicals include using small wins and taking local, spontaneous, authentic action (Meyerson & Scully, 1995) as well as undertaking collective action (Meyerson, 2001). Small wins, or conducting small change experiments, allow us to "uncover resources, information, allies, sources of resistance, and additional opportunities for change" (p. 595). These incremental attempts to nudge the status quo snowball into a much larger change strategy than what might have been acceptable to the organization if the entire change strategy had been proposed all at once. Spontaneous, authentic action is when tempered radicals express their dual commitments authentically, voicing their beliefs, identities, and feelings spontaneously in their everyday interactions, even when they run counter to what is acceptable in the institution's culture. This is also characterized as "disruptive self expression" (Meyerson, 2001, p. 41). Collective action, or strategic alliance building, is when tempered radicals work with like-minded individuals to wield greater legitimacy, power, and resources than they could on their own, and it often leads to change even when the tempered radical does not have the formal authority to direct those changes (Quinn & Meyerson, 2008).

Leading from the middle is an academic leadership concept advanced by Bolman and Gallos (2011) in which they describe higher education administrators, who occupy middle management, as experiencing a duality in their positions. On the one hand, there is power and potential in the boundary-spanning nature of our work. CEPs are well positioned to create consensus and build collaboration across disciplines, units, and community-campus entities. On the other hand, the expectations and pressures of more senior leaders diverge from those of our colleagues and constituents. Further, others' expectations of us differ between community and campus cultures. As middle administrators, we typically have large portfolios of responsibilities, yet limited resources and little formal authority. As a result, we influence change by "facilitating, selling, and encouraging rather than controlling and implementing" (Bolman & Gallos, 2011, p. 146) and mostly "propose, recommend, negotiate, and nudge" (p. 154). To respond to the divergent expectations and pressures, we often use our diplomatic skills, goodwill, and strength of relationships as buffers between senior administration and faculty or student realities and between campus and community cultures. Take a moment to reflect more deeply on the concepts of tempered radical and leading from the middle by responding to the prompts in Box 3.2.

BOX 3.2
Compass Point: Leading Change–B

List the strategies and behaviors of a tempered radical and those of an administrator leading from the middle. Which of these come naturally to you? Can you find examples of these in your own work? What strategies and approaches discussed here do you find challenging? Which might you want to develop? Think of an administrator who holds a similar institutional position to your own. Which strategies and approaches from these frameworks has he or she used? Consider discussing with that person their approach to facilitating and stewarding change.

Using these frameworks as touchstones can help us maximize the potential we have to steward change, given our unique boundary-spanning identities and institutional locations as CEPs. Yet we are not alone. Throughout this section, the concept of collective leadership has been mentioned. Sandmann and Plater (2009) describe the four stages of (formal) leadership in an engaged institution as interpreting the campus mission to reflect engagement with multiple communities, defining goals and objectives to realize this interpretation of the mission, articulating the means and priorities to realize the goals, and bolstering this commitment through the leader's personal interactions. Plater (2011) explained that in a collective leadership frame, through a "conspiracy of the concerned" (p. 107), these stages can be accomplished by the collaborative work undertaken by the many people who are the infrastructure that supports engagement. Such collaborative work, or collective action, doesn't magically happen. It requires a catalyst and a set of knowing contributors. We suggest the CEP is one such person who can rally others to exert collective leadership in the service of community engagement. The ensuing sections lead readers through consideration of how they develop familiarity with the institution's mission as it reflects community engagement, think systemically about change, and convene and curate change. All of this is done in a collaborative and democratic way, thus helping readers to develop a sense of their role as a change agent who employs collective leadership.

Developing Deep Knowledge of Mission, History, and Purpose

The change agenda we are proposing for CEPs is the strategic integration of community engagement as an animating priority in an institution of higher education. This encompasses the recognition and realization of community engagement as an institutional priority and the implementation and enhancement of community engagement activities as a means to realize that priority. In her vast work with institutions of higher education that seek to embrace community engagement, Holland (1997, 2005) has determined that "different institutional responses to engagement are predictably logical and compatible with the mission, history, purpose, and capacity of different types of institutions" (Holland, 2005, p. 253). We believe that a CEP must begin by cultivating deep knowledge of the institution's mission, history, purpose, and goals to develop insight into the ways community engagement amplifies these institutional commitments.

Morphew and Hartley (2006) suggest postsecondary mission statements have two functions: to instruct us on what activities support the institution's imperatives and to establish a shared purpose that is motivational and inspirational. It is critical to understand how the institution's mission shapes its civic calling and the norms that support community engagement practices. Understanding the intention of the phrasing of the statement is important, whether it is producing civic-minded graduates, addressing society's challenges, promoting the welfare of the region, or any number of other statements. The nature of the mission-based commitment often feeds into the campus's expressed as well as implicit institutional goals. These expressions are also often influenced by the institution's type (e.g., land grant, private liberal arts, private religious, public comprehensive, public regional).

As an example, let's say a college's mission statement declares that it will be of service to the city, region, state, and nation. If that institution was a public research university, the expression of service might be through strategic partnerships in health, education, or environmental sustainability, and faculty research productivity would be prioritized as part of these partnerships. Alternatively, let's say the institution is a private religiously affiliated college. In this case, the expression of service might be through volunteer activities that encourage reflection on spiritual formation, justice-based collaborations, and community-engaged teaching. Further, the history of the institution matters a great deal. Take, for example, Duquesne University, which was founded to educate the children of immigrant mill workers who were typically quite poor and disenfranchised. As a result, the expression of engagement at Duquesne University is heavily oriented toward working with people and communities that lack educational opportunities and are experiencing economic disenfranchisement.

BOX 3.3

Compass Point: Leading Change–C

Investigate the grounding for community engagement at your institution by collecting artifacts of your institution's mission, identity, goals, and key initiatives and then reflect on a series of questions about those artifacts. Note: If you are not currently at an institution or if you are hoping to make a change, gather artifacts for the institution you wish to learn more about. For example, collect the following:

- Institutional mission and vision statements
- History of the institution's founding and any major historical moments
- Most recent strategic plan
- Recent accreditation self-study documents (the statements institutions write about themselves for the purposes of regional accreditation). There are six regional accreditation bodies: New England Association of Schools and Colleges, Middle States Commission on Higher Education, Higher Learning Commission, Northwest Commission on Colleges and Universities, Southern Association of Colleges and Schools, and Western Association of Schools and Colleges. Figure out which one accredits your institution and seek the documents written to assert your institution should maintain its accreditation.
- A list of institutions that are considered peer institutions
- Copies of presidential or chancellor speeches from the past year
- A copy of the institution's publicity pieces that are sent to alumni, donors, and prospective students
- The engagement unit's website, promotional materials, and key documents

Questions

- How is community engagement expressed as part of the mission or vision statement? (See mission and vision statements.)
- Is this expression a current portrayal of the ways the institution is involved with its larger communities? If not, what led to the different ways it is involved? (See history, accreditation documents, speeches, and publicity pieces.)
- What are the institution's strategic priorities and goals? (See strategic plan.) Are these different from what is expressed elsewhere? (See accreditation documents, speeches, and publicity pieces.)

(*Continues*)

BOX 3.3 (*Continued*)

- What is it about the schools included in the list of peer institutions that the campus wishes to emulate?
- Is the engagement unit's work aligned with the ways in which the institution expresses the role of engagement in its mission, goals, and priorities? If not, why? Is there widespread support for the unit's differing interpretation?
- How would or could you use their artifacts to articulate or justify engaged teaching and scholarship to an administrator or faculty member?

Able to Articulate Connection of Institutional Mission to Community Engagement

The context of the institution's mission, institutional type, and history figures heavily into the expression of engagement that is acceptable under the institution's norms and can also help us to call on the institution to more fully embrace community engagement. Attending to this context helps us align our work with what matters at the institution and also helps us to think strategically about what is possible. Deep knowledge of the campus mission, history, and purpose also allows the CEP to develop an informed critique of current expressions, and such a critique can be used to drive changes in practice, if desired, or resist an unintentional trend that is possible or beginning to happen.

Knowledge of Relevance to Other Campus Goals

Once you deeply understand your organizational context, you are able to determine how community engagement might fit in other change agendas at your institution and how it could enhance the strategies available to the institution as it responds to trends and external pressures. Too often, and to its detriment, we propose the implementation of some form of community engagement without knowing how it fits in the overall evolution of an organization and how the goals of community engagement integrate with the goals of other campus initiatives. It's critical for CEPs to be able to work in fluid environments, sense what changes are happening, and learn how community engagement fits with those changes. Take a moment to reflect on how community engagement fits with other priorities of your environment by responding to the prompts in Box 3.4. Understanding the relationship between community engagement and the metadrivers of

BOX 3.4

Compass Point: Leading Change–D

Review and reflect on the following questions. Consider how the intersection (and resulting proposed involvement) between community engagement and others' priorities and agendas also (a) serves the civic mission of your institution so the campus is not working off mission; (b) serves preexisting goals for the community engagement initiative to not take it off course; and (c) is doable in the current capacity of your operation, or if not, how can you leverage the intersection between community engagement and a specific highly visible priority for additional resources?

1. What is important to your campus leadership right now? What key initiatives or problems are leaders pursuing or asking the campus to embrace? How does community engagement tie into those initiatives or problems?
2. What is important to your surrounding geographic community right now? What key agendas are being pursued, and what challenges are civic leaders rallying around? How could your campus contribute to such agendas or problem solving?
3. What is important to your immediate supervisor right now? What key issues or opportunities is he or she working on? How does your work fit in with what has his or her attention?

change in higher education (Kezar, 2014) and the agendas the institution's leadership is choosing to pursue helps the CEP to think systemically and strategically.

Among the myriad pressures and opportunities facing our campuses, we think community engagement is particularly relevant to the ever diversifying membership of our campuses, the search for relevance and significance in the local context, and demands for accountability in our educational delivery. Box 3.5 offers three case studies for your consideration of how community engagement fits with the goals and opportunities of other change agendas present at an institution.

Using Data to Create the Case for Change

Once you have a good grasp of what role community engagement plays in the institution's mission, history, and goals and the ways community

BOX 3.5
Compass Point: Leading Change–E

Case A: The campus desires to create a more equitable and welcoming environment for underrepresented students, faculty, and staff. It would like to attract and retain a more diverse group of students. (Recommended reading: Sturm, Eatman, Saltmarsh, & Bush, 2011)

Case B: The campus desires to develop greater regional recognition and financial stability by forging better relationships with regional and state legislators, funders, and employers and to increase its enrollments among talented students in the region. (Recommended reading: Dubb, McKinley, & Howard, 2013)

Case C: The campus desires to strengthen its educational offerings, ensuring students are well-prepared for the road ahead. The campus has learned that students feel employment postgraduation, quality of education, and overall student experience will most influence their enrollment decision. (Recommended reading: Hoy & Johnson, 2013)

- What sorts of community engagement would fit best with the goals of each scenario?
- Can you think of a community engagement activity that would be distracting or irrelevant to the campus goals? How might implementation of community engagement strengthen the institution's approach to meeting its goals?
- What evidence of success would be most important to collect in each instance?

engagement can be aligned with other change agendas at the institution, you can determine if change is needed and at what level. As said earlier, the change agenda might be to influence the institution to make community engagement a greater priority (ideological change) or it might be to enhance or strengthen community engagement initiatives (structural change; Hartley, Harkavy, & Benson, 2005). One way to know what kinds of adjustments are needed and to effectively persuade others that change is necessary is to gather data about the current state of affairs. The use of data or information and processes used to convene people around those data as a change method is sometimes called *organizational learning* (see Dee & Leišytė, 2016, for a current review of organizational learning in higher education). External program or unit reviews, program evaluations, and student learning assessments can be used to generate useful data, which can help the user to note weaknesses, unfulfilled hopes of producing impact, and opportunities to improve practices or to rally the campus around a change agenda.

Peer review is deeply ingrained in the culture of higher education. We typically place high value on having others, whom we deem to be knowledgeable peers, review our work to determine its merit. This is most recognizable in the systems we use to propose academic conference presentations, publish journal articles, and evaluate one another's teaching and research. It is also used at programmatic and institutional levels when we conduct external program reviews or external unit reviews. Teams of reviewers who have relevant knowledge and practice conduct these reviews, which are evaluation processes used to assess the quality of a program, department, or initiative. The reviewers are generally from aspirant institutions (or in the case of community engagement programs and centers, from aspirant programs or units) and sometimes include stakeholders from the local community. Typically, external reviews begin with the development of guiding questions (sometimes determined by the unit leaders, by campus administrators, or in collaboration with the external peers who perform the review), and then these questions structure an internal study of the program or unit that is being evaluated. That internal study, often called a self-study, is then given to the external reviewers, who prepare additional questions and schedule a visit to campus to meet with a wide variety of stakeholders who provide input and relay their experiences. The external reviewers take some time to render what they have observed, read, and been told into a summary document that usually concludes with recommendations to maintain and improve the quality of the program or unit.

Short of having peers evaluate the quality of a program or unit, CEPs can use a variety of tools to conduct a self-study. A number of frameworks might be used, depending on the initiative being studied. If you were interested in assessing the institution's commitment to service, you could use Holland's (1997) matrix that establishes levels of institutional commitment to service across a series of organizational factors. If you were interested in evaluating the institution's performance as an anchor institution, you might use the anchor institution dashboard (Dubb, McKinley, & Howard, 2013). If you were interested in a comprehensive and thorough institutional review of community engagement practices, you could use the Carnegie Community Engagement Classification's application framework. A number of state Campus Compacts such as Iowa and North Carolina have developed institutional self-study frameworks built on the Carnegie application. If you were interested in assessing the degree to which service-learning is institutionalized on a campus, you might use the Rubric for the Self-Assessment of the Institutionalization of Service-Learning (Furco, 2003). The National Inventory of Institutional Infrastructure for Community Engagement, developed by Welch and Saltmarsh (2017), is a tool to assess the state of community engagement centers and helps compare a center to others among institutions that have achieved the Carnegie classification. In addition to large-scale evaluations, you might be interested in changing practices at the program or curricular level, which would necessitate the use of a contextually specific program evaluation or student learning outcome assessment.

Convening and Curating Change Processes

It is possible to convene stakeholders and curate change even from the middle level of an organization. Revisiting the frames of tempered radical (Meyerson, 2001) and leading from the middle (Bolman & Gallos, 2011) give us ideas of how it is done. We use our relationships and authentic, spontaneous expression of our commitments to facilitate growth and change (sometimes through making proposals, other times through perseverance and nudging small changes along). Both require taking risks to involve our colleagues in a consideration of what the future could be, albeit in small and immediate ways.

It is unlikely that we will find ourselves with robust networks of colleagues to call on if we remain isolated in our own narrow channel of work. Rather, it's important for us to become full citizens of our institutions, fluent in its holistic array of priorities, goals, concerns, and opportunities. Being a full citizen means participating in the governance of the institution, contributing our service on committees and task forces that administer the future of the campus, and raising ethical concerns when we encounter them. For example, this book's coauthor, Lina, as a very new staff person, was asked to serve on one of her university's accreditation committees. Although it was a lot of work to fit into her already overwhelming schedule, it was one of the best institutional service commitments she ever made. In the course of the committee work, she learned more about the goals and priorities of the campus than she could have ever guessed at on her own, and she had the opportunity to show how community-based learning could fit into a great number of other institutional priorities. By working competently and speaking honestly, she earned the interest and respect of her faculty colleagues. From that service commitment grew close working relationships she later called on when she had the chance to initiate some campuswide change processes that required large-scale acceptance from faculty and administrators.

When CEPs eventually do have the opportunity to initiate change processes, it is vital for us to be mindful of building a diverse cadre of thought partners and stakeholders and that we help those who are involved to feel that their time has been valuably spent, their viewpoints are authentically considered, and the process is leading to action not just talk. Curating change is about creating a venue in which a diversity of views can be heard and considered and the best course of action can be devised. Doing this takes two levels of competence: a true embrace of democratic ideals and a mastery of conducting meetings and following through.

Democratic engagement is a framework that centers the cocreative and participatory ideals that underlie community-campus engagement (Saltmarsh & Hartley, 2011; Saltmarsh, Hartley, & Clayton, 2009). Saltmarsh and Hartley (2011) and Saltmarsh, Hartley, and Clayton (2009) remind us we cannot hope to achieve deeply reciprocal partnerships with communities that are inclusive, participatory, and predicated on valuing many different ways of knowing and doing without cultivating the same in campus-based processes. When we approach change work with the ideals of democratic engagement, it means that we seek diverse collaborators, develop processes that are inclusive, prioritize cocreation and construction of the ideas that will move us forward, and focus our work on change that makes a more equitable institution and in turn enables us to foster the same qualities in our community-campus engagements.

When the preliminary competency model was being validated, *good facilitation of meetings* did not meet the cutoff score to be included as one of the competencies. It was only when we looked at the open-ended responses that we saw people felt there was more to the story. Respondents indicated that meetings and programs being facilitated by CEPs had to be inclusive, participatory, and reflective—no small task. In these ways, we think facilitation can be supportive of democratic engagement. Indeed, the kinds of meetings that keep people coming back are well structured and meaningful. We've seen many instances in which the people being asked to invest their time in a change agenda or implementation process devalue the process (and often disengage) because their first interaction was time badly spent, or they felt their perspective wasn't truly valued and their voice was not being heard during the meeting. We offer a meeting facilitation checklist in Box 3.6 that you may find useful.

Even when a process is well facilitated, if people don't believe their views and input truly matter, divestment quickly happens. The ability to craft questions and experiences that elicit rich on-topic input needs to be

BOX 3.6
Compass Point: Leading Change–F

Facilitating Inclusive, Participatory, and Reflective Meetings That Catalyze Organizational Change

This exercise offers a checklist that can help build an inclusive and participatory context for a meeting concerned with organizational change. Using the following checklist, reflect on a meeting you recently facilitated or attended. Which of these elements were present? Which were absent? What would you add to this list? How did the presence or absence of these steps affect attendee inclusion, participation, and reflection?

Premeeting

- Invitations and agendas should be extended several weeks before the meeting (rule of thumb: three weeks for invitations, one to two for the agenda).
- Prepare an invitee list that is inclusive of the diverse perspectives held on the topic. Think carefully about who holds information or opinions that will inform the group's holistic understanding of the issue at hand. Ask yourself who is not included among the draft list of invitees? Why? What is the downside of not inviting them? If there are very good reasons not to extend an invitation, is there a way to solicit their thoughts or information and share it with the group?
- For those invitees not normally included in this conversation, prepare them for full participation. Have a discussion with them in advance of the meeting, perhaps as part of inviting them, that provides the context and the goals of the meeting, emphasizes your respect for their participation and contribution, orients them to what has happened prior to their inclusion, and informs them who will be at the meeting. In case some might feel intimidated or reticent to provide input, tell them the specific questions you hope they will answer during the context of the meeting and explain that you will facilitate the meeting in such a way to make room for their contributions. If they don't feel comfortable voicing their input directly, offer an alternative to have that input shared with the group. For instance, we have facilitated meetings in which the meeting leaders tell the group that they had a prior discussion with so-and-so who

(*Continues*)

BOX 3.6 (*Continued*)

shared something particularly relevant to the meeting. The leaders describe the idea or thought and then ask the person to correct them if necessary. Of course, prearrange this kind of intervention before the meeting.

- At times it might be important to tell people who cannot attend to send a proxy in their place. This is particularly helpful when trying to gather input and participation from multiple departments, organizations, or schools. However, ask them to prepare their proxy and offer to have an introductory conversation with the proxy prior to the meeting.
- Assemble an agenda and send it out in advance of the meeting. Use language that is easily understood by everyone in the group. When you assemble the agenda, have a process for soliciting items from among the group. If someone proposes an item that seems irrelevant to the conversation, take the time to ask about it. If it is, indeed, off topic, be straightforward in explaining that. More often than not, the item is related, and you will need to work with the contributor to accurately describe its link to the overall agenda.
- Schedule ample time on the agenda for real discussion and input. Resist the temptation to cram as much as you can into the meeting. If full participation and reflective engagement are your goals, schedule the time necessary for rich conversations to happen. If your meeting is simply updates (no discussion), a meeting format might not be necessary and could be accomplished through some other form. Consider leaving the last points on the agenda for other business from the group and parking lot items (items that arise during the meeting but cannot be addressed and are set aside for another time). If you choose to do this, make sure there is actual time budgeted for these items.
- Decide on the best venue and time for the meeting; do the venue and time allow sufficient access to the meeting or do they preclude people from joining?
- Provide adequate information about how to get to the meeting, including location, directions, parking, building entry requirements, child care, refreshments, and so on.
- Ask if any special arrangements might be necessary (people coming late or leaving early might affect the order of the agenda; dietary restrictions or preferences will affect the menu; if children need to

(*Continues*)

BOX 3.6 (*Continued*)

be present it might affect the tone or language used in the conversation). Ask about any specific support or assistance that is needed to enable someone's attendance and active participation. Create a meeting culture where requesting and arranging accommodations (whether they are dietary requests or working with an interpreter) are the norm and not perceived to be an inconvenience. Underscore that you want each attendee to have what he or she needs to fully participate in the meeting.

- Ask for attendees' preferred format for receiving meeting materials in advance of the meeting. Do not skip this step or give it short shrift. Some people might want the materials electronically, and others might want them in hard copy. Distribute accordingly and be sure to leave adequate time for review if there are materials attendees need to consider before the meeting. If there is reason to believe that not all attendees will be comfortable reading materials, offer a way to have the materials discussed or read aloud in advance of the meeting or as part of the meeting.

During the meeting

- If you do not have good facilitation skills, consider arranging for someone else to run the meeting while you are still learning how to facilitate. Seek professional development for facilitating reflective meetings. It's invaluable to the work of a CEP.
- Set up the meeting for comfort. Arrange seats so people can see each other, ask people to introduce themselves at the beginning, and ensure people know what's on the agenda and the core purpose of the meeting. If the meeting will center on one goal for discussion, consider posting it somewhere visible and reading it aloud periodically.
- If this meeting will become a regularly occurring meeting, consider drawing up ground rules that prioritize inclusion and authentic participation. If this is a one-off meeting, but the content is contentious, take the time to draw up group norms for the discussion.
- Keep the meeting focused, but don't dismiss people's concerns out of hand. You can use a parking lot, which is typically a place in the room where concerns are written down (like a flip chart or whiteboard) that need to be put aside while the conversation continues.

(*Continues*)

BOX 3.6 (*Continued*)

However, create time in the agenda at the end to address the parking lot. You don't need to have a full discussion for each parking lot item, but you do need to decide with the group how each parking lot item will be handled. For example, some items are simply for follow-up by individuals at a later date. Some might require you to meet with the contributor for a lengthier conversation. Some might determine points for the next meeting's agenda and some might require gathering and sending information to the group.

- Check for understanding throughout the meeting. After materials have been presented, ask if there are questions and wait a solid five to seven seconds before moving on. Ensure that everyone has the opportunity to provide feedback. If it's not possible to do so orally, invite people to record questions or concerns on index cards for a postmeeting follow-up.
- Consider using traffic light cards if it's a big meeting. Print a set of three index cards for each person. On a red card, print "I have a question." On a green card, print "I agree." On an orange card, print "Slow down please." Give each attendee a set of cards and talk about how to use them at the beginning of the meeting.
- Leave one empty chair in a highly visible position. At appropriate times, point to the chair and ask, Whose perspective is not being considered in this conversation? or ask, Whom did we not think to invite who may be important to this conversation?
- Employ summary statements once input has been given. "So what I heard the group say is—" and then ask if you heard correctly. Don't recount each individual point but provide a summary that captures the themes of the conversation. Practice finding themes and summarizing them quickly in various settings. Staff meetings are a great place to hone this skill.
- Drive the meeting toward action: Once the group agrees that its feedback is summarized accurately, either propose what actions you as leader will take as a result; catalog the actions that require volunteers; ask the group to list the actions that need to be taken as a result of the discussion and who is best to take those actions; or, if no action is possible because more information is needed, determine what that is, who needs to get it, and how it will be distributed. Record the actions and those responsible for them somewhere visible and also in the meeting notes. Be clear about the outcomes of the meeting.

(*Continues*)

BOX 3.6 (*Continued*)

Postmeeting

- Circulate notes with action steps highlighted and provide opportunities for participants to offer corrections and revisions. Just as with the meeting materials, ask for the best way to provide attendees with the meeting notes.
- It is hoped that your meeting facilitation will prevent having attendees' contributions being sidelined in the conversation. If you suspect someone may have been excluded from the discussion, was not fully heard, or was otherwise limited in their participation, follow up to ask how the person experienced the meeting and if there is anything that can be done to include his or her contribution in the meeting notes or meeting follow-up.
- As part of the notes, offer your reflection on the meaning of the meeting and invite others to do the same. Invite suggestions on how to improve the next meeting.

coupled with strong facilitation and practiced reflective listening. Being able to accurately reflect the diverse input of the group and then lead the group through a consensus-building process to determine what the next steps need to be are key. Making those next steps actionable and following up as necessary will keep people invested from meeting to meeting.

Good meetings, however, are unlikely to catalyze institutional change if they aren't supportive of an overarching strategic plan that outlines change goals. In addition to participating in large institutional strategic planning efforts, CEPs are increasingly using strategic planning to guide the direction of their centers or initiatives. For example, 84% of engagement centers in a study at Carnegie-classified institutions indicate that community or civic engagement is included in their institutional strategic plans (Welch & Saltmarsh, 2013), and strategic planning for the institutionalization of service-learning significantly influences long-term sustainability of such programs (Vogel, Seifer, & Gelmon, 2010). Knowing how to conduct strategic planning is important for CEPs who see themselves as institutional change agents. Strategic planning is a specialized kind of process and skill sets. If sufficient resources are available, we encourage CEPs who lead engagement initiatives or units to hire a consultant skilled in strategic planning to facilitate such efforts. Even if such resources are available, and especially if not, the CEP needs to be familiar with strategic planning (see Box 3.7).

BOX 3.7
Compass Point: Leading Change–G

Suggested Readings

The Society for College and University Planning is a practice community for those who are responsible for implementing and supporting planning processes on campuses and provides a step-by-step guide on strategic planning. See https://www.scup.org/page/index for more resources.

Hinton, K. E. (2012). *A practical guide to strategic planning in higher education.* Ann Arbor, MI: Society for College and University Planning.

Strategic doing: Developed in the context of U.S. regional economic development partnerships, strategic doing helps stakeholders form strategic collaborations that rapidly move through plan, do, learn, adjust cycles.

Morrison, E. (2013, December). *"Strategic Doing": A new discipline for developing and implementing strategy within loose regional networks.* Paper presented at the annual conference of the Australian-New Zealand Regional Science Association International, Hervey Bay, Queensland, University of Southern Queensland, Australia.

Future search, used in many different cultural contexts, is a planning method that brings together large groups of stakeholders over the course of a few days to plan for collaborative, future-focused action.

Weisbord, M., & Janoff, S. (2010). *Future search: Getting the whole system in the room for vision, commitment, and action.* San Francisco, CA: Berrett-Koehler.

We close this chapter with a case study in Box 3.8 to pull together the competencies of change work discussed here.

Deepening Our Critical Commitments: Questions to Ask

Despite knowing a great deal about change methods or planning approaches or despite their degree of familiarity with innovative programs, some people might not have the wisdom to know what change a situation demands. We propose that CEPs have not only technical ability (knowledge and skill) but also critical consciousness that guides their

BOX 3.8
Compass Point: Leading Change–H

Seeking to better infuse the institution's mission throughout the general education experience of its students, campus administrators chose to implement a service-learning requirement for all undergraduates. The requirement was spearheaded by a campuswide committee of faculty and had high support from the Faculty Senate. The Office of Service-Learning was established to support service-learning classes, of which more than 80 were offered each academic year. The office staff were able to point to examples of rich, high-impact service-learning but were also frustrated by some classes that served as a way for students to check the box for a graduation requirement. A student learning outcome assessment study was conducted with service-learning classes across campus. The assessment found that students' disciplinary learning was flourishing in service-learning classes, but students demonstrated minimal civic learning or social responsibility gains. The campus also conducted an interview project with community agencies that worked with service-learning classes and learned that the students helped to build agency capacity, but the agencies wanted more collaboration with faculty and didn't feel the students always had the necessary preparation to be effective in community work. These findings were shared widely among faculty who taught service-learning classes, agencies that worked with those classes, and key administrators. Shortly thereafter, the campus provost chose to retire and a new provost took office. The Office of Service-Learning and its advisory committee felt that the issues with the service-learning requirement warranted a change and needed a compelling way to convince the new provost to pursue a change process. With the provost's support, the Office of Service-Learning and the committee initiated an external review.

The external review involved bringing two peer experts to campus who conducted an exhaustive two-day visit with faculty, students, staff, administrators, community partners, and institutional leaders. Their report confirmed that the quality in service-learning classes was uneven and uncovered underlying issues many people felt were preventing success. Because service-learning was a graduation requirement, some students and degree program directors dismissed it as one of a long list of perfunctory requirements rather than a signature learning experience. There was limited faculty development.

(Continues)

BOX 3.8 (*Continued*)

Greater resources were needed to support partnership coordination and transportation. Perhaps most important, there was lack of clarity about the civic goals of service-learning. The Office of Service-Learning, the advisory committee, and the new provost decided that the service-learning graduation requirement would be discontinued and a new pedagogical model of community engagement would be developed.

Over the next academic year, the office engaged faculty, community partners, and students in a process to develop a new pedagogical model. They began by meeting as a large group to speak about the external review findings. They were asked to offer existing examples of rich, civically oriented service-learning in which partners felt valued and the community and student learning outcomes were strong. They read a series of research briefs about civic learning, civic professionalism, developmentally appropriate student learning, and democratic engagement. They met with field experts who provided them with narratives about what community-based learning looked like at other institutions. Then they split into teams and began drafting a new model. The model was refined through committee discussions. A short video presentation about the model was produced and circulated widely. Then, the director of the office held open forums about the model with each school at the university and with a group of long-time community partners. Forum attendees were asked to come with questions, critiques, and ideas for improvement. Based on that input, the model was further refined.

The new model prioritized civic learning outcomes, learning from and with communities about community concerns, and democratic engagement. The model featured two levels: introductory and advanced. The classes were no longer part of a graduation requirement but were embedded in degree programs that touted the importance of civic learning.

The new model was proposed to the provost eight months after work had begun. It was strongly supported throughout the university and was formally adopted within months. Implementation began quickly thereafter with the launch of a new grant program (modeled after the engaged department work of Kecskes, 2006) offering teams of faculty, administrators, students, and community partners four years of funding to support their planning, course-related costs, transportation, and assessment activities.

(*Continues*)

BOX 3.8 (*Continued*)

- What were the cultural changes embedded in this example? What were the structural changes?
- Describe the organizational learning used in this example.
- What evidence of inclusion, participation, and reflection are present here?
- How did the process ensure that members felt their time and input were valued?
- Think of a condition in your context that requires change. Using this case as an example, imagine the process you would use to implement that change.

work. We close this chapter by offering a list of questions, adapted from Hernandez and Pasquesi (2017), designed to prompt your critical reflection. We encourage you to think about these questions at whatever level of practice (institutional level versus programmatic level) you prefer.

1. Whose agendas determine the development of community engagement programs? Who is included in change processes? To what degree is their input considered alongside those with institutional authority?
2. Are your community engagement practices aligned with the agendas, strengths, challenges, and opportunities of the communities you seek to work with?
3. Is there awareness of the differences among forms of engagement such as charitable activity and community-responsive or collaborative projects with social change work? Are different forms used appropriately?
4. Who benefits from your engagement? Intellectually? Economically? Politically? Socially?
5. Examine the language used to describe engagement at your institution. Does it evoke paternalism? Commodification? Patronization? Does it evoke participation? Collaboration? Equity?

Chapter Four

INSTITUTIONALIZING COMMUNITY ENGAGEMENT ON CAMPUS

I try to be the fixer of situations and I gravitate to people who are institutional misfits. (Jenkins as cited in Guthrie, 2003)

Institutionalization of community engagement is an interesting and complex process that is unique on individual campuses. Weaver and Kellogg (2017) describe the institutionalization of community engagement as "establish[ing] the goals and values of community engagement as norms within the well-established organizational culture of a university campus" and "embedding community engagement within the university as a whole" (p. 119). Over time the role and responsibility of the community engagement professional (CEP) has evolved to include advocating for and facilitating institutionalization. After completing this chapter, those working in the field of community engagement or currently working as CEPs will be able to reflect on the areas (see Table 4.1) in which they are competent and identify areas related to the institutionalization of community engagement they would like to develop further. Those who are new to supporting community engagement or who aspire to enter the community engagement profession will demonstrate awareness and an emerging understanding of these areas of competence.

TABLE 4.1
Competencies and Critical Commitments Associated With Institutionalizing Community Engagement on Campus

4.1 Knowledge of institutional and program evaluation methods 4.2 Knowledge of benchmarks or artifact of institutionalization 4.3 Knowledge of potential funders, grant seeking 4.4 Able to advocate for community engagement and communicate its value, vision, and goals in your context 4.5 Able to communicate institution's brand of engagement (e.g., orientation and animating mission)	4.6 Able to advocate for development of policies that support community engagement 4.7 Able to conceive and implement institutional structures to support engagement 4.8 Able to cultivate a critical mass of supporters for engagement 4.9 Able to empower people within the institutions they serve and to hire and develop good staff	4.10 Able to leverage resources and advocate for community engagement as an institutional priority 4.11 Able to navigate the institution's political environment 4.12 Able to report data to strengthen institutional support 4.13 Able to balance multiple priorities and to plan for short-term and long-term goals 4.14 Embrace respect for community perspectives
Critical Commitments • Able to unveil, name, and challenge contradictions in practice • Able to work within the structural constraints of the institution toward social change		

Working on institutionalization represents a significant shift from a pedagogical framework that is primarily focused on teaching, learning, and scholarship involving faculty and students to a political context working with administrators and other leaders on campus and in the community. Consequently, the CEP must be astutely aware of the cultural, systemic, and top-down and bottom-up political dimensions of institutionalization (Welch, 2016). Welch (2016) described an "institutionalization compass" (p. 64) comprising an array of cultural and systemic factors coupled with "top down" and "bottom up" (p. 65) influences (see Figure 4.1). The CEP can use this compass to navigate the pathway leading to institutionalization by being aware of and understanding these dynamics (see Box 4.1).

Figure 4.1 Institutionalization compass points.

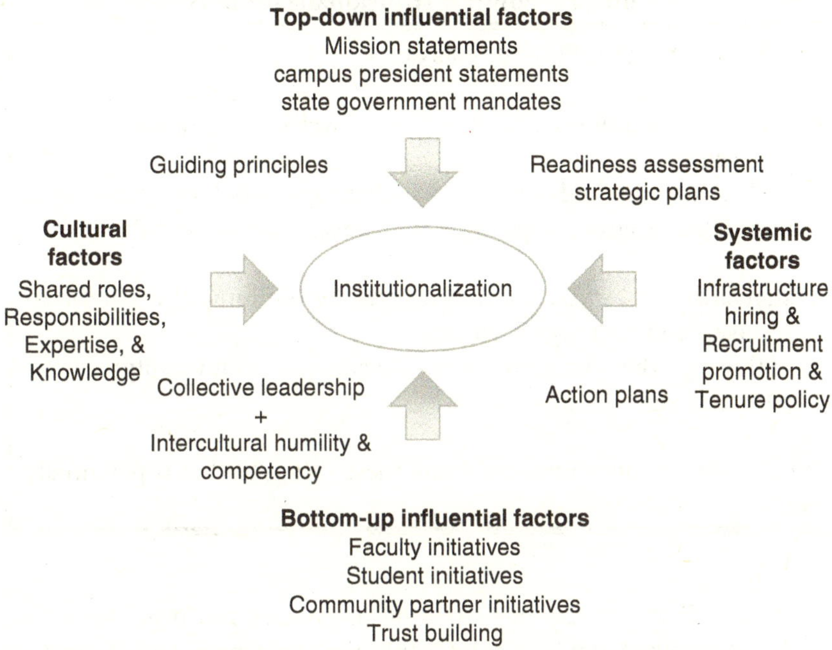

Note. From *Engaging Higher Education: Purpose, Platforms, and Programs* (p. 65), by M. Welch, 2016, Sterling, VA: Stylus. Copyright 2016 by Stylus Publishing. Reprinted with permission.

BOX 4.1

Compass Point: Institutionalization–A

Review the institutionalization compass points in Figure 4.1. Identify and list information and resources already known or readily available to you. Conversely, identify and list information and resources unknown to you and consider how you might obtain them. Share and discuss your two lists with others or with a mentor to help you plan how to navigate institutionalization on your campus.

As effective as institutionalization is, some practitioners fear that institutionalizing will lead to the loss of the work's soulful nature. In some respects, our work and field as a whole have become victims of their own success as manifested in the exponential growth and adoption of community engagement on campuses. Expansion requires administrative and logistical coordination. Similarly, the world has become a much more complex and dangerous place since the advent of the field a generation

BOX 4.2

Compass Point: Institutionalization–B

Think about the benefits and costs of

- creating institutional policy to govern community-campus engagement,
- replicating a method or program so that more people can participate,
- bringing a program or process from a peer's campus onto your own campus,
- standardizing service-learning classes by outlining the criteria to receive a course designation, and
- outlining the process for developing community-campus partnerships.

What is potentially gained by doing these things? What is potentially lost?

ago. This reality now requires attention to policies and procedures that ensure safety for students, faculty, community partners, and those they serve. Our litigious society demands risk assessment and attention to liability that often seems to trump the pedagogical focus and mission of this work. Indeed, the bureaucratic roles and responsibilities associated with institutionalization can seem to overshadow the transformative impact community engagement can have. Once again, an effective CEP must carefully balance the art and science of this work. CEPs must, in essence, do a bit of a dance in weighing potential advantages and disadvantages to formalizing community engagement in the institution. We suggest you reflect further on the costs and benefits of institutionalization by responding to the prompt in Box 4.2.

Now that we have a fundamental understanding of the institutionalization process, we explore the competencies that CEPs must have to facilitate institutionalization.

Knowledge of Institutional and Program Evaluation Methods

Evaluation occurs at the macro and micro levels in an institution. At the macro level, every accredited institution of higher education must successfully go through an external review by knowledgeable colleagues using specific benchmarks and criteria. Likewise, all professional preparation programs (e.g., education, nursing, pharmacy, psychology, and social work) are based on licensure or certification that requires demonstration of specific competencies to be accredited by professional associations and state licensing boards. Research reveals that some form of community or civic engagement is included in all the regional accreditation commission standards (Paton et al., 2014), so be sure to become familiar with the specific wording in your accreditation standards and work to meet them as you advocate for continued institutionalization on your campus.

An effective and strategic CEP will be able to explain to administrators the ways engaged teaching and scholarship meet or address the review standards that are being used. An example is the core values and guiding principles of the Association to Advance Collegiate Schools of Business (2016), which state,

> The school must demonstrate a commitment to address, engage, and respond to current and emerging corporate social responsibility issues (e.g., diversity, sustainable development, environmental sustainability, and globalization of economic activity across cultures) through its policies, procedures, curricula, research, and/or outreach activities. (p. 6)

It is highly unlikely that a dean or program coordinator in a school of business can readily provide that type of documentation, and so it is incumbent on the CEP to assist in this process. The institutional and programmatic review process generally requires an internal or in-house review first followed by a formal review by objective experts outside the institution. The CEP must know, understand, and participate in the process and time lines.

In addition to traditional accreditation review, institutions are now seeking recognition for their community engagement efforts through formal review by outside entities. Four common examples are the application process for the Carnegie Foundation for the Advancement of Teaching's elective classification for community engagement, programmatic evaluation across disciplinary departments and administrative units, external reviews for engagement centers or programs, and internal evaluations of specific programs such as the unit's faculty development program or overall institutionalization efforts. The application process for the Carnegie Community Engagement Classification entails a comprehensive evaluation review that provides additional prestige for the institution after receiving the recognition. Entire institutes and academies hosted and sponsored by Campus Compact and affiliates of the Carnegie Foundation have been devoted to preparing institutions as they apply for these designations. Most institutions employ a team of administrators and faculty to compile a comprehensive set of evidence to demonstrate that institutions meet the criteria and benchmarks.

Similarly, institutional and programmatic evaluation occurs at a microlevel within specific disciplinary departments as well as administrative units across academic affairs and student life, including the campus center for community engagement. An effective CEP is at the ready to assist these offices by providing important data and information related to engaged teaching and scholarship to critically assess the operations and functions. A straightforward example of this is providing the number of courses, students, faculty members, and community partners involved with community engagement as well as the number of hours allocated to engaged teaching and learning. Providing evidence of the impact engaged teaching and scholarship have on students, faculty, and the community is equally important. Specific validated survey instruments used to quantify impact are described in chapter 6. CEPs should consider consulting and working with their Office of Institutional Research to use these measures as part of the regular, annual campuswide assessment process. Related to this, the CEP as a scholar can offer citations and references to research related to the discipline or context being evaluated.

Campus centers for community engagement often undergo external evaluation by preparing a self-study and then inviting peers from the field to perform an external review. Typically, external reviews are motivated by an institutional policy dictating that academic centers or programs undergo external peer evaluation every five or ten years. If this policy does not pertain to your unit, it is still a good idea to propose to your supervisor that an external review will help enhance your unit and the institutionalization of community engagement on the campus. Typically, an external review is guided by a set of questions developed at the unit and institutional level, which are then investigated by two or three peers from outside the institution with knowledge and experience in the field of community-campus engagement. In addition to examining the sufficiency of staffing, funding, unit efficacy, and the ability of the unit to enhance the institution's core mission, other areas for external evaluation include the degree to which the unit embraces and promotes diversity and inclusion, and the degree to which the unit promotes equity in its community engaged work. The National Inventory of Institutional Infrastructure for Community Engagement provides an excellent road map for evaluating engagement centers' functionality when compared with engagement centers at Carnegie classified institutions (Welch & Saltmarsh, 2018).

An effective CEP can provide a comprehensive program evaluation that encompasses a variety of interrelated contexts, settings, and stakeholders. Welch and Plaxton-Moore (in press) proposed a holistic framework of assessing professional development that can be adapted to assess the overall impact of community engagement programs coordinated by campus centers. Because community engagement extends beyond the four walls of the classroom to various settings and constituencies, a holistic framework must explicitly name the elements that should reflect impact. Their holistic framework provides multiple methods that directly and indirectly assess the impact of community engagement. Direct impact assessment provides descriptive statistics such as number of hours, students, courses, partnerships, as well as pre- and postmeasures of faculty or student knowledge of content related to engaged pedagogy or social issues addressed through engaged teaching and scholarship. Indirect assessment involves determining impact in other settings and contexts with participating stakeholders such as students or community partners. Welch and Plaxton-Moore (in press) conceptualized a model that consists of two domains of contexts and stakeholders, four domains, four stakeholders, conceptual framing factors, locus of change and impact, level of expertise, and an impact assessment matrix (see Table 4.2).

Various matrices focusing on the institutionalization of service-learning developed over the past 20 years can be adapted and applied under the broader umbrella of community engagement (McRae, 2015). Holland (1997) developed a matrix consisting of seven factors that can be used to help the institutionalization process. Furco (1999) also developed a developmentally based rubric incorporating five components associated with service-learning beginning with building a critical mass to sustained institutionalization, which he later revised (Furco, 2002). Campus Compact created an institutionalization rubric consisting of 12 characteristics of an engaged campus (Hollander, Saltmarsh, & Zlotkowski, 2000). Pigza and Troppe (2003) enumerated nine indicators and mechanisms for enabling engagement on a college campus. Driscoll (2009) indicated the Carnegie classification of community engagement was designed to provide great flexibility in conceptualizing and institutionalizing community engagement. Some institutions have actually used the application process for the Carnegie classification as a blueprint for institutionalizing community engagement (Welch, 2016). Based on her earlier work, Holland (2009) developed a set of benchmarks tied to the Carnegie classification that could be used

TABLE 4.2
Holistic Framework for Professional Development to Advance and Assess Community Engagement.

Domains	*Factors to Consider*	*Necessary Faculty Competencies*	*Locus of Change*	*Measures of Impact*
STAKEHOLDERS				
Faculty	Discipline Social identity and background Prior life experiences Nature of faculty role (e.g., tenured, adjunct, etc.) Level of professional experience with CES Other professional commitments	Describe CES concepts, terms, and principles (novice) Familiar with CES history and seminal literature (novice) Identify personal motivations and commitments that drive interest in CES (novice) Apply CES principles, theoretical frameworks, and pedagogical strategies when implementing CES (intermediate) Identify potential CES outcomes and a plan for assessing them (intermediate) Develop and deepen cultural competence and critical consciousness (intermediate) Effectively describe CES activities for promotion and tenure review (advanced) Engage in reflection about professional practice and identity through the lens of CES (advanced)	Course design and pedagogical practice Scholarly identity Sense of belonging to community with other CE scholars Behaviors and beliefs rooted in cultural competence and critical consciousness P and T preparation Reflective practice	Pre- and postmeasure of knowledge Course syllabus and related documents that meet designation and incorporate benchmarks of best practice Focus groups and interviews Awards (e.g., Lynton, Ehrlich) Written and oral reflection Faculty participation in PD communities

Students	Social identity and demographics Prior life experiences Developmental stage or level (Constraints on) time (Constraints on) funds Perception of purpose of higher education or degree attainment Perception of community Values and beliefs	Understand need for community-engaged experiences, reflection, and assessment that align with course content and outcomes (novice) Attend to student diversity of student developmental stages, social identities, and life experiences when designing course (intermediate) Integrate community engagement into a class as an integral component of learning process (intermediate) Supplement community experience with content that allows students to reflect on systems of power, privilege, and oppression (intermediate) Effectively facilitate oral and written critical reflection (intermediate) Implement authentic assessment of student learning from CE (advanced)	Student achievement of disciplinary outcomes Student achievement of civic outcomes (knowledge, skills, and dispositions) Students' sense of connection to community Student self-efficacy as a civic actor and social change agent Student civic behaviors Student vocational calling and professional trajectory	Scholarly work products Project deliverables for CP Reflections Surveys Interviews and focus groups Community partner evaluation of student performance
Administrators	Organization structure (chart) Individual roles and responsibilities Power dynamics Disciplinary field Professional pathway and aspirations	Describe community-engaged practices happening across campus (novice) Describe history, principles, and practices of CES in higher education (intermediate) Use data to advocate for funds, policies, and practices that support CES (advanced)	Articulate public purpose of higher education, and specifically CES Know and value existing CEL activities happening at institution Know and value CEL principles, practices, and trends Promote and support CEL	Oral and written public statements Allocation of funds and awards Discussions and interviews Participation in committees, working groups, meetings about CEL

(*Continues*)

TABLE 4.2 (*Continued*)

Domains	*Factors to Consider*	*Necessary Faculty Competencies*	*Locus of Change*	*Measures of Impact*
Community partners	Mission of organization Staffing and leadership Services provided Nature of service (e.g., advocacy, direct service, education) Capacity to form partnerships with courses and host students Community and clients served Funding and budget considerations Partnerships and collaborations with other institutions	Knowledge of potential community partners, their missions and services (novice) Understand community partner role as coeducator (novice) Understand concept of reciprocity (novice) Communicate effectively with community partners about expectations, needs, and challenges of partnership (intermediate) Integrate community partners into course planning, content delivery, and assessment (intermediate) Maintain equitable balance (reciprocity) between student and community outcomes in achievement of CES partnership activities (advanced) Collaborate with community partners to cocreate knowledge, learning experiences, and capacity building opportunities (advanced)	Build capacity to provide services or assess impact Partnership reciprocity Shift power dynamics toward equity Grow awareness of and advocacy for CP work	CP-generated data on outcomes or impact for organization Surveys Focus groups and interviews Written narratives and reflections Student reflections on CP Grants and awards for CE work

CONTEXTS				
Higher education and academic discipline	Existence of journals, texts, conferences, and so on National awards and recognitions Accreditation and assessment Research, reaching, service paradigm History and nature of discipline Relative value of discipline as perceived by various groups	Familiar with CES history and seminal literature (novice) Write and speak about CES work in a compelling way for grants, scholarly articles, and conference presentations (intermediate) Collaborate with colleagues across institutions, disciplines, and communities to produce innovative scholarship on CES (advanced)	Dissemination of CE practices and research across CE field New paradigms of engaged research, reaching, service Transinstitutional and transdisciplinary collaborations More equitable, inclusive, democratic higher education spaces (campuses, conferences, etc.)	Publications Conference presentations Grants National awards and classifications (e.g., President's Honor Roll, Carnegie) Host convenings and conferences
Institutional	Mission and vision Logistics and administration of CE Policies and procedures Culture and values Accreditation status Departmental politics Budget and funding	Connect with campus CE center and other colleagues doing CES (novice) Evaluate scholarly content of CES narratives and scholarship in RPT portfolios (intermediate) Act as a mentor and resource to novice CE faculty (intermediate) Understand institutional support structures and barriers that affect the practice of CES (intermediate) Work in coalition with other CE stakeholders to bring about institutional changes that sustain and enhance CE practices and outcomes (advanced)	Policies and procedures Organization culture and values P and T review guidelines, policies, and practices Funding priorities Whose voice matters Infusion of CE across departments and schools Incentives and reward for CE Recruitment and retention of CE faculty and administrators	Funding for CEL Awards and compensation for faculty Existence of a center or office supporting CEL Engaged departments Survey of faculty, staff, administrators National awards and recognitions (e.g., Carnegie Community Engagement Classification)

(*Continues*)

TABLE 4.2 *(Continued)*

Domains	*Factors to Consider*	*Necessary Faculty Competencies*	*Locus of Change*	*Measures of Impact*
				Community partner representation in decision-making bodies and processes Reports and white papers Institutional self assessment (e.g., NIIICE)
Classroom	Layout of classroom Number of students Structure, format, and timing of course sessions Quarter or semester system Disciplinary content and outcomes	Organize the classroom space to reflect multidirectional teaching and learning (novice) Invite diverse voices by including underrepresented narratives, and community partners and members as guest speakers (intermediate) Recognize and navigate inherent classroom power dynamics based on role, race, class, and other aspects of identity (intermediate) Use a range of techniques to facilitate group discussion and reflection (intermediate) Identify and use appropriate community spaces as classrooms for student learning and integrate community members as course participants and colearners (advanced)	Student engagement Integration of content that reflects diverse voices and perspectives Shift classroom power dynamics toward more democratic, inclusive, equitable paradigm Create space for multiple epistemologies and learning styles	Tracking student participation and completion of service commitments Student reflections Observation of teaching Review of course content Review of course activities and assignments

Community	Assets and resources, challenges and barriers Social justice issues History and current status Demographics and juxtaposition of diverse groups Nature of relationships between service providers and residents or recipients	Recognize community as a collection of diverse groups and individuals with both converging and diverging interests, needs and assets (novice) Understand complex systemic nature of social justice issues (novice) Develop and act in accordance with a commitment to fostering social change (novice) Work effectively with diverse community constituencies (intermediate) Transfer or apply skills to the community to build capacity (intermediate) Leverage CES to support community empowerment and social change (advanced)	Address community-identified priorities and needs Build trust and sustained partnerships between town and gown Build individual and collective capacity of community to drive positive social change	Community presence on campus Faculty and student presence in community Feedback from community members and leaders from surveys, focus groups, interviews Sustained collaborative projects and programs Asset maps Public policy, economic development metrics or interventions resulting from CES collaborations

Figure 4.2 Division of Community Engagement organizational framework at Virginia Commonwealth University.

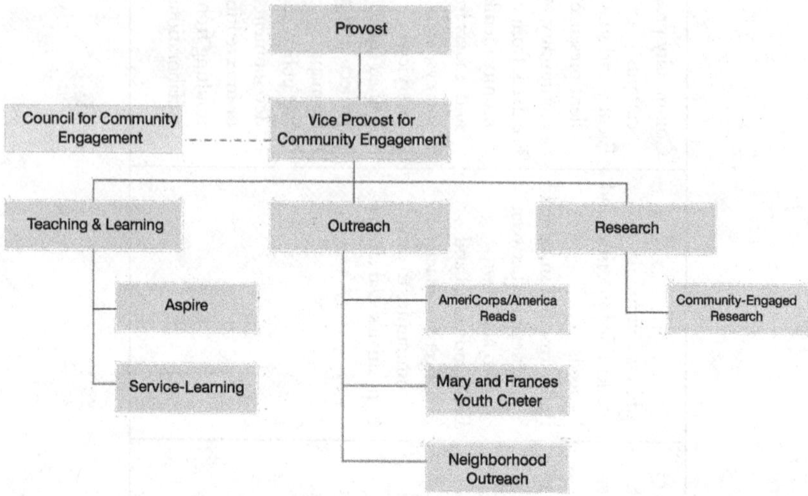

Note: "The University Next Door: Developing a Centralized Unit That Strategically Cultivates Community Engagement at an Urban University," by V. L. Horton, J. L. Early, M. Resler, A. Trussell, & C. Howard, 2016. *Metropolitan Univesities*, 27(1). 101. Reprinted with permission.

to sustain institutionalization efforts. Horton and colleagues (2016) used Kotter's (1995) framework for change to develop a centralized unit and strategic plan to institutionalize community engagement. In Horton and colleagues' model, they created a Division of Community Engagement coupled and affiliated with a Federation for Community Engagement Research to coordinate community engagement at Virginia Commonwealth University, which could serve as a structural template or example for other institutions (see Figure 4.2).

Knowledge of Potential Funders, Grant Seeking

Some large, highly resourced campus centers for community engagement have a staff member dedicated to fundraising and grant writing. However, most centers do not, requiring the CEP to either take on this role and responsibility or to work with a representative from the institution's central offices that support funding, such as offices labeled development, institutional advancement, sponsored research, or grants coordination. If working with another campus unit, it is advisable for the CEP to conduct regularly scheduled meetings, perhaps on a monthly basis, with the liaison from that office. These meetings focus on identifying potential funding agencies, grant opportunities, and donors. Although the CEP is gaining information and insight into funding strategies, the CEP must in turn educate and inform the development officer about the role, responsibilities, and programs of the campus center for community engagement. This provides the CEP and development officer with an opportunity to work together to create a plan for grant writing to foundations and government agencies as well as cultivating potential donors who may make contributions that sponsor or subsidize various programs in the campus center. In the meantime, the CEPs should allocate time and energy to learn more about foundations and grants on their own as a prerequisite step to meeting with the development officer. Two useful online resources are Foundationcenter.org and grantspace.org.

Able to Advocate for Community Engagement

As discussed earlier, it is important to know, understand, and use the institution's mission to make a case for advancing community engagement. Likewise, the CEP must continuously obtain support and advocate for community engagement as an institutional priority. One way to use resources is to obtain and use descriptive data and empirical evidence not only on the impact of community engagement on multiple stakeholders ranging from students to faculty and institution to the community but also on data-informed best practices derived from the literature and professional associations. This approach equips CEPs with empirical evidence and professionally grounded information rather than merely their own personal opinion and desires when negotiating with a direct administrative supervisor. The benchmarks of excellence that manifest themselves in the application for the Carnegie Community Engagement Classification would be perceived as a legitimate and credible source for leveraging resources as well as appealing to the institutional commitment to and desire for external recognition. Results from annual Campus Compact membership surveys can also be used to compare and contrast the types and amounts of resources comparable (and competitive) institutions have. The Council for the Advancement of Standards in Higher Education provides a comprehensive description of standards and guidelines for civic engagement and service-learning programs. Finally, as part of your role as a practitioner scholar, peruse the professional literature for articles that report best practices. Welch and Saltmarsh (2013) provide a comprehensive

BOX 4.3

Compass Point: Institutionalization–C

Obtain a copy of your institution's mission statement. What aspect of the narrative could be used to develop a brief statement, sometimes referred to as an *elevator speech*, that provides a rationale for advancing community engagement in the institution's mission, which could be succinctly presented in the course of an elevator ride between floors? Commit this to memory as well as incorporate it into various documents and your center's website.

yet succinct overview of best practices and infrastructures of campus centers for community engagement.

Every institution has a mission statement, and a CEP must be able to articulate how community engagement reflects and incorporates the mission of the institution as well as the overall public purpose of higher education (Welch, 2016). Some institutional mission statements explicitly describe the role and value of community engagement. Outreach is inherent in the mission of land-grant institutions, which can be incorporated into a more focused emphasis on community and civic objectives. Many faith-based institutions use narrative from their tradition that reflects basic tenets of community engagement. Conversely, some institutions have rather vague statements or language that may actually have a condescending tone that does not reflect mutuality or partnership. Take a moment to reflect on the ways in which your institution's mission informs your approach to advancing community engagement by responding to the prompt in Box 4.3.

Additionally, a CEP should consider incorporating Etienne's (2012) pragmatic arguments for advancing community engagement. He argued that community engagement helps recruit and facilitate the roles and responsibilities of the new faculty who likely experienced some form of community engagement as students themselves and now endeavor to do this work as scholars. He also suggested that community engagement helps to serve the community because the academy is indeed part of the community and a beneficiary of the community's growth. Finally, community engagement advances the overall prestige of the institution as a committed partner to the community while advancing the scholarship of engaged faculty.

Able to Advocate for Policies That Support Community Engagement

For an example of policy and how policy is described on a campus, refer to your faculty handbook. The ability to affect and drive institutional policy is a bit of dance.

On the one hand, arguments must be sound, based on mission, and grounded theoretically. Facts and figures from the literature are powerful tools. Keep in mind, most faculty and administrators are experts and scholars in their fields and therefore have limited knowledge or understanding of key concepts and empirical evidence related to the growing field of community engagement. Do your homework and be prepared to present empirically based information to support your argument. Likewise, scholars are likely to seriously consider accreditation standards or other professional organizations that establish standards that can influence policy and procedures.

On the other hand, persuasion is also effective when it appeals to philosophical tenets and values of the institution and key stakeholders. This is when interweaving the institutional mission into the discussion is important. Thus, an effective CEP must carefully balance and combine the two dynamics when advocating for policies that support community engagement.

An additional challenge is CEPs who are not faculty and therefore have little to no voice in shared faculty governance on curricular matters. Thus, they must incorporate collective leadership in which they marshal influential faculty allies to champion policies determined by shared governance. Members of a faculty advisory board for a campus center for community engagement can legitimately take this role.

Effective advocacy for any cause requires compelling evidence to justify the investment of limited resources to operationalize programs and policy. In essence, a strong advocate must make a strong case not only for why but also for how as well. A good idea by itself is not good enough if the process of implementing it is too daunting or complicated. Ineffective implementation of a policy can backfire and provide argumentative ammunition later to naysayers who will respond, "We told you so," when and if a policy is poorly implemented procedurally.

A fundamental rubric for conceptualizing any argument for or against a policy is to consider and articulate information according to who, what, where, when, why, and how in a brief written proposal or an oral report.

To prepare, strategic CEPs will meet one-on-one with key stakeholders to identify their goals and concerns. The CEP will seek input of faculty, students, community partners, and other key players such as legal counsel or the fiscal officer who are often behind the scenes to gain insight into the pros and cons associated with policy and procedures. We offer a case study for your consideration in Box 4.4.

Able to Cultivate a Critical Mass of Supporters

The CEP must have cheerleaders, especially well-respected faculty who advocate and advance engaged teaching and scholarship (Fisher, 1998). An array of critical constituencies ranging from students, faculty, administrators, families and parents, and community partners can play this important role. Convening a faculty advisory group, partners panel, or student leadership group does more than simply provide advice to the CEP. A group of committed faculty also becomes a liaison and champion of engaged teaching and scholarship in their own departments and disciplines as well as in other committees and settings such as the Faculty Senate. Over time after a trusting relationship has been established, a cohort of community partners can speak publicly about the value of working with the institution and help shape the ways engagement serves the institution's and community's interests. Student leaders will attest to the impact their participation and involvement has had on them and help prioritize student leadership efforts.

Therefore, it is imperative for a CEP to know and use what matters to each of these groups to help obtain support. For example, a university president is likely to be interested in the recognition and prestige associated with community engagement and how pedagogical forms of community engagement enhance student persistence and employment after graduation. The CEP must be prepared to educate the president or provost on the Carnegie Community Engagement Classification as well as provide

BOX 4.4

Compass Point: Institutionalization–D

> Your Faculty Senate is reviewing a proposal to allocate a portion of student fees to support cocurricular community engagement programs. You have been invited to make a five-minute presentation to the senate on the proposal and respond to questions. How would you prepare to present a compelling argument? What would your presentation advocate and why?

empirical evidence on the trend of women faculty and faculty from diverse backgrounds leaning toward pursuing engaged teaching and scholarship (Eagan et al., 2014), which in turn may help recruit a more diverse faculty. Once these factors are known, the CEPs must carefully and repeatedly articulate the value of engaged teaching and scholarship in their institution. They become champions for this work because of the impact it has not only on learning, scholarship, and the community but also on pragmatic and political fronts. See Box 4.5 to consider what matters to various stakeholders and constituencies.

Able to Empower People and Hire and Develop Good Staff

Empowering an engagement center staff nicely embodies the integration of discrete supervisory skills and the art of leadership. It is important to have competent professionals working at the campus center who can carry out the duties clearly and carefully articulated in job descriptions. Over time, a CEP may encourage staff members to identify a project or initiative related to their job description that could be incorporated into their roles and responsibilities. Although this may initially appear like more work, this type of empowerment often actually improves the overall quality of work production, as the staff member is professionally stimulated and invigorated. After a pilot period, this new role and responsibility may be included in the staff member's job description.

Above and beyond the supervision of staff, an effective CEP nurtures the personal and professional development of the individuals working in the center through mentorship. Ideally, a portion of the center budget is allocated to staff members' professional development, allowing them to attend a local, regional, national, or even an international conference. After returning to the office, staff members are invited to report on their takeaways during a staff meeting or explore specific ideas heard at the conference during a one-on-one weekly check-in meeting that could be part of their role and responsibilities. Similarly, and at a smaller, microlevel scale, effective CEPs allocate time and resources for in-house professional development activities that benefit the entire office, either through shared reading of an article or books or watching short videos during staff meetings. Many campus centers allocate time in the summer just prior to the beginning of the academic year for a staff retreat either on or off campus. Take a moment to reflect on supervision and mentorship by responding to the prompts offered in Box 4.6.

BOX 4.5
Compass Point: Institutionalization–E

Take a moment to think about and make a list of what matters to each of the following constituencies. Then reflect on how you might explain the value of engaged teaching and scholarship to that specific group that would garner their support. Some examples in the context of a campus president have been provided to help you begin.

Constituency	*What Matters?*	*Response*
President and provost	Prestige and recognition Recruiting diverse faculty interested in community engagement	Carnegie classification Etienne (2012) pragmatic arguments Eagen and colleagues' (2014) study documenting growth of engaged scholarship by faculty of color
Administrators		
Faculty		
Students		
Parents and families		
Donors and alumni		
Community partners		

BOX 4.6

Compass Point: Institutionalization–F

Compare and contrast *supervision* and *mentorship*. What are the essential features of each? How does one go about mentoring staff in ways that empower them and inspire them to do this work?

The process of empowering staff is an art that involves a delicate balance of avoiding the overbearing micromanagement of personnel activities and instead promoting open communication and coaching. Staff want and need feedback and support on a regular basis. They desire to be valued and heard as well as have an opportunity to contribute and grow. Conversely, they rightly resist and resent behaviors that appear to be micromanaging. Two effective strategies that promote mentorship while maintaining oversight of roles and responsibilities include weekly one-on-one check-in meetings and weekly staff meetings.

One-on-one check-in meetings are typically 30 to 60 minutes long. They are consistently scheduled for the same day and time of week to instill a routine and convey to a staff member that this time is important and devoted specifically to that person and his or her work. It helps to maintain notes or a record of each meeting with each staff member either in a digital file or hard copy format in a three-ring binder, for example. This not only serves as a record of what was discussed but also helps to monitor the progress of certain projects as well as keep track of next steps (see Figure 4.3 for an example template).

Regularly scheduled staff meetings at the same time, on the same day, and at the same location each week provide an opportunity to cultivate an office culture and sense of community. Despite everyone's busy schedule, this is one time when everyone in the office is at the same place at the same time. The science of effective staff meetings involves agendas and efficient use of time. The art of effective staff meetings entails a safe climate for discussion and celebrating each other and each other's work. Although it may initially seem like an inefficient use of limited time, beginning a staff meeting with quick round robin check-ins and updates of everyone's personal and work life sends them a message of their personal importance. Likewise, allocating 5 to 10 minutes for collective reflection activities models and demonstrates not only your commitment to the practice of reflection but also your willingness to invest time and care in cultivating a culture of self-care in the office. The reflection activity can be rotated and can range from a poem, song, video clip, essay, or photograph that is inspirational and encourages a discussion. These activities and approaches are illustrated in the case study contained in Box 4.7.

Figure 4.3 Template for weekly one-on-one check-in meeting with staff.

Name ____________________ Date ______________

Program ____________________

Discussion Items:
Report Notes:
To Do/Follow Up:

Able to Leverage Resources

Navigation of politics, advocacy for community engagement, and development of resources have been addressed in other sections of this chapter. Competence in those areas is crucial to the CEP's ability to advocate for community engagement as an institutional priority. Typically, campus priorities are set by the institution's leaders and shared governance processes,

BOX 4.7
Compass Point: Institutionalization–G

Identify specific concepts and practices of empowering staff in the following example.

The Walden Center coordinates the curricular and cocurricular community engagement programs at a medium-size public institution with a staff of seven: one full-time director, one full-time administrative assistant, two full-time cocurricular program coordinators, two full-time curricular program coordinators, and one part-time development officer shared with another office. The elected student president of the center also attends and participates in the weekly staff meeting.

A week prior to the academic year, the entire staff meets off campus at a nearby park that includes an indoor meeting space. Using a potluck approach, the staff plan and share a lunch along with midmorning and afternoon refreshments. The group reviews a master calendar of key events and tasks for the year. Each staff member names his or her personal and professional goals and seeks input and suggestions from coworkers. They collectively identify a book they will read and discuss together during a staff meeting on the first week of the month.

The director begins each Monday morning meeting with the administrative assistant to review the week's activities, prepare the weekly staff meeting agenda, and discuss progress regarding ongoing projects. By midmorning, the director meets with the cocurricular staff for an hour for updates on their activities followed by another meeting with the curricular staff for their updates. Following lunch, the director meets with the development officer for an hour. The director maintains records and notes for each meeting and encourages staff to do the same so they are all on the same page. The director reviews notes from past check-in sessions for updates on previous discussions regarding specific actions.

Each Wednesday, the entire staff meets at 1:00 p.m. in a conference room outside the center for a 90-minute staff meeting. The staff does not schedule other appointments, meetings, or site visits during this time. Phone and other electronic devices are turned off to create and promote presence at the meeting. Each meeting begins with a brief reflection activity that individual staff members take turns facilitating. The topic and format vary and typically reflect the personality and interests of the individual. Following the reflection activity, the staff quickly gives updates on their professional and, at times, personal

(*Continues*)

BOX 4.7 (*Continued*)

lives. This also provides an opportunity for celebration of birthdays or giving condolences for a family member's death. About 20 to 30 minutes are allocated during the first Wednesday of the month to continue the book discussion. The office culture also has a tradition of passing around a stuffed toy owl named Woo Hoo! to recognize and celebrate the work of their coworkers. For example, the stuffed animal was awarded to the new administrative assistant who successfully and quietly coordinated her first luncheon event for community partners. The trophy will sit on her desk until she forwards it in the same spirit and fashion to another coworker in the office.

The remainder of the meeting follows the agenda that was developed by the director and administrative assistant following an invitation or request for agenda items from the staff during their weekly one-on-one check-in meetings.

The Walden Center staff meetings always begin and end on time, even if all the agenda items were not covered. Staff rarely miss a staff meeting and do so only if they are ill or have an urgent family or health matter that interferes with the scheduled meeting.

In what ways does this demonstrate empowerment to nurture competent staff?

- What, if anything, surprised you? Are there aspects of this case study you currently incorporate or would like to incorporate? If so, what are they and why?
- What aspects of supervision and mentorship would you add?

We suggest reviewing and reflecting on this case study with your team.

most frequently as some form of strategic planning. Institutional priorities are also shaped by the institution's accreditation process and when new institutional leaders are hired. It is critical for the CEP to seek opportunities to be included in institutional strategic planning, institutional accreditation self-studies, and interviewing or orienting new leaders for the institution. This may require some form of self-advocacy such as asking a supervisor to be included or seeking approval to meet with newly hired institutional leaders to inform them of the importance of community engagement at the institution. CEPs who don't have access to these opportunities can approach the key institutional influencers who are connected to community engagement. For example, faculty leaders are often part of hiring, accreditation, and strategic planning processes. Community leaders often meet with new institutional leaders for orientation purposes. Student leaders often hold seats on hiring committees and strategic planning committees.

Likewise, it is also useful and strategic to be creative in using limited and coveted resources on campus and be willing to come up with different ideas and share resources. This might include proposing using a half-time administrative assistant from another office or graduate students to fulfill internship requirements to help meet internal office operations. Finally, consider seeking additional financial resources to support programs and operations. Work with your development office to identify grants as well as potential donors and sponsors. A specific type of program may appeal to and resonate with an alumnus or a donor.

Able to Navigate Institution's Political Environment

Similar to partisan politics, institutional politics involves access and the use of limited resources to advance a specific agenda. Beyond the ability to navigate the organizational structure of the institution, the CEP must be able to traverse the political waters and currents on campus, which requires knowing who the formal and informal leaders are. Formal leaders are typically high-level administrators such as the president or provost as well as midlevel administrators such as deans and department chairs. An additional and related factor is an awareness of the degree to which the campus culture is centralized or decentralized. Although administrators wield a degree of power, the Faculty Senate and other shared governance procedures drive virtually all curricular and academic program decisions. Therefore, CEPs must have their finger on the pulse of not only the Faculty Senate but also the people across campus who influence shared governance decisions. This enables the CEP to ascertain what matters to specific constituencies. The only way to accomplish this kind of political reconnaissance is to attend Faculty Senate meetings when possible and engage in informal conversations with midlevel administrators or informal faculty leaders on a regular basis. A key legitimate use of a CEP's time and budget includes conversations over coffee and lunch. Conferring with a faculty advisory group is another efficient way to monitor campus politics. A classic and long-standing political tension has existed between academic affairs and student affairs (Jacoby, 2015) in which the latter is often perceived by faculty as less relevant to teaching and scholarship (Welch, 2015). It is incumbent on the CEP to be in contact with colleagues in student affairs and explore ways to share resources and possible partnerships that meet the priorities of both units in times of limited funds and resources.

Able to Report Data

The CEP must be able to document the impact of and return on the investment the institution makes to community engagement, which includes providing quantitative and qualitative data. Documentation data can be provided through an annual report made available to the administration, faculty, community partners, alumni, and donors. Documentation can also be reported on the center's website and newsletters.

Quantitative information may include the number of students, faculty, hours, community agencies, and clients involved in community engagement each semester. These numbers can be represented as dollars invested by multiplying the number of hours by the current federal hourly rate and value of volunteer service (see https://independentsector.org/resource/the-value-of-volunteer-time/). These types of data will be useful in annual reports and grant proposals. This pragmatic bottom-line information is what many administrators need and want. It also appeals to various stakeholders in business and finance.

Gathering other quantitative data might involve a partnership with your Office of Institutional Research, which typically conducts an array of surveys and demographic analyses related to aspects of community engagement. Quantitative data includes result from student surveys that document important nonacademic development in areas such as attitudes and behaviors toward diversity, civic engagement, and even spirituality. Useful instruments for this purpose include the Civic Attitudes and Skills Questionnaire (Moely et al., 2002) and the National Assessment of Service and Community Engagement (Johnson, Levy, Cichetti, & Zinkiewicz, 2013; Sienna College Research Institute, 2018).

Another form of quantitative data can be derived from correlational analysis on various factors such as student retention, grade point average, graduation rates, and employment by comparing students involved with community engagement through courses or cocurricular programs with students who are not enrolled in those courses or participating in those activities.

Faculty, administrators, and CEPs tend to focus on cognitive or academic measures to assess impact on students. Sterk-Barrett (2015) offered a unique and alternative approach to traditional cognitive factors by assessing the impact community engagement had on students' spiritual development. Students at Boston College, a Jesuit university, are required to take a course in philosophy and theology. Sterk-Barrett conducted a mixed-methods study to document the impact of service-learning participation on spiritual growth among 272 undergraduates in the Boston College PULSE Program, a service-learning program designed to educate students on social injustice by working with marginalized populations and community organizations through courses in the departments of philosophy and theology. The study was designed to answer the following: Did spiritual growth occur among undergraduates participating in service learning? Which aspects of the service-learning experience related to the occurrence of spiritual growth? What role did challenge and support play in the process of spiritual growth? Similarly, Sterk-Barrett also used the College Students' Beliefs and Values instrument (Astin, Astin, & Lindholm, 2011) as pre- and postmeasures in which the components of the service-learning experience related to spiritual development were analyzed quantitatively. Interviews were also conducted with 11 study participants whose results revealed high or low levels of change on the spiritual development factors. Quantitative and qualitative results revealed significant spiritual growth for students who participated in the PULSE program.

On a microlevel, simple pre- and postmeasures conducted in community engagement courses or cocurricular programs can document student growth. If possible, those measures can be compared with non-community-engagement courses and programs for a quasi-experimental study to determine if there is a significant difference among students' self-reported attitudes, behaviors, and knowledge.

It is also important to quantify and document the impact on faculty and community partners. Unlike the student measures described previously, there are few standardized instruments to use with faculty and community partners. Consequently, it is important for CEPs to gather and maintain a database of important indicators of impact such as a list of faculty publications and presentations to demonstrate contributions to a disciplinary field. Similarly, a CEP should consider archiving a list and abstract of service-learning course projects and other forms of engaged scholarship that have contributed to capacity building in the community. This includes compiling a list of community partner objectives for service-learning courses and community-based research initiatives that have been undertaken.

BOX 4.8
Compass Point: Institutionalization–H

> What are some tangible examples and evidence of soft data on the impact of community engagement you could use to solicit continued support at your institution?

Qualitative data can consist of anecdotal reports, reflection entries, a report of deliverable products that community partners received through community engagement, and interviews or focus groups. Excerpts from student reflection are an often neglected yet powerful indicator of impact. Although it is important to incorporate quantifiable documentation of impact, including human stories that put a face on the data is equally effective. This includes testimonials or satisfaction reports from community partners and those they serve. The adoption of a product developed by students and faculty is a form of tangible evidence of impact. Other forms of soft data include reporting publications and presentations made by faculty doing engaged teaching and scholarship. For example, a computer science class worked with a local wildlife center and sanctuary to develop a cell phone application through a Science Education for New Civic Engagement and Responsibility grant that could be used by local residents to identify wildlife. Providing a hands-on educational and service-learning experience for students, the product was readily adopted by the organization and widely publicized, giving the college and community agency increased visibility documenting its public relations impact (Lindsay Wildlife Museum, 2015). Reflect further on these sorts of data by responding to the prompt in Box 4.8.

Able to Balance Multiple Priorities and Plan for Goals

An engagement unit has many things going on at once, all of which need coordination by the CEP. Added to this are the priorities and activities of the institution as well as community partners who interact with engagement activities and involve the CEP. This requires the CEP to be able to balance a variety of internal and external priorities while planning to meet short- and long-term goals using three key tools and skills.

The first is an action plan that consists of a goal statement and a series of steps framed by who does what, when, and where (e.g., see Figure 4.4). A written plan literally puts everyone on the same page to monitor the

Figure 4.4 Sample action plan.

GOAL:	Develop and implement a semester-long faculty development learning community for 6 to 10 instructors consisting of three half-day retreats to develop a course proposal/syllabus for a new service-learning course to be incorporated into the new core curriculum next academic year.

WHO	Does WHAT	With What	WHEN	OUTCOME & DATE	Done
Center Director + VP for Faculty Development	Identify & obtain $500 per participant for honorarium	Meeting to review faculty development plan & budget	April 2016	$5K obtained & committed by end of fiscal year	X
Center Administrative Assistant	Review calendar for possible half-day retreats	Campus facilities venue website	April 2016	Venue identified and reserved	
Center AA	Meets with catering to plan lunch & snacks	Campus catering on-line menu & fees	May 2016	Menu & snacks selected	
Academic Program Coordinator	Prepares curriculum materials	Center library resources	May 2016	Completed packet of training materials	
Center Director & Academic Program Coordinator	Draft RFP inviting faculty participants		May 2016	Draft reviewed & approved by VP	

progress of the work. The action plan serves as a checklist, periodically monitored and reviewed. Developing an action plan involves brainstorming a list of necessary resources and tasks and then arranging them in chronological order.

The second tool and skill is a personal or master calendar for the center or program related to the action plan. A calendar provides a short and long view of things to do and things to come. It is important to use a bookend approach when looking at and identifying a specific date for a scheduled event or meeting, looking at not only the date in question but also the day before and after the tentative date to determine if other time- and resource-intensive tasks are already scheduled that may interfere with the new calendar item. For example, April 5 might be currently open for a meeting with the vice provost, but the deadline for a major grant is due the next day. A strategic CEP anticipates stress as well as last-minute work and will attempt to schedule the important meeting for the following day if possible.

The CEP and staff should also refer to the campus master calendar to note important dates, tasks, and events that will affect center operations. An efficient campus center staff plans for incremental steps and mini deadlines to provide ample time to complete tasks. A useful exercise is to mark all standing events, tasks, and deadlines on a master calendar, which often reveals interesting patterns or factors worthy of consideration. For example, spring tends to be a very busy time as programs and projects wrap up, coupled with annual end-of-year celebration events and activities such as preparing annual reports, assisting faculty and community partners as service-learning projects draw to a close, and interviewing to recruit new student leaders for the upcoming academic year. In reviewing the master calendar, the staff collectively identified the cluster of important tasks and activities in the month prior to final exams at the end of the academic year. One of those was an annual celebration event recognizing outstanding student leaders, faculty, community partners, and alumni. Although important, it competed for time and energy on other critical work. The group collectively decided to move the event to February, which provided not only breathing room for other end-of-year work but also a bright spot during the winter doldrums and low energy that students often experience nearly two weeks into a new semester.

The third key and the most difficult skill is the ability to say no. There are times and situations when the best thing a CEP can do to help is to recognize that limited time and resources may actually be detrimental to other initiatives. It may very well be in the best interests of everyone to acknowledge the importance of the work while explaining why it is not possible or feasible to participate in the initiative or project at this time.

More important is how one says no. Always explain why and offer to participate at a later date when other competing priorities have passed.

Respect Community Perspectives

Although institutionalization of community engagement is primarily concerned with how it becomes pervasive and core at a campus, institutionalization also affects the communities that will be involved in the results of institutionalization. It is critical for CEPs to remind campus stakeholders that community perspectives need to be taken into account as the campus institutionalizes community engagement. A significant paradigm shift toward mutuality and democratization in the practice and ethos of community engagement is embracing and including community perspectives. In this way, we view community partners as public scholars with a unique expertise that makes a meaningful contribution to cocreating new knowledge that can be applied in authentic settings to promote social change. This manifests itself as a partnership in which community partners have a voice in the engaged work. Historically, the academy has imposed a positivistic, expert model that often smacks of charity that presumably helps those in need at best or perpetuates oppression and injustice at worst. Students often come away with valuable learning experiences to complete courses or requirements for their majors leading to a career that may be at the expense of the community. Likewise, faculty often conduct research on the community that leads to their own professional advancement, but the community receives little or no benefit from the efforts. Such practice reflects a deficit-based perception of the community that can be readily exploited for the unilateral benefit of students and faculty. As a result, community agencies and residents are often suspicious of the academy's motives. Representatives from community agencies and even residents of neighborhoods are invited to the proverbial table for discussion regarding implementation and institutionalization of community engagement. Chapter 9 provides a detailed look at cultivating high-quality community-campus partnerships.

Deepening Our Critical Commitments: Questions to Ask

Two critical commitments include being able to unveil, name, and challenge contradictions in practice and being able to work within the structural constraints of the institution toward social change. As a CEP endeavors to honor these critical commitments, two deep and related questions emerge. One is philosophical and the other is pragmatic.

First, it is important for you as a CEP to not only know and understand the public purpose of higher education as a whole and of your institution in particular but also to know how to articulate this to others on your campus. The commodification of higher education and the array of complex factors affecting colleges and universities make it difficult, if not impossible, for educators to recall and honor their mission to serve society. These issues include financial challenges, student enrollment and retention, diversity and equity, and reputation, to name a few. Therefore, it is incumbent on the CEP to identify and point out contradictions between the public purpose of higher education and the practices that undermine efforts to advance community engagement. How can and will you articulate the importance of community engagement in this framework of challenges that has captured the attention of administrators? How can you diplomatically and skillfully challenge these practices?

Second, it is important to realize that your goal of institutionalizing community engagement is in direct competition with other important initiatives across campus also vying for limited resources. How does one make a strong, data-based argument for institutional support and resources when there is so little to go around? How does one make the case for a concept and approach that as presented earlier is largely unknown or misunderstood by faculty and administrators? What are the benefits and who benefits from this work? Speaking broadly and philosophically is as important as it is passionate, but realistic and pragmatic arguments must also be presented.

Chapter Five

KNOWING COMMUNITY ENGAGEMENT ADMINISTRATION

Although focusing on the administrative structure of engagement is less appealing to many faculty and others on the front lines of community interaction, and indeed abhorrent to some, it cannot be denied that the way institutions align leadership responsibilities and their authority over strategy and resource allocation will in many ways determine where engagement fits into higher education's future. (White, 2016, p. 243)

There are two aspects to administration: knowing and doing. Knowledge of this work is multifaceted and multidimensional. At a core foundational level, effective community engagement professionals (CEPs) must know who they are, what guides them as engaged professionals, and how they arrived at this vocation. This knowledge and insight will guide you on your journey as engaged professionals. With a greater understanding of themselves, CEPs expand their knowledge and perspective to include a theoretical understanding of the methods of community-campus engagement coupled with insight into their institution's mission and infrastructure and how it achieves the public purpose of higher education and reflects the history of engagement as presented in chapter 2. In other words, knowing, as this chapter argues and demonstrates, is a prerequisite to doing, as described in chapter 6. Knowing

TABLE 5.1
Competencies and Critical Commitments Associated With Knowing Community Engagement Administration

5.1 Knowledge of context, self, institution, environments external to institution, history of engagement 5.2 Knowledge of community-engaged pedagogies, including history, methods, underlying theories, and community challenges that may be addressed through community-engaged pedagogies	5.3 Knowledge of community-engaged scholarship, including history, methods, underlying theories, and community challenges that may be addressed through community-engaged scholarship 5.4 Knowledge of civic skills	5.5 Knowledge of infrastructure and program models for community engagement 5.6 Knowledge of institutional policies that may effect community engagement (e.g., faculty handbook, student handbook, etc.) 5.7 Embrace critical thinking 5.8 Embrace visionary thinking
Critical Commitments • Able to unveil and disrupt unequal power structures • Able to name injustices and power differentials		

includes an awareness and acknowledgment not only of the benefits and qualities of this work but also of its potential limitations and liabilities.

After completing this chapter, those working in the field of community engagement or currently working as CEPs will be able to reflect on the areas in which they are competent (see Table 5.1) and identify areas they would like to develop further. For those who are new to supporting community engagement or aspire to enter the community engagement profession, they will demonstrate awareness and emerging understanding of these areas of competence.

Developing Deep Context Knowledge

The kind of clarity necessary to balance attention to administrative details while emphasizing the purposeful change work of community engagement comes from intentional practice. Harper (2011) characterizes intentional

BOX 5.1
Compass Point: Knowing Administration–A

Reflect for a moment on how disciplinary training and community practice knowledge inform CEPs' approaches to their work. For example, a CEP has a bachelor's degree in sociology, a graduate degree in community mental health counseling, and a doctoral degree in educational leadership. These disciplinary frames orient her thinking in significant ways. Systemic and social theories draw her attention to the ways social problems are multideterminant and to the importance of critical social analysis, the attention to process and group dynamics influences how she understands collaborative ventures, and learning theory and organizational development influence her construction of programs and initiatives. Imagine how different her work might be if her disciplinary preparation had instead included history, multimedia design, and student affairs. Her work would still be high in quality and civic in nature, but the understandings, emphases, and tools she brings would be different from those she currently employs. What is your disciplinary training? What community practice knowledge do you draw on? How do these shape your approach to the work?

practice as "reflectively and deliberately employing a set of strategies to produce desired educational outcomes" (p. 288). He goes on to say that intentional practice is reflective and actionable, and it results in effective practice. We propose that cultivating a deep knowledge of the foundational concepts that animate our work is the first step in establishing the kind of intentional practice that yields effective administration in the midst of the whirlwind.

The foundational concepts include knowing about the specific context we find ourselves in, including our own preparation, history, and strengths as well as those of our institution and the communities with whom the institution is working. It also includes knowing the history of community-campus engagement.

In regard to self-reflection, CEPs must be clear about the disciplinary training as well as the "community practice knowledge" and its embedded civic capacities that have shaped their approach (Dostilio & McReynolds, 2015, p. 114). Those of us who have postsecondary education have some form of disciplinary or interdisciplinary training, which influences how we understand (theoretical perspectives) and approach (framework of skills and methods) our work.

However, CEPs are not fully shaped by their disciplinary training or academic preparation. Having "community practice knowledge and its embedded civic capacities" (Dostilio & McReynolds, 2015, p. 114) is equally important. Community practice knowledge is knowing how communities and community development work firsthand. The civic capacities associated with community development include knowing how to develop familiarity with a community, how to have a dialogue, how to build consensus, how to collaboratively make decisions, and knowing a community's political and resource landscape. A CEP can emerge from any number of professional backgrounds, academic or otherwise. As such, each of us brings a rich and diverse array of experiences and perspectives. For example, imagine what a returning Peace Corp volunteer or community organizer and activist can contribute to academia. Conversely, CEPs emerging from community contexts must become aware of and incorporate aspects of academic culture to be effective. Specific civic skills are discussed in chapter 6, but knowing one's disciplinary lenses and community practice history is critical in understanding how to approach engagement and perhaps even knowing the blind spots. Reflect further on how your background may inform your approach to your work in Box 5.1 and Box 5.2.

Knowing the history of your institution and the communities it works with is vital to work that is responsive to its cultural context. You need to know the mission of your institution, its institutional type (land grant, comprehensive, community college, liberal arts, research intensive, faith tradition, etc.), the story of its founding, and the history it has with its broader communities. At first blush and from a perfunctory technical approach, this can and should be easily accomplished by reviewing your institution's website. However, an additional nuanced approach that reflects the art and craft of this work is to carve out time to meet with formal and informal leaders on campus and in the community to gain historical and cultural insights. As discussed in more detail later in this chapter, the storytelling process not only paints a portrait of place but also

BOX 5.2

Compass Point: Knowing Administration–B

> What formative experiences have shaped your approach to community engagement? What civic skills do you possess? Which might you need to further develop?

lays the important relational foundation necessary to effectively work with these individuals later in your role as a CEP.

Communities your campus seeks to engage might include geographic communities (neighborhoods or regions), communities of identity (e.g., senior adults or vulnerable children), or communities of shared interest (e.g., stakeholders who seek the economic vitality of your region). Knowing the history of how your institution has engaged with these communities as well as the community's history means consulting data as well as developing relationships, having conversations, and collecting stories. The grand tradition of the listening tour cannot be understated. Often CEPs will arrange to meet with a variety of campus-based stakeholders when they are new to a position or about to undertake a new initiative. We have found it is also important to do the same with members of the community you are hoping to engage. This approach is further enhanced by requesting a walking tour of the neighboring communities, which could include meeting formal and informal community leaders at a nearby diner or a community or religious center. You can find additional information sources to help augment your listening tour in Box 5.3.

BOX 5.3

Compass Point: Knowing Administration–C

1. Review your institution's Carnegie Classification (its basic classification, undergraduate or graduate instructional program, enrollment profile, size, and setting). What does this institutional profile tell you about the ways community engagement is positioned to support the institution's purposes and identity?
2. Where can you find a history of your institution, including the story of how it was founded? What is your institution's mission statement? How do the history, founding, and mission provide support for community engagement?
3. What is the history and mission of your unit?
4. List the communities people on campus seek to work with. Does this list differ from unit to unit, or is there consistency across campus? Now list the communities your unit seeks to work with. Are there other units on campus that work with these same communities?
5. Where can you collect data and from whom can you collect stories about the history your campus has with the communities your unit chooses?

Knowledge of Community-Engaged Pedagogy and Scholarship

It is important for you as a CEP to have a fundamental knowledge of the forms and methods of community engagement associated with the academic mission of higher education, namely, teaching and research. In this section, we offer some introductory information about community-engaged approaches and scholarship, including the histories of how they developed, underlying theories that inform them, and how they might be applied in your local community context. If your profile of responsibilities is focused on cocurricular work with students, the development of strategic partnerships, or the work of place-based programs, cultivating deep knowledge of student development, partnership development, or place-based strategies is critical (see chapters 7, 9, and 10).

Community-engaged scholarship refers to an array of scholarly work (including teaching, research, and creative activity) that involves community engagement. Boyer (1990) coined the term and the concept of scholarship of engagement as teaching or research methodologies that incorporate the rich knowledge and resources of higher education to address social and community needs. There are many names for these pursuits: community-engaged research, community-based participatory research, public scholarship, service-learning, and community-based learning, among others. It is critically important for you to be well versed in these methods if you are working with faculty or colleagues who are planning learning experiences for students or conducting community-based forms of inquiry.

Community-Engaged Pedagogy

The rich history and tradition of experiential education have played an important role in the evolution and emergence of community engagement. Swaner (2014) acknowledged Dewey's (1938) conceptualization of learning as an active process rather than passively assimilating information as a key tenet of experiential education designed to promote a democratic society. Deans (1999) invokes Freire's (1970) concepts of praxis and the development of critical consciousness as central to the ability of experiential education to connect individual learning to social change. Some theories that underlie the exact design of such learning experiences include constructivism (Vygotksy, 1980), in which individuals use language and experience as "tools" to construct meaning, which leads to higher thinking skills; active learning (Kolb, 1984), in which a cycle of experience, reflection, integration, and application is employed to integrate knowledge and experience; and transformation learning (Hart, 2009), in which students' attitudes and behaviors are changed along with their cognition through a sequential process of pursuit and accumulation of information, direct application that leads to mastery of concepts, integrating intuitive and analytic behavior, understanding, and wisdom by blending truth with ethics on how to be. The transformative process that occurs through experiential education can be expanded from a traditional student-centric focus to include a mutual benefit to communities that reflects and embodies the public purpose of higher education when those stakeholders are included as coëducators and public scholars (Welch, 2017).

Community-engaged pedagogy can be conducted in a variety of ways and contexts (see Table 5.2). Furco (1996) identified five approaches: volunteerism, community service, internships, fieldwork, and service-learning. Many course or credit-bearing approaches have been characterized by Kuh (2008) as high-impact practices because of the pedagogical significance they can have for students' learning and include service-learning or community-based learning, undergraduate research, internships, first-year experiences, learning communities, diversity or global learning, and capstone courses. Research suggests these high-impact practices facilitate and promote deeper learning as well as self-reported personal and practical development (Kuh, 2008). Engaged pedagogy can also occur in cocurricular experiences through volunteer service and a variety of established non-credit-bearing programs (Hoy & Meisel, 2008).

For a detailed examination of curricular and cocurricular approaches to engaging students, see Welch (2016, chapter 6), which includes the importance of helping students understand the public purpose of their engaged learning experiences.

Community-Engaged Research

Community-engaged research, which involves the broader community, is distinct from research on community questions or concerns but disengaged from those affected by the concerns. This research has many names, often indicating the degree to which the community participates in the development of the research. Minkler and Wallerstein (2002) trace the roots of community-based participatory research to two traditions: northern and southern. The northern tradition is exemplified in Lewin's (1946) method of action research; in social science the methods used investigate how to make improvements or changes in processes such as those found in the workplace and in intergroup relations. In the southern tradition, chronicled by Fals Borda (1987), research is used to challenge

TABLE 5.2
Cocurricular and Curricular Approaches

Cocurricular Approaches	
Alternative breaks	Student leaders and faculty and staff supervisors spend their fall or spring break doing volunteer service as an alternative to the traditional semester break vacation.
AmeriCorps	A federally funded program in which students receive an educational voucher or pay to help defray the cost of college education by working with community organizations through various programs such as Jumpstart and America Reads.
Bonner Leaders and Scholars	A program and curriculum designed by the Bonner Foundation to nurture students' civic leadership through sustained service with a community agency.
Volunteer Experiences	Students spend time doing service with no academic credit or financial payment to work on a community project.
Curricular Approaches	
Fellowships	Students receive academic credit or a modest financial stipend to work on a project with a community partner agency.
First-year experience	A formal program designed to help students adjust to college life, which often includes service projects coupled with readings, reflection, and other assignments. Some programs offer academic credit or meet various forms of graduation requirements.
Immersion experience	Students live and work in supervised settings on a community project with a community agency supervised by the community partner or faculty or staff and often includes readings and reflection.
Learning communities	Students are assigned to academic groups that focus on a specific topic or series of related topics often associated with a disciplinary focus that may include service activities.
Living-learning communities	Residential settings where students focus on a specific topic or series of related topics often associated with a disciplinary focus that may include service activities usually supervised and coordinated by staff from the Office of Residential Life.
Service-learning	A credit-bearing course in which instructional objectives are tied to service activities designed to meet community partner goals coupled with ongoing critical reflection.

(*Continues*)

TABLE 5.2 (*Continued*)

Undergraduate research and community-based research	Students independently or in a class work with community partners to collaboratively create a research question, design and implement a methodology, and analyze and interpret the findings to the community partner to promote capacity building for the agency while developing research skills and reinforcing key concepts from course work.

Note. Adapted from Welch (2016).

the distribution of political and socioeconomic power and is a highly participatory endeavor. Those who are the subject of the inquiry participate in the design and implementation of the inquiry. From these roots, we find an array of approaches to community-engaged or community-based research. According to Israel, Eng, Schulz, and Parker (2013),

> Although there are differences among approaches, they all involve a commitment to conducting research that to some degree shares power with and engages community partners in the research process and that benefits the communities involved, either through direct intervention or by translating research findings into interventions and policy change. (p. 6)

Community-engaged research differs from traditional research in that the goals of the research are relevant to the community, the source of the research question is a community-identified question or need, community members collaborate with the research team, the relationship between the researcher and research participants is often long term and interdependent, the value of the research is measured by its usefulness to the community and to social change, the owners and beneficiaries of the research are multiple and include community stakeholders, and the modes of presentation and dissemination are relevant to the community (Strand et al., 2003).

The handbook by Fitzgerald, Burack, Seifer, and Votruba (2010) provides a wealth of information on the various forms of engaged scholarship as well as an examination of issues such as promotion and tenure. They explore engaged scholarship in various types of institutions and settings as well as the nurturing of students as scholars and civic leaders. Strand and colleagues (2003) should also be on the bookshelf of every CEP. Finally, a useful and succinct brushstroke of engaged teaching, learning, and scholarship is provided by Welch (2016). To further enhance your knowledge of community-engaged pedagogy and community-engaged research, we recommend completing one of the exercises in Box 5.4.

BOX 5.4

Compass Point: Knowing Administration–D

Consider pursuing one of the following exercises:

1. Find a colleague on campus who does community-based pedagogy or research, and ask the following:
   a) Why did you choose this form of engaged pedagogy or research as opposed to traditional methods?
   b) How did you go about establishing a partnership to conduct this experience?
   c) If this is an engaged teaching and learning experience, how did you articulate the meaning and purpose of this work to your students, who may have been expecting traditional teaching and learning methods?
2. Visualize or imagine a community-based project in which you are interested. How would you approach a community agency to explore the possibility of establishing a partnership?
3. There is no substitution for experience. If you have not used community-engaged pedagogy as an instructional leader (not as a student), is it possible for you to coteach or assist with a class or learning experience in which the leader uses community-engaged pedagogy? If that is not possible, seek someone who has the reputation on your campus as being an outstanding community-engaged teacher. Ask to see the syllabus and if you may observe a few classes. For those of you who have used community-engaged pedagogy as an instructional leader, review the syllabus or learning goals and associated activities.
4. Reflecting on the definitions and qualities you read about in Welch (2016) or Fitzgerald and colleagues (2010), in what ways did the learning experience you are examining match what was described in the readings?
5. In what ways was it different? What were the strengths of the learning experience? What might have been improved?

Knowledge of Civic Skills

Knowledge and application of civic skills are important for the CEP and for students. Here, we turn our attention to and provide a brief introduction of the fundamental concepts of civic skills with which CEPs must be familiar, all of which are presented in more detail in chapter 7. The National Task Force on Civic Learning and Democratic Engagement (2012) convened scholars and CEPs from around the country to collectively conceptualize how to promote civic education in higher education, resulting in a framework for twenty-first century civic learning and democratic engagement. The framework provides a foundation of knowledge, skills, values, and collective action that can be used in civic education.

Knowledge of Infrastructure and Program Models

Knowing about various program and infrastructure models used to support engagement is absolutely key knowledge for you to build as part of your foundation. Institutional structures and supportive units are often cited as benchmarks of institutionalization (Furco, 1999; Holland, 1997). As described previously and elsewhere in this guidebook, a CEP must have a thorough understanding of the systemic structures of the institution. In this way, the CEP can strategically use existing structures as well as advocate for the development of new ones.

It is helpful for the CEP to use systems theory in this process, which has been used by those in many disciplines such as biology, business, education, and sociology. A *system* is defined as a constellation of interrelated actions, resources, individuals, and groups interacting in an organization (Arbnor & Bjerke, 2009). Maher and Bennett (1984) developed a model for educational settings consisting of five domains: human, physical, information, operational tools, and finance. These five domains effectively characterize and frame the infrastructural systems of institutions and campus centers for community engagement.

Human resources obviously consist of people in the institution, engagement center, and community. Physical resources are buildings, offices, and geographical locations on campus and in the community. Informational resources are written or unwritten ideas, data, and knowledge used to carry out operations central to the organization. Cultural values of how and why things are done a certain way fall under this category. Information often manifests itself within operational tools used to meet specific goals. Operational tools range from computers to paper clips and include documents such as promotion and tenure policy and procedure manuals. Finally, financial resources pay for programs, personnel, and equipment, which may be part of the institutional budget or flow-through dollars from governmental, corporate, or private sources.

Using a systems approach, the CEP must conceive of and implement institutional structures that support and advance community engagement at the institutional level and in a campus center for community engagement. Just as an athletic director must know and name the resources and facilities necessary for winning teams, the CEP must conceptualize and advocate for resources that can be used for an effective campus center to support community engagement across campus. In essence, the CEP must know and obtain human, physical, informational, operational, and fiscal resources to run a center and support campuswide initiatives for community engagement. Administrators are generally more receptive to requests that are based on a sound rationale and empirical information. The benchmarks in the application of the Carnegie Community Engagement Classification, the standards of the Council for the Advancement of Standards in Higher Education (2015), and the research by Welch and Saltmarsh (2013) provide a CEP with a strong foundation for garnering and establishing an infrastructure. Welch (2016) provided a detailed description of basic components that facilitate institutionalization and constitute a campus center, which are offered in Table 5.3 as a systems framework checklist that can be used to plan and support the institutionalization of community engagement.

Knowledge of Institutional Policies

Most campuses have standard operating procedures, perhaps known as administrative policies, as well as legal policies and policies that apply specifically to the work of faculty. Being familiar with these policies is critical to your work as a CEP. Typically, administrative policies may include rules and processes for student and class-based fundraising; what the institution considers to be a center, institute, or partnership; how media requests are handled and by whom; and policies that govern the use of institutional transportation resources.

Legal policies include memoranda of understanding among the institution and key partners (e.g., clinical agreements, community-university partnership agreements, and grant subcontracts); institution-specific policies related to risk management; processes for reporting discrimination, harassment, and sexual misconduct; and protocols for hosting youths under the age of 18 on campus and for faculty, staff, and students working with youths under the age of 18 in campus or community settings. If you have not already met with your institution's legal counsel, ask your supervisor if it would be possible. Having a conversation with the institution's

TABLE 5.3
Systems Framework Checklist for Implementing the Institutionalization of Community Engagement

Resources	*Examples*	*Need*	*Have*	*Seek*	*N/A*
Human	Midlevel administrative oversight (e.g., chief administrative officer, engagement officer, vice provost for engagement) Development officers and communications office representatives Center, institute, and program directors Program staff Executive directors of community organizations Advisory board or steering committee Faculty Students and student leaders Alumni Community members Parents and families Other?				
		Need	*Have*	*Seek*	*N/A*
Information and Policy	Institutional mission statement Asset maps and assessment rubric results Policy and procedural manuals (e.g., course designation process) Promotion and tenure criteria Professional literature Professional development Operational definitions Campus Compact (state or national) Other?				

(*Continued*)

TABLE 5.3 (*Continued*)

Resources	*Examples*	*Need*	*Have*	*Seek*	*N/A*
Physical	Center office space on campus Residence halls Classrooms Community partner sites Community centers, schools, and parks Shared annex space in the community Other?				
		Need	*Have*	*Seek*	*N/A*
Fiscal	Institutional funds and operational budget Grants Development office and gifts and in-kind resources Tuition tiers Special fees Other?				
		Need	*Have*	*Seek*	*N/A*
Operational Tools	Organizational alignment flow chart and reporting lines Asset maps and assessment rubrics Strategic plan Risk management assessment and policy Memos of understanding Data management systems and information-technology services (e.g., phones, computers) Other?				
		Need	*Have*	*Seek*	*N/A*
Office and Unit Partnershps	President's office Academic affairs Student affairs Residential life Campus communications Advancement and development Mission and ministry Athletics Other?				

BOX 5.5
Compass Point: Knowing Administration–E

> Locate a copy of the faculty retention, promotion, and tenure policies, usually found in the faculty handbook. Ask a trusted faculty colleague who is familiar with community-engaged scholarship to discuss the policies with you and how these policies facilitate or inhibit faculty involvement in community-engaged scholarship.

risk management officers or legal counsel about the work of your unit may uncover additional supportive policies and resources that are applicable to your work. More on the topic of risk management is included later in this chapter.

The last category of institutional policies you should review provides the expectations for faculty workload, review, promotion, and tenure. Typically, faculty work is governed by these policies and dictates (to some degree) faculty's willingness to be involved with community engagement in their roles as faculty. Typically, in U.S. tenure-granting institutions, faculty who are on the tenure track, in contrast to those who are not on the tenure track or are considered clinical faculty or faculty of practice, enter as assistant professors and demonstrate their capacity to be effective teachers and scholars during a certain period of time. The exact criteria for this demonstration is specific to your institution's policies.

Generally, pending a successful demonstration of their capacity, typically called a review, faculty work for a few more years as an assistant professor until they are eligible to be considered for promotion to the rank of associate professor and eligible to earn tenure. At some institutions the associate rank is coupled with tenure, and at others rank and tenure are earned separately. Eventually, faculty have the opportunity to be considered for promotion to full professor, a status indicating excellence in all categories of faculty work. These policies are especially important for CEPs to understand if their work involves faculty. The policies outline exactly what kinds of work are deemed acceptable and encouraged at the institution. At some institutions, particularly those where community engagement is a priority, the review, promotion, and tenure policies explicitly address the nature and value of community-engaged scholarship as part of faculty work. Rarely will an institution expect all of its faculty to undertake community-engaged scholarship. However, at some institutions, there is no mention of community engagement in faculty workload policies, and its value (if there is value attributed to it) is then determined informally in faculty and institutional cultures. We recommend the exercise in Box 5.5 as a means to become more familiar with these policies at your institution.

Embrace Critical Thinking

The concept and practice of critical thinking are grounded in principles of critical theory that lend themselves well to community engagement. Guba and Lincoln (1993) summarized critical theory as a reformative, transformative, and emancipative inquiry that reconsiders and reexamines historical contexts that promote reform and restitution. In this way, we are invited and encouraged to reconsider the way something has always been and why. Critical thinking challenges us to ponder how cultural, political, and institutional structures and assumptions influence actions and beliefs as well as consider the ways they may intentionally or inadvertently perpetuate the status quo, which includes injustice and oppression. This requires scholars to transcend their traditional academic boundaries and perspective to include the perspective of others. At a microlevel, this might include revisiting our assumptions and approach to teaching and

BOX 5.6

Compass Point: Knowing Administration–F

In looking at the following typical scenarios, consider what matters. To whom? Why? What is the impact? Explore what you might do or say so each scenario could be inclusive and mutually beneficial to multiple stakeholders.

1. Students take on leadership roles in cocurricular programs in the campus center for community engagement, which they can include on their résumé when they apply for law school.
2. A faculty member is interested in having her students observe and critique community garden programs in underresourced neighborhoods and write an article on their experiences.
3. A community agency is hoping a group of students will help at a fundraising gala by setting up tables and chairs, providing child care, and coordinating parking.
4. A department has embraced the notion and practice of experiential learning and has implemented a requirement that students must complete 20 hours of service to graduate.

learning. At a broader macrolevel, critical thinking invites scholars and practitioners to reexamine their traditional positivistic approach to epistemology coupled with how they generate and disseminate new knowledge. It involves the inclusionary practice of giving voice to the community. This approach reflects what Saltmarsh and Hartley (2016) refer to as public scholarship that has emerged from feminist, postmodern, postcolonial, and critical race theories in which the traditional positivist approach to scholarship has been called into question as complex social and cultural factors are considered from a democratic and inclusive lens. Succinctly put, critical thinking involves asking, What matters? To whom? Why? and What is the impact? We can ask these questions in our staff meetings, classrooms, campus committees, and neighborhood advisory groups. To reflect further on these important questions, we recommend you respond to the prompts about each scenario offered in Box 5.6.

Embrace Visionary Thinking

Individuals and institutions can easily become trapped in and comfortable with the status quo. At one time in history, a particular approach or perspective may have made a great deal of sense as well as address a need or meet a goal. Over time, contexts and factors change, requiring a new vision and approach. Change is difficult and stressful. As CEPs we must embrace visionary thinking. When a new idea or approach is proposed, it is important to begin the discernment process with "We can't if," rather than "We can't because." This liberates us to weigh the pros and cons and perhaps even pilot a new idea or program knowing we are not committed to it until it has proven itself or can be modified.

Hickman and Silva (1984) said, "Vision is a mental journey from the known to the unknown, creating the future from a montage of current facts, hopes, dreams, dangers, and opportunities" (p. 151).

Deepening Our Critical Commitments: Questions to Ask

CEPs must continue deepening critical commitments by unveiling and disrupting unequal power structures as well as naming injustices and power differentials. Historically, institutions of higher education have engaged in unilateral interactions with communities, often in the form of placing preprofessional students into practicum settings with little to no benefit for the cooperating agency. The ethos and practice of community engagement requires mutuality and parity to form true partnerships, a relatively new approach for the academy and community. It requires a new way of thinking, doing, and talking with communities and encourages us to ask the following questions:

1. What does it mean or look like to engage in critical dialogue with community?
2. What power differentials exist between campus and community?
3. What injustices does your institution seeks to remediate?
4. Are institutional initiatives and efforts just? Do they unintentionally embody or impart injustice or oppressive practices?

Chapter Six

DOING COMMUNITY ENGAGEMENT ADMINISTRATION

Execution is the ability to achieve a critical goal while living in the midst of a raging whirlwind. (McChesney, Covey, & Huling, 2012, p. 78)

Chapter 5 discussed the knowledge community engagement professionals (CEPs) need to carry out their administrative responsibilities. This chapter focuses on the actions, or doing, embedded in administration. Prior to chapters 5 and 6, this book focused on the tasks of leading change from the middle spaces of an institution and institutionalizing community engagement in an institution, both of which require leadership competence. In comparison, the competencies of CEPs who administer community engagement programs are concerned with the tasks of management and execution. Bolman and Deal (2008) concretized this distinction by saying, "Managers focus on execution, leaders on purpose" (p. 343). In the typical work of a CEP, we do not feel these roles are taken by different people, that is, some people are responsible and suited for leading, whereas others are responsible and suited for managing. Rather, we suggest that different categories of work, such as leading change, institutionalizing engagement, or administering engagement programs, require different competencies, which, often, a single CEP has. Doing community-engaged program administration demands competence in a variety of areas, often on the same day and frequently at the same time. The life of an engagement program administrator is wonderfully hectic, bursting with bridge building and creative work. The administrative role presented in this chapter is generally focused on using various tools, not only to tighten the nuts and bolts of operations but also to do so in an artful way. This includes leadership whereby the CEP is thrust into the middle and sometimes to the rear of the whirling activity, gently shepherding colleagues and stewarding resources to advance this work rather than being out in front. Take a moment to consider the case study in Box 6.1 and respond to the reflective prompts we offer there.

The pace of days like the one in the following case study can be exhausting, and administering the associated work can be Sisyphean. Although it is true that administering an engagement unit requires a range of competencies to manage a large number of tasks, and these competencies are developed over time, effective CEPs know the value of self-care and stepping back from time to time.

After completing this chapter, those working in the field of community engagement or currently working as a community engagement professional will be able to reflect on the areas in which they are competent

BOX. 6.1
Compass Point: Doing Community Engagement–A

Read and reflect on the following case study of a CEP.

A CEP begins her day checking in with staff (some of whom are full-time professionals, others undergraduate or graduate students), then meets with a dean to discuss her school's community engagement work with a local middle school that has been difficult, and heads off campus to attend a steering committee meeting for a local economic redevelopment project that it is hoped would establish new partnerships for the university in the surrounding neighborhood. When she returns to campus, she closes her office door and sits down to review the draft of a research-to-practice brief being written about a new program evaluation strategy. Later she convenes a few of her staff to begin planning for the center's next substantial website revision. Her late-afternoon appointment is with a faculty member who is seeking her thought partnership as he develops his third-year review materials for promotion and tenure. At 5:30 p.m., she quickly submits a business expense report before flying out the door to continue on with the rest of life for the day.

To what extent does this scenario reflect your typical day? Do you think your staff, faculty, or administrators have an understanding of the work demands of a CEP? Why or why not?

TABLE 6.1
Competencies and Critical Commitments Associated With Doing Community Engagement Administration

6.1 Able to manage a portfolio of work that is dynamic and relationship oriented 6.2 Able to cultivate and maintain relationships 6.3 Able to collaborate and work across roles and disciplinary silos 6.4 Embrace community partners as coeducators	6.5 Able to communicate effectively 6.6 Able to plan effective programs 6.7 Able to cultivate and manage multiple funding streams and budgets 6.8 Able to develop and supervise staff 6.9 Able to manage risk	6.10 Knowledge of assessment and evaluation methods 6.11 Able to collect and analyze data 6.12 Able to assess and evaluate impact of community engagement on its stakeholders
Critical Commitments • Committed to a dialogue with communities • Able to recognize one's subject position in connection to privilege and oppression		

and identify areas they would like to develop further. Those who are new to supporting community engagement or who aspire to enter the community engagement profession will demonstrate awareness and emerging understanding of these areas of competence (see Table 6.1).

Able to Manage a Portfolio of Work

In their work on the disciplines of execution, McChesney, Covey, and Huling (2012) have examined how thousands of organizations execute strategy. They suggest that when a strategy feels vague or too big, we often resort to busyness or invest our time in busywork. For example, consider working on a campus that has set a goal of becoming a national leader in civic engagement or developing people of conscience equipped to build a more just and equitable world. It is easy to let the day-to-day functions of your unit become overwhelming in these contexts. It is important for the CEP not to fall into believing the engagement unit is solely responsible for community engagement. Typically, CEPs operate from a space

BOX 6.2

Compass Point: Doing Community Engagement–B

Presently in your unit, what is the one wildly important goal that when executed has the potential, more so than any other goal, to help your unit focus its contributions on the engagement strategy of your institution? What would lead to your unit's achieving this goal?

that provides the support and resources for *others* to carry out the work of community engagement. Releasing ourselves from sole ownership or a proprietary perspective for our institution's community engagement allows us to focus on the very specific contributions we need to help our units make the larger institutional picture. Winnowing broad strategies to achievable but truly important goals is the key to execution, particularly in a hectic and complex campus environment. These kinds of goals, called *wildly important goals* (McChesney et al., 2012), involve incremental administrative tasks to achieve deep, substantive change. We suggest taking a moment to consider wildly important goals within your practice context by answering the prompts in Box 6.2.

Able to Cultivate and Maintain Relationships

The nature of community engagement work, whether we are thinking of tasks on campus or in communities, is highly collaborative. The administration of community engagement can only occur through relationships with stakeholders in the engagement unit, across the campus, and in many different spheres in the community, such as forming relationships with residents, key leaders, and organizational staff. Outreach to intentionally establish relationships is key to the work of a CEP (Welch & Saltmarsh, 2013). The collaboration in these relationships often rubs against the prevailing higher education culture in which one stakeholder group, often administrative leaders or faculty, sets the rules or processes to be followed and other stakeholder groups are affected by those decisions.

Able to Collaborate and Work Across Roles and Disciplinary Silos

One of the defining characteristics of contemporary models of civic engagement is *mutually beneficial collaboration,* in which everyone

BOX 6.3
Compass Point: Doing Community Engagement–C

A CEP has morning coffee with a faculty member from the Department of Chemical Engineering who is also eager to have students, who are developing solar-powered hydrogen cells, work with the local municipality's motor pool to create sustainable, solar-powered golf carts as maintenance vehicles in city parks. The CEP has lunch in a nearby neighborhood with a community organization leader hoping to work with the School of Business to create microloans and business plans that build the capacity of local women in under-resourced neighborhoods who are interested in creating a popup catering business of local cuisine. The CEP ends the day in a conference with the provost and Faculty Senate to explore establishing a place-based anchor partnership between the medical school and a community health and wellness clinic.

To what extent have you as a CEP engaged in these types of strategic conversations with your faculty colleagues, community partners, administrators, or Faculty Senate? Do others view these types of collaborations as part of your work?

Reflecting on the various interactions the CEP has with others in these cases, make a list of all the relationships the CEP will need to initiate or maintain to be effective. Make a list of the additional stakeholders the CEP might involve, or introduce to one another, to move each initiative forward. How does the volume of relationships the CEP has in the case studies presented in this chapter compare with the volume of your relationships? In what ways do you nurture relationships as part of your work? What strategies do you use to participate in the worlds of your stakeholders?

contributes knowledge, skills, and experience in determining the issues to be addressed, the questions to be asked, the problems to be resolved, the strategies to be used, the outcomes that are considered desirable, and the indicators of success.

The focus on collaborative work in which everyone contributes has led to a proliferation of colanguage in community engagement circles. We often refer to engagement initiatives as coconstructed, partners as coeducators, and knowledge as coproduced to indicate the highly participatory and collaborative orientation embodied in our work. In the context of working with community partners, the CEP must view these individuals as "public scholars" (Ramaley, 2010, p. 355) with a unique perspective and expertise coupled with the scholarly expertise of faculty.

A unique and rewarding aspect of CEPs' work is the opportunity to work with faculty from an array of disciplines. We have the opportunity to learn about a host of topics, skills, and issues when we collaborate with colleagues. Likewise, we are fortunate to venture into vibrant neighborhoods energized by leaders with a vision to build capacity, which creates the border crossing and bridge building in our roles and responsibilities described in chapter 2. The case study in Box 6.3 illustrates the relationship-oriented work of a CEP, which often involves matchmaking, capacity building, and networking.

Embrace Community Partners as Coeducators

The case study in Box 6.3 shows how CEPs introduce and connect faculty from various disciplines to explore interdisciplinary projects as well as broker potential partnerships with community leaders and organizations. Therefore, it is important for the CEP and program staff to understand that the practice of informal conversations and meetings is a critical component of this work and instrumental in forging authentic relationships.

How then do CEPs form authentic relationships? From a personal and philosophical context, Hernandez and Pasquesi (2017) suggest CEPs cultivate a *critical consciousness,* defined as authentic, dialogic relationships based on acknowledgment of power difference, mutuality, and deliberative collaborative effort, and form collaborative relationships "rooted in a sense of belonging and human connection" (Kinefuchi, 2010, p. 67). This means CEPs must listen with the intent of forming connections with others through dialogue and reflect on their positionality in regard to those they work with so they can be aware of power dynamics at play in their relationships and of the potential for cultural inauthenticity and invasion to creep into their work. This also requires intentionality in how we see others (whether students, faculty, or community members) and how we refer to the work. Embracing an asset-based mind-set is key. From an applied perspective, forming authentic relationships requires actually meeting face-to-face, ideally in others' spaces, for conversation. The engagement unit cannot become an island. It is so important for CEPs to participate in the activities, meetings, and environments of the other people they work with. Attending the neighborhood's monthly community meetings, participating in student events, being present at Faculty Senate meetings, and volunteering to speak in department meetings are all examples of strategies that help CEPs understand their partners' worlds and create opportunities for relationships.

Able to Communicate Effectively

CEPs must use effective written and oral communication when interacting with a variety of stakeholders. Correct grammar and spelling go without saying, and proofreading all documents is an absolute must. The focus here is on the affective and relational aspect of communicating, listening, and speaking. E-mail and phone calls remain the primary forms of communication. It is critical for a CEP to respond to e-mails and voicemails in a timely manner. Refrain from sarcasm, especially in written forms of communication, as it can often be misconstrued and misunderstood. Avoid using higher education and disciplinary jargon or acronyms when communicating with community partners.

Listen with intentionality when working with others. Put on your effective communication caps: *C* is for clarifying questions to help understand what has been shared; *A* is for attending skills through effective and appropriate body language, eye contact, and facial expression during one-on-one conversations; *P* is for paraphrasing what has been shared to check for understanding as well as convey your intentional listening; and *S* is for summarizing with a wrap-up sentence to capture the essence of what has been said or decided (Welch & Sheridan, 1995).

Able to Plan Effective Programs

Too often CEPs will hear about an interesting program at a neighboring campus and decide to replicate the program without a clear rationale for doing so. For example, the Bonner Scholars Program (Bonner Foundation, 2018a) has been replicated in countless variations as student service corps or community engagement fellowships for student cohorts. Despite the exemplary success of the Bonner Scholars Program, without a clear understanding of what purpose a student cohort program would serve for your particular campus, efforts to replicate the program are likely to have unsatisfactory results. Knowing the unique purpose of the program for your campus (and its associated outcomes and goals) is key. Is the purpose to build a stakeholder's capacity for engagement? Is it to make opportunities for community engagement more widely available to a particular audience? Is it to incentivize participation or to bolster the support for those already engaging in this work? Is it to enhance a particular stakeholder group's leadership or voice in the design and delivery of engagement initiatives? The answers to these questions provide the starting point for the program's purpose. From there, the planning model may vary.

The following models are particularly helpful for community engagement program planning:

1. Backward design (for designing learning experiences)
2. Theory-of-change modeling (summarizes change work at a strategic level)
3. Logic modeling (for program planning and evaluation)

Each model functions at a different level, but all use some variation of backward planning, in which you determine the outcome and then plan how you will get there. For programs that are most concerned with a particular stakeholder group's learning and development, such as building faculty familiarity with participatory research methods or enhancing students' civic empathy, backward design is instructive (Wiggins & McTighe, 2011). For multifaceted change efforts, theory-of-change modeling is helpful. Originating in program evaluation work, theory-of-change is focused on strategy and context as a means to explain a particular pathway of change (Weiss, 1995). For planning efforts focused more on a specific program or time-bound initiative, logic modeling may be a good fit (Kellogg, 2004). Initially used in the philanthropic and evaluation communities, logic models link a program's short- and long-term outcomes with the program's activities and processes. Logic models can help you gain clarity about how your planned work relates to your intended results.

Able to Cultivate and Manage Multiple Funding Streams and Budgets

Six budget models are commonly used in American higher education today, each with its own benefits and drawbacks (Hanover Research, 2012):

1. Incremental budgeting: This year's budget proposals and allocations are largely based on last year's budget levels.
2. Zero-based budgeting: A process that starts from zero; each unit must justify its requested funding levels and expenditures each year.
3. Activity-based budgeting: A system that monitors which activities drive the greatest revenues for the institution and awards financial resources to those activities.
4. Responsibility center management: An approach that gives decision-making authority for how to spend the revenue and income

generated by a unit to that unit while also asking units to share a portion of the expenses incurred by the institution's general operations.

5. Centralized budgeting: A process in which all decision-making (proposals and allocations) is made by central administration.
6. Performance-based budgeting: A process that awards funds based on performance determined by defined outcomes standards.

In addition to institutional budgetary allocations, engagement units typically receive funding from grants, donations, endowments, and contracts, otherwise known as fees for service. If you are not already aware of how your unit's funding is determined and the proportion of funding that comes from the institution (often referred to as *hard funding*) and funding that comes from other temporary sources such as grants, sponsorships, and gifts (often referred to as *soft funding*), it is very important to learn this right away.

Once you understand your institution's budgeting model, where your unit's funding comes from, and how it is distributed across funding types, you can better understand what opportunities exist for cultivating additional funding. This is assuming, of course, that additional resources are necessary to sustain and enhance the programs and initiatives of the unit. More money is not necessarily a direct correlate with better quality programs. Resources (fiscal and staff) need to be aligned with the number of participants, complexity of programming, priority given to the initiative institutionally, and evidence of desired outcomes and impacts. However, if you do find yourself in need of additional resources, the old adage about an institution's priorities are reflected in where it spends its money is particularly useful. Typical rationales that work in concert with each other are the following:

1. Synergy with institutional priorities. Calculate the per-participant investment the institution is making; that is, the amount of institutional funding divided by the number of participating students or community members or faculty, and so on. Is this per capita investment on par with the rhetorical priority the institution places on community engagement? Does your engagement initiative support or join with other key institutional priorities (e.g., retention rates among particular students, interdisciplinarity, etc.)?
2. Financial need. Based on your program's outcome and impact data, are additional resources necessary to sustain, enhance, or repair initiatives? Can you articulate clear goals for sustaining or enhancing

the program that require additional resources?

3. Clear positive results. Using your program's outcome and impact data, what positive impacts does community engagement make on the institution? These data may include program participant outcomes, reports of reputational goodwill created through the institution's engagement initiatives, alumni survey responses, and improvements to key metrics of community vitality, among others.

Once you have refined your rationale for increased resources, study the institution's strategic plan and budgeting process, and then get ready to make your case. Holland and Langseth's (2010) three-part recipe for making a funding case is to contextualize your case in the larger institutional or community issues people view as critical, make the connections clear between your program and one or more of the critical issues, and show why your program is particularly well suited to address one or more of the critical issues.

As external funding is concerned, in addition to grant programs that typically circulate requests for funding proposals and notices of funding availability, you may consider approaching private foundations, corporate foundations, community foundations, and individual donors. Typically, your institution will have advancement and development staff who are liaisons with these stakeholders. Always work with your institution's advancement staff to initiate conversations with these funders. Often, institution administrators know which foundations and donors they will approach to support specific programs. Going it alone will undermine the institution's strategy and portray you as someone who either doesn't have the institution's support or is naïve about the ways of the funding community. Advancement staff are wonderful guides through the funding world. However, it is becoming more and more common for the CEP to take on development roles and responsibilities. Some centers, especially larger and endowed units, have a staff member whose sole responsibility is writing grants and coordinating fundraising. Finally, many centers are now establishing a development committee that provides advice on fundraising strategies, cultivates donors, and makes a financial commitment to the center. Consult with your institutional development office or alumni office to generate a list of potential committee members.

Regardless of which funding streams you choose to cultivate, knowing your institution's budgeting model, your annual budgeting process, and how your initiatives support and enhance the institution's priorities. In addition, having a good grasp on how your funding is distributed will equip you with the information you need to work with others at your institution to secure the resources necessary to sustain and enhance your work. Take a moment to reflect on your unit's budget by responding to the prompts in Box 6.4.

CEPs not only manage funds but also are often expected or required to procure them. Some directors of campus engagement programs are fortunate to have the development office staff take the lead on this. However, not all programs have that luxury. Therefore, effective CEPs have a basic understanding and level of skill in grant writing and fundraising. Valuable information on this topic can be found in the professional literature. Weerts and Hudson (2009) argue how strong advancement and development programs are critical to gain necessary resources for programming. Holland and Langseth (2010) is also a valuable resource. Finally, Masterson (2016) encourages CEPs to "go big, build relations, and think long term" (p. 8A) when approaching private foundations for funding.

Able to Develop and Supervise Staff

Collins (2001) wrote, "Great vision without great people is irrelevant" (p. 42). Despite the fact that developing a highly skilled and motivated staff is one of the most important areas of work you will ever perform as a leader, very little has been written on this topic specific to community engagement initiatives. A great range of staff size, responsibilities, and backgrounds is found in community engagement units. According to the membership survey by Campus Compact (2014), respondents indicated an average of 3.6 full-time staff, 1.5 part-time staff, and 12.6 student workers in these units. Some units also include hybrid positions in which faculty have administrative responsibilities. Engagement initiatives also include fellows or scholars such as community scholars who build capacity for campus partnerships among community groups or take on specific community initiatives in partnership with the engagement unit. Faculty fellows can build capacity among their faculty colleagues for community-engaged

BOX 6.4

Compass Point: Doing Community Engagement–D

> Review the line items in your current budget. What do they reveal about your unit's values, priorities, and operations? For example, what does a line item for food suggest? Does your budget include professional development opportunities for you and your staff? Why or why not?

scholarship, and postdoctoral fellows or visiting scholars can assess, evaluate, or research questions of importance to the campus, community, and field. Periodically, engagement units include graduate student interns who are hoping to become a CEP one day. In summary, engagement unit staff are quite diverse.

Staff come from a variety of backgrounds and preparation pathways. For some people, working in a community engagement unit is their first position after college. Others may have had careers in the social sector or as community organizers before stepping into the role of a CEP. Increasingly, staff are sculpting careers as CEPs, progressing through various staff roles with increasing responsibilities and leadership tasks. Hiring, developing, and promoting these staff are critical responsibilities of CEPs. Typically, their concrete functions include recruitment and selection, orientation, supervision, performance appraisal, staff development, and separation (Winston & Creamer, 1997).

Most institutions have human resource (HR) departments that can provide assistance with hiring processes such as creating job descriptions and using behavioral techniques during interviews. HR typically conducts standardized employee orientations to campuses. HR staff often use a structured process for performance appraisals and can counsel you if you feel one of your staff members isn't a good fit for the unit and needs to be guided out of the position. Working closely with HR is an important starting point.

One of the unique characteristics of the professionals you will recruit, hire, supervise, and develop is that they must pair effectiveness with a keen and deepening commitment to the civic purposes of the work. Consulting this book and reviewing the competency model (Dostilio, 2017a) will help you identify the sphere of work each of your staff members is responsible for, its constituent elements, the critical civic commitments of the work,

BOX 6.5

Compass Point: Doing Community Engagement–E

> Meet with a community engagement colleague or two who manage staff and ask them to tell you some of their strategies for hiring and developing their staff. Ask what processes they use to supervise staff. Do they meet individually with them on a weekly or biweekly basis? Do they meet as a whole team? What are the context and format of the meetings? What resources have your colleagues consulted to help them with their approach to staffing?

and opportunities for professional development. Likewise, review ways to couple the nuanced act of mentoring with the technical aspect of supervision of your staff described in chapter 4. You can further hone your staff supervision skills by learning how others approach these tasks. See Box 6.5 for prompts that can guide a consultative conversation with a colleague or mentor about staff supervision.

Able to Manage Risk

Community engagement involves campus stakeholders interacting face-to-face or virtually with community stakeholders and noncampus entities and vice versa. Because of the diversity of activities and interactions involved in community engagement, risk is not a singular, defined thing. There is risk of harm in community engagement that spans personal, reputational, financial, physical, or environmental impacts to the individuals and organizations involved. Risk is inherent in all we do, and we cannot eliminate it. We can, however, manage excessive risk to the well-being of those involved and alert stakeholders to the practices and processes that will help them to manage their own participation and well-being.

Each campus has its own legal counsel and risk management personnel who should be consulted when constructing a risk management plan. When one of the authors was first establishing a service-learning program and met with the risk management officer on campus, the officer explained that his job was not to say no but yes, which is how the institution can enhance the safety and well-being of those involved. Although not all risk management officers may be familiar with community engagement practices and have varying degrees of risk tolerance, it is simply not an option to keep details of your initiative hidden from them. Doing so exposes you, the institutions and organizations, and people involved to greater risk of harm.

Your campus already has processes in place to manage the risk and impact associated with a variety of occurrences such as hosting minors (youths under the age of 18) on campus; having campus stakeholders work with you in off-campus settings; screening and managing drivers for campus transportation; reporting discrimination and harassment; determining travel advisories for destinations across the globe; establishing agreements for large-scale partnerships; and protecting students, staff, and faculty when they volunteer in the community. You need to be knowledgeable of these processes and comply with them. If they do not exist, then you should discuss these activities with your risk management officer or institution's legal counsel to develop standard practices and processes. Likewise, keep in mind that more and more community organizations and their boards of directors have their own risk management procedures and policies that institutions of higher education must follow. Unlike earlier approaches to community engagement, today it is rare for students to enter a community agency on their own to find a partner to work with them to complete engaged learning assignments.

In addition to the kinds of activities most engagement programs are involved in, many unique projects and initiatives require individualized risk management plans. One approach to developing such plans is the relational approach to coconstructed risk management (Dostilio & Molchan, 2015), in which stakeholders including risk management professionals map the severity and frequency of potential risks involved in a particular activity at the institutional and program levels. By developing scenarios that characterize likely harms and responses for each type of risk, unique risk reduction and prevention procedures are developed for the initiative. Then a mutually agreed-on scope of work is outlined, community-based orientations for the task and work are offered, and a communications plan is put in place for telling stakeholders which standard practices and procedures will be used to manage risk and what they should do if harm has occurred.

Knowledge of Assessment and Evaluation Methods

Knowing how to assess and evaluate our work and its impacts on communities, students, faculty, institutions, and staff is critical to our work as CEPs. The data and insights gained from assessment and evaluation are invaluable to strategic planning, monitoring the depth and quality of key relationships such as community-campus partnerships, program planning and implementation, determining impact, and budget planning and fundraising. However, these terms, *assessment* and *evaluation*, are often used interchangeably and as synonyms, revealing some confusion on their meanings and purposes. Therefore, it is important to understand how they are related and yet serve different purposes. In the context of our work as CEPs, our conceptualization of these two terms is based on a hybrid combination of principles derived from education and organizational development.

Assessment is an ongoing process of establishing goals coupled with obtaining, reviewing, and using information about someone or something to monitor performance or operations to make necessary modifications and improvements. Assessment is typically formative in nature, meaning it occurs before and during an activity to review and consider things like efficiency (e.g., How much time or how many people are involved? Are current procedures effective?). Evaluation involves methods of observing and measuring someone or something to determine and judge its value based on a standard or criteria. Evaluation, therefore, is often considered to be summative in that the outcome or product derived from the activity or operation is judged in terms of its quality and whether or not it achieved the desired goal (Angelo & Cross, 1993; Duke University Office of Assessment, 2018).

In her advice on establishing and sustaining a community service-learning office, Jacoby (2010) implores us to go for quality over quantity. Although she is referring to service-learning classes, we can use this advice for all community engagement initiatives. We feel assessment is instrumental in enhancing the quality of our work and ensuring that our civic values animate our initiatives. CEPs frequently object, saying they don't have the time or capacity to evaluate programs or assess participant outcomes. We believe these tasks are the bedrock of the job of a CEP. How else will we know whether or not our work is quality work? How else will we know whether or not we are actually pursuing the civic purposes of community engagement as opposed to providing activities simply for activities' sake? Because assessment and evaluation are so important, questions about an institution's assessment and evaluation methods and the impacts of engagement on various stakeholders are included in the application for the Carnegie Foundation's Community Engagement Classification.

Able to Collect and Analyze Data

We offer a few working ideas here as an introduction and then point you toward resources that will help you deepen your familiarity with assessment and evaluation. Linda Suskie (2009), a student learning assessment guru, makes these suggestions for people first attempting assessment: Start small and produce quick results; start by focusing on a small number of important goals, not by trying to assess too many things; start with easier assessments, such as those outcomes and qualities that are easiest to define and measure; focus on assessment tools and strategies that yield the greatest dividends for the time and resources invested; and keep things simple, start with the information you have and only collect information that is useful.

We suggest you begin with documenting and tracking what is happening, where, with whom, by whom, and for what purpose as a kind of inventory. Systematizing the collection of this information is important and can be done in low-tech and high-tech ways. A number of software packages and relational databases available for purchase can perform these tasks. Many focus on student engagement in communities, and a few offer more comprehensive tracking across a breadth of public-facing activities. Although the information generated through an inventory may not give you insights into what could be done to improve the quality of initiatives or how you could strategically advance community engagement on your campus, it will certainly allow you to respond when you are asked what is happening and who is involved. As discussed in chapter 7, establishing measurable and observable objectives or benchmarks is useful in determining whether or not programs and activities are effective and achieve their goals.

To gain more strategic insights and measures of quality, you need to identify what you're trying to learn. As with program planning, this begins by outlining your desired outcomes or the changes you hope to see as a result of your work. Generally, it is insufficient to ask "What impact have we had?" That doesn't direct your assessment and evaluation efforts and will likely lead you to measure outcomes in ways that aren't very meaningful. Rather, begin with a very specific question or goal, such as, Have the residents of X neighborhood experienced increased access to health services as the result of the XYZ initiative? Now you have a very clear idea of what you are measuring: increased access to health services among residents in a particular neighborhood. This in turn can be used to develop measurable and observable objectives for summative evaluation, such as the pilot program for health services in the neighborhood clinic will achieve a 20% increase from initial baseline data in service delivery to residents.

Able to Assess and Evaluate Impact of Community Engagement

Whenever possible, develop an assessment plan as you conceptualize the program rather than trying to evaluate program outcomes after the fact. This will help to drive the success and quality of the initiative. Align the goals of your assessment, what you are interested in knowing, with those that also matter to the campus and community. It's worth mentioning that the assessment targets and methods most often discussed in community engagement books and journals are primarily focused on outcomes and impacts relevant to the campus and its faculty and students. Less frequently, and with far less specificity, are community outcomes and impacts measured, and when they are, it is typically uninformed or guided by community development theory and rarely does the assessment get at social change (Stoeker, Beckman, & Min, 2010).

Once you've selected your assessment targets or your driving questions or outcomes and impacts, select strategies to collect data relevant to those targets. You can collaborate with people on your campus to help plan your assessment and help you access information you need. Often campuses have assessment directors or institutional research units that routinely collect data about enrollments, retention, graduation rates, alumni perceptions, organizational climate, faculty ranks, institutional financial investments, and so forth. These people are typically experts in designing institutionally focused assessments. For assessment targets focused on community questions, expert partners are also available. In addition to organizations that may be working with your particular initiative and likely collect information about the clients they serve and the issues they seek to address, other regional bodies routinely collect data about the issues communities face, for example, governmental bodies like divisions of health and human services and housing and urban development, and nongovernmental groups like the United Way. Program evaluation is arguably more embedded in the culture of the nonprofit sector than in postsecondary education, and you will find assessment experts in community partnerships.

Finally, as you plan and carry out your assessment and evaluation, have a communication plan for providing the findings to key stakeholders and how they will be used to improve the work. As said earlier in this chapter, the insights you gain from assessments and evaluation are powerful information to include in funding requests and strategic planning, and they can provide your unit with credibility among leaders at the institution and in the community. The key to a good assessment approach is being proactive. It's important to regularly collect information in structured and systematic ways (Bringle, Hatcher, & Multhiah, 2010), rather than find yourself reacting to requests. Increasingly, institutions are using scorecards and dashboards to routinely share the outcomes and impacts of their engagement initiatives in a transparent way.

CEPs should also be aware of standardized, formal tools that can be used to assess various aspects of community engagement, including students' civic development and growth (see Figure 6.1). CEPs should consult with the institutional research on campus to discuss and identify surveys, if any, currently used on campus to assess student impact in civic and community engagement. These offices typically have a standard list of surveys used on a regular basis. Therefore, it is important to determine whether or not any of the standardized tools in Figure 6.1 could be included in the queue of surveys.

Figure 6.1 Formal and standardized tools to assess student impact of community engagement.

Civic Attitudes and Skills Questionnaire
The Civic Attitudes and Skills Questionnaire (Moely et al., 2002) is a robust and validated instrument that assesses students' attitudes toward and application of skills in civic engagement. The survey was used to assess the impact of Tulane University's institutional commitment to civic engagement following Hurricane Katrina.

Civic-Minded Graduate Scale
The Center for Service-Learning at the Indiana University Purdue University at Indianapolis (IUPUI) developed the civic-minded graduate model and an accompanying survey (Hatcher, 2008). This model and survey identify and assess the specific knowledge, skills, and dispositions to describe how students develop civic mindedness (IUPUI, 2018).

National Assessment of Service and Community Engagement
This assessment measures the rate, frequency, and depth of student community service across nine dimensions of human need and assesses student perceptions of, motivations for, and obstacles to service, as well as institutional structures that affect service participation (Levy & Johnson, 2009).

National Survey of Student Engagement (2018)
This survey collects information from four-year colleges and universities about first-year and senior students' participation in programs and activities that institutions provide for their learning and personal development. It provides participating institutions with a variety of reports that compare their students' responses with those of students at self-selected groups of comparison institutions. The survey includes 10 engagement indicators and 6 high-impact practices.

CEPs may be asked or required to either conduct research or at least be knowledgeable of existing research on civic and community engagement. A "must have" resource is the four-volume series of Research on Service-Learning: Conceptual Frameworks and Assessment. The books are part of the IUPUI Series on Service-Learning Research. Volume 1 is focused on international service-learning (Bringle, Hatcher, & Jones,

BOX 6.6

Compass Point: Doing Community Engagement–F

List the various methods and instruments used on your campus to conduct assessment and evaluation. What, if any, methods or instruments do you currently use in your center? Consider scheduling a meeting with staff at your institutional research office to discuss current institutional mechanisms for assessment and evaluation. Explore possible ways you and your office might work with institutional research to combine efforts.

How would you respond to a faculty member or administrator on your campus who is dubious about how community engagement is assessed and evaluated?

2010), whereas volume 2A presents research on students and faculty (Clayton, Bringle, & Hatcher, 2013a) and volume 2B reports studies on community and institutional impact (Clayton, Bringle, & Hatcher, 2013b). Volume 3 examines research on civic outcomes for students (Hatcher, Bringle, & Hahn, 2016). We recommend considering the assessment and evaluation practices used at your campus in Box 6.6.

Deepening Our Critical Commitments: Questions to Ask

An effective CEP is able to unveil and disrupt unequal power structures. Unfortunately, these are rampant and sometimes subtle in the academy and the community. It is difficult, if not impossible, for individuals in an organization or setting to unveil and disrupt oppressive power structures if they don't even know these conditions exist. Likewise, those with power are often oblivious when it simply seems inherent in their positions. This requires critical reflection and consideration.

1. What are some of the existing or potential power structures?
2. How do those structures influence different stakeholders' participation, authority, and decision-making in interactions?
3. CEPs must be committed to and able to recognize their subject position in connection to privilege and oppression. In what ways and at what times do you hold power? Conversely, in what ways and at what times are you subject to someone else's power?

Chapter Seven

FACILITATING STUDENTS' CIVIC LEARNING AND DEVELOPMENT

To be a good citizen, it's important to be able to put yourself in other people's shoes and see the big picture. If everything you see is rooted in your own identity, that becomes difficult or impossible. (Pariser, n.d.)

Directly and indirectly facilitating students' civic learning and development is part of the community engagement professional's (CEP's) role and responsibilities. In many ways, civic skills are embedded in community engagement experiences, sometimes explicitly as a set of discrete activities and other times implicitly as a type of hidden curriculum that accompanies traditional disciplinary content and instructional objectives. After completing this chapter, those working in the field of community engagement or as a CEP will be able to reflect on and apply the basic principles designed to advance students' civic development that address the following competencies and critical commitments presented in Table 7.1.

As mentioned briefly in chapter 5, the National Task Force on Civic Learning and Democratic Engagement (2012) provides a framework for twenty-first-century civic learning and democratic engagement consisting of a set of knowledge, skills, values, and collective action that can be used in civic education (see Table 7.2). Although useful, this framework is not a

TABLE 7.1
Competencies and Critical Commitments Associated With Facilitating Students' Civic Learning and Development

7.1 Knowledge of civic learning pedagogies (as potentially distinct from community-engaged pedagogies) 7.2 Knowledge of students' developmental trajectories and expression of civic learning and development	7.3 Knowledge of the ways in which students' identities inform and frame their community engagement experience, particularly those students from historically marginalized groups 7.4 Able to collaborate with and support historically marginalized students	7.5 Able to facilitate peer-to-peer discussion that positively affects student learning 7.6 Able to construct solid learning outcome goals 7.7 Embrace an asset-based mindset that guides students 7.8 Embrace the value of contributing to the larger community as a role model for students
Critical Commitments • Committed to cultivating authentic relationships with students • Committed to developing students' critical consciousness		

curriculum. CEPs must be aware of various resources, materials, and curricula that incorporate the skills, knowledge, values, and collective action strategies enumerated in this document that can be applied to cocurricular programming and courses. Likewise, CEPs must have other competencies related to students' civic learning and development.

Knowledge of Civic Learning Approaches

When we seek to learn and teach students about civic matters, we are hoping to foster the desire to be an active and engaged citizen and to acquire the knowledge, skills, and abilities that enable us to thoughtfully discuss public issues, work collaboratively with many others (including those with different perspectives and worldviews than our own), and navigate systems and structures in our country to bring about change. This civically focused teaching and learning is called *civic learning pedagogy*. Community-engaged approaches are potentially different from civic

TABLE 7.2
A Framework for Twenty-First-Century Civic Learning and Democratic Engagement

Knowledge	*Skills*	*Collective Action*
• Familiarity with key democratic texts and universal democratic principles, and with selected debates in U.S. and other societies concerning their applications • Historical and sociological understanding of several democratic movements, U.S. and abroad • Knowledge of the diverse cultures, histories, values, and contestations that have shaped U.S. and other world societies • Exposure to multiple religious traditions and to alternative views about the relation between religion and government • Knowledge of the political systems that frame constitutional democracies and of political levers for influencing change	• Critical inquiry, analysis, and reasoning • Quantitative reasoning • Gathering and evaluating multiple sources of evidence • Seeking, engaging, and being informed by multiple perspectives • Written, oral, and multimedia communication • Deliberation and bridge building across differences • Collaborative decision making • Ability to communicate in multiple languages • Values • Respect for freedom and human dignity • Empathy • Open mindedness • Tolerance • Justice • Equality • Ethical integrity • Responsibility to a larger good	• Integration of knowledge, skills, and examined values to inform actions taken in concert with other people • Moral discernment and behavior • Navigation of political systems and processes, formal and informal • Public program solving with diverse partners • Compromise, civility, and mutual respect

Note. From *A Crucible Moment: College Learning and Democracy's Future*, by National Task Force on Civic Learning and Democratic Engagement, 2012, Washington, DC: Association of American Colleges & Universities. Copyright 2012 by AAC&U. Adapted with permission.

learning methods in that the community-engaged pedagogy is concerned with teaching and learning that applies community-based experiences and partnerships to a broad array of student learning, which may or may not explicitly include civic elements. As a caveat, there is a high degree

BOX 7.1
Compass Point: Civic Learning–A

> Civic knowledge does not simply and suddenly manifest itself in students; it must be overtly taught. Think of a disciplinary-based service-learning class on your campus or one you know of. How could you integrate civic learning into the design of the class? Look at the learning objectives for the class, often listed early in the syllabus document. Which of these overlap with the elements in the twenty-first-century civic learning framework in Table 7.2? Which could be enhanced by integrating elements from the framework?

of overlap between the two kinds of teaching and learning, but it is possible to have civic learning experiences without personally engaging the public beyond a campus, and so not all civic learning experiences are community-based.

Over the past decade, a number of curricula, materials, and approaches have been developed to nurture students' civic skills and sense of citizenry. The Higher Education Research Institute at the University of California, Los Angeles developed a leadership curriculum that can be used to foster students' civic learning. Astin and colleagues' (1996) guidebook has become a classic over the years and is still used on many campuses. The model incorporates three perspectives or levels: the individual, the group, and the society or community. Seven critical values drive the model toward social change: collaboration, consciousness of self, commitment, congruence, common purpose, controversy with civility, and citizenship.

The public achievement model, created by Boyte (2018), focuses on promoting civic agency and can be implemented in schools, community organizations, or faith-based institutions using a set of core elements and principles threaded through six developmental stages. Students form a team about an issue, supervised by a coach, either a peer or teacher. The teams design action projects to address the identified issue based on three guiding principles: the issue the team picks has to serve the common good, the team's actions to resolve their issue are nonviolent, and the team's actions are legal or lawful. The public achievement model has been used at Augsburg College and the University of Denver to integrate civic education into their cocurricular and curricular programs to develop "citizen professionals" (D. Donovan, personal communication, 2015). The Sabo Center for Democracy and Citizenship at Augsburg College has created materials and offers training on the use of the public achievement organizing model (see http://inside.augsburg.edu/publicachievement/).

Battistoni (2002) describes eight specific civic skills: political knowledge and critical thinking, communication, public problem-solving, civic judgment, civic imagination and creativity, collective action, community or coalition building, and organizational analyses.

Similarly, Schutt (2001) published a comprehensive workbook that begins by exploring elements of a good society. Subsequent chapters include an examination of obstacles to progressive change and elements of an effective strategy for democratic transformation. The workbook also provides extensive figures and forms that can be used in a course devoted to developing civic skills.

Gottlieb and Robinson's (2006) workbook defines and describes the practice of *civic responsibility*. It includes assessment strategies and an appendix containing reflection resources as well as lists of films, quotations, and articles. The guidebook also enumerates essential competencies and skills along with a civic responsibility rubric. Rimmerman's (2006) text is essentially a narrative of civic activism that provides an academic foundation for civic education that could accompany other resources that provide specific skill sets. McTighe Musil's (2015) curriculum can be used across disciplines to explore the public purpose of disciplines.

The Bonner Foundation Network Wiki site (http://bonnernetwork.pbworks.com/w/page/13112067/Bonner%20Program) provides a list and short description of several civic learning pedagogies. One article by William M. Sullivan (2012) recommended professional education incorporate an apprenticeship of knowledge, skills, and purpose. In another passage, Hackett (2016) argued engaged learning is not merely for promoting the common good but also helps students learn how to be effective and good citizens in their vocational life by framing academic experiences through "semi-structured, interdisciplinary, holistic group work based on a civic problem, issue, or passion" (p. 1).

A decade ago, Wake Forest University launched a comprehensive program designed to prepare a cohort of students as democracy fellows to advance civic engagement. A study was conducted 10 years after the graduation of that cohort (Harriger, McMilan, Buchanan, & Gusler, 2017). Results indicated the democracy fellows had a greater understanding of civic responsibility than their peers in a comparison group and were more likely to be politically active with an interest and willingness to interact with individuals who hold different beliefs. In Box 7.1, we recommend practicing the integration of civic learning outcomes with community-engaged classes.

Knowledge of Students' Developmental Trajectories

As educators, CEPs are cognizant of the fact that students are at various developmental stages in terms of assimilating and applying civic skills. Therefore, it is useful to have heuristic frameworks to identify the developmental levels and trajectories of students' civic development. This assists CEPs and faculty they work with to make informed instructional decisions based on students' level of knowledge and understanding. McTighe Musil (2002) conceptualized and described what she characterized as the faces and phases of citizenship. Her framework depicts progressive phases of students' civic development in the context of community, scope, levels of knowledge, and benefits. Phases run from a spectrum of being exclusionary to generatively interdependent. The concept of community is framed from one unilaterally beneficial context to an interactive network. Similarly, the scope of civic development ranges from disengagement to civic prosperity framed in levels of knowledge ranging from a singular, unilateral perspective to multiple interactive connections. Her model outlines the beneficiaries for each phase. She expanded this framework in McTighe-Musil (2009), working with a team of scholars to create the civic learning spiral that represents a developmental scheme. The spiral consists of six elements, each including specific skills, attributes, and behaviors: self, communities and cultures, knowledge, values, skills, and public action. Each element includes civic learning outcomes.

The Bonner Foundation created a model for civic development that is used in the Bonner leader development programs (Hoy & Meisel, 2008). It consists of five development levels focusing on common commitments for cocurricular and curricular experiences: expectations, exploration, experience, example, and expertise (see Table 7.3). The curriculum includes a scope and sequence of skills for civic leadership in Table 7.4.

TABLE 7.3
Bonner Foundation Model for Civic Development

Level	*Experience*	*Commitment Examples*
Precollege	Expectation	Ethic of care as a cover value for engagement and service
First year	Exploration	Involvement in a variety of service projects
Second year	Experience	Focus on a set of issues, neighborhood, or agency
Third year	Example	Emerge as a leader of peers and begin to manage discrete projects
Fourth year	Excellence	Continue as project leader in a specialist capacity

TABLE 7.4

Bonner Foundation Civic Leadership Training Scope and Sequence

Bonner Training Calendar (A Developmental Sequence)

The following is an illustration of how a Bonner Program can intentionally support student skill and knowledge development, implementing the student development model. This chart represents how students' service positions, skill building, and areas of knowledge might evolve over four years.

	Year 1	*Year 2*	*Year 3*	*Year 4*
Types of roles and placements	**Exploration:** • Learning about issues • Learning about the community; discovering one's passions and talents • Settling into primary site and position	**Experience:** • Commitment to an issue, agency/site, and place • Expanded position and responsibility, such as coordination, organization, and planning	**Example:** • Project coordinator or leader role; managing of project or volunteers • Expanded leadership roles in the Bonner Program or at sites • Capacity-building service positions	**Expertise:** • Planning team or specialist; project or site leadership • Capacity-building service positions • May link to academic major, minor, certificate, or coursework
Knowledge and commitments to emphasize	• Knowledge of self and ability to reflect • Knowledge of community • Exploration of diversity • Community building • Introduction to civic engagement	• Analysis of diversity issues • Knowledge of poverty • Understanding of piace and ability to think critically around community • Introduction to other forms of civic engagement	• Engagement in other forms of civic engagement (advocacy, public education) • International perspective • Critical thinking and systems analysis (understanding root causes) • Leadership skills and application through practice	• Exploration of social justice • Vocation and career exploration/ preparation • Spiritual exploration • Connection to academic study (capstone/ thesis)

(*Continues*)

TABLE 7.4 (*Continued*)

	Year 1	*Year 2*	*Year 3*	*Year 4*
Skills distribution	• Active listening • Communication • Goal setting • Organization • Reflection • Time management • Understanding of place and community assets	• Balance and boundaries • Budgeting • Conflict resolution • Facilitation • Project planning • Teamwork • Understanding an issue (choose focus)	• Delegation • Project management • Volunteer management • Event planning • Fundraising and grant writing • Planning and running a meeting • Understanding root causes and systemic solutions • Public speaking	• Decision making • Evaluation and program assessment • Marketing and public relations • Career networking • Public education and advocacy (i.e., town meeting) • Public speaking
Linking to high-impact practices	• First-year seminars • First-year trips • Learning communities	• Second-year exchange • Learning communities • Service-learning	• Third-year leadership • International/global immersions • Undergraduate research • Policy research/issue briefs	• Senior capstone courses and research projects • Policy research/issue briefs
Potential courses (civic engagement minor)	• Lead-in course (e.g., Service-Learning 101 or issue oriented)	• Poverty/economic development • Research methods (CBR or service-learning)	• Policy/democratic engagement (policy or government internship) • International course	• Capstone/individually or problem- or issue-focused research

Note. From *Bonner Student Development: Goals and Framework*, by R. Hackett, 2018, http://bonner.pbworks.com/w/page/105850659/Student%20Development%20-%20%20Goals%20and%20Framework. Copyright 2018 by Bonner Foundation. Reprinted with permission.

The six common commitments and approaches in the model include civic engagement, social justice, community building, diversity, international perspective, and spiritual exploration.

The Association of American Colleges & Universities (2010) developed a civic engagement value rubric "intended for institutional-level use in evaluating and discussing student learning, not for grading" (para. 1). In this way, CEPs might use the rubric to identify and determine students' level of civic development to assist in programmatic and instructional planning. The rubric examines six dimensions of students' civic life: diversity of community and culture, analysis of knowledge, civic identity and commitment, civic communication, civic action and reflection, and civic contexts and structures. Milestones at four levels of demonstrated outcomes are used to determine students' developmental progression.

Welch and Koth (2013) combined principles from developmental psychology with faith formation to develop an innovative metatheoretical

BOX 7.2

Compass Point: Civic Learning–B

Which of the civic learning models or curricula described in this chapter resonate with you and why? Which one might be a best fit given the culture and mission of your institution? Civic development is not usually included in an explicit curriculum, learning objectives, or course work other than perhaps the field of political science. In essence, students rarely take a formal course to promote their civic development. How then can civic development be infused into engaged course work? How can or would instructors with expertise in an academic discipline other than political science even visualize or incorporate civic development into their course? How might a CEP play a role in helping instructors explore and include civic development into their courses? Can, should, how, or could a CEP explicitly teach civic skills to students? We have described a number of curricula in this chapter that could help you integrate civic learning into your campus. If you didn't have access to one of these predesigned curricula, how would you integrate some or all of those components of the twenty-first-century civic learning framework into cocurricular leadership programs or curricular credit-bearing courses? When, where, and how might you do this at your own center with student leaders or by providing technical support to faculty members teaching a course?

model of spiritual development of students through service-learning, which could also be applied to other forms of civically engaged educational experiences. Welch and Koth define and explicitly delineate *spirituality* from *religion*, characterizing it as "a dynamic process in which an individual forms personal meaning and purpose of his or her sense of self and it transcends relationships with others and the world at large" (p. 616), which aptly complements elements of a civic ethos. The model offers a spiraling framework that charts the space students find themselves in and navigate as they move through three levels of experience described by Youniss and Yates (1997) as transactional, transformative, and transcendental during service or civically engaged activities. The model has been used with students as they reflect on and determine their spiritual as well as civic trajectory through their personal experiences. Educators can also use the model as a heuristic framework to identify and monitor student movement from space to space, which informs instructional decision-making. We recommend you reflect further on approaches to civic learning by answering the prompts offered in Box 7.2.

Knowledge of How Students' Identities Inform and Frame Their Experience

CEPs must be aware of the various ways students' identities are framed by their experiences, settings, and circumstances. The dominant epistemological paradigm in higher education is grounded on a male Euro-American perspective. This framework has begun to shift and be questioned with the expanding presence and participation of students and faculty from historically marginalized groups and settings. Mitchell, Donahue, and Young-Law (2012) provide a compelling perspective of service-learning as a "pedagogy of whiteness" (p. 612) that serves as a normative approach of teaching and learning that has a limited, if not potentially detrimental, impact on students from diverse backgrounds. Whiteness is conceptualized as a social construct that prioritizes and imposes "cultural understandings, mores, and values of European immigrants to the United States" (Mitchell et al., 2012, p. 614) in ways that empower Euro-Americans with privilege and opportunities while excluding and oppressing members of other racial groups. Their argument can and should be expanded from a focus on service-learning to consider the other ways and lenses that are used to promote students' civic learning. Mitchell and colleagues (2012) propose three strategies for challenging a pedagogy of whiteness: checking assumptions and taking a reflective stance, framing service-learning and other structures to promote thoughtfulness, and teaching and talking about race.

Checking Assumptions and Taking a Reflective Stance

CEPs and instructors incorporating civic learning and community engagement are invited to reflect on the following questions: Who are my students? How do I know? Do I imagine students will share my assumptions about service and the community? Do I assume students will learn what I learned or would have learned from similar experiences? Do I presume students will have the same needs as learners like me when I was a student in college?

If the answer to any of these questions is yes, CEPs should ask, Who might think differently? Who might have different learning needs? CEPs should then begin to design their courses, activities, and training from the perspective of meeting diverse perspectives and needs rather than a single perspective or set of needs that is assumed to be universal.

Framing Service-learning and Other Structures to Promote Thoughtfulness

As discussed elsewhere in this chapter, CEPs and instructors must use an asset-based approach to frame any and all activities and experiences. This approach communicates that the community can make a meaningful contribution to the overall learning experience rather than assume the role of passive recipient of charity provided by college students and instructors. This framing includes incorporating readings that employ an asset-based approach. Using leaders from the community as guest speakers and coeducators gives the community voice as well as presents them as public scholars with public expertise. This also circumvents the potential burden of having students from these settings taking on the uncomfortable role of spokesperson on behalf of a specific group to educate the CEP and peers on the complexities of these settings. Finally, CEPs and instructors must understand and appreciate the complex demands of juggling school, work, and family to allow scheduling flexibility to meet service requirements.

Teaching and Talking About Race

CEPs and instructors must proactively and preemptively frame discussions about race that are directly related to the objectives of the course or experience and minimize ill-informed assumptions or comments by students. This entails intentional planning and structured dialogue as opposed to inviting radio talk show comments that rarely include critical listening and civil discourse. Specific strategies for implementing peer-to-peer discussion are presented next. Similar to the first strategy of reflecting on one's assumptions, a CEP and instructor can redirect miseducative statements by asking, What do you mean by that? and How do you know?

Able to Collaborate With and Support Historically Marginalized Students

CEPs must have intercultural humility and cultural competence to work effectively with students from historically marginalized groups and settings. Civic learning and community engagement often place students and faculty in settings that offer different contexts of race, class, culture, gender, sexual orientation, and educational levels (Ross, 2010). Beyond assimilating facts about cultural differences and practices, cultural humility promotes an understanding of the social, political, cultural, and economic dynamics that affect beliefs and behaviors of members in a particular community. As noted earlier, this requires an understanding of power and privilege through self-reflection and self-critique to recognize unintentional and intentional racism and classism that can and often occur (Ross, 2010). This provides CEPs with the opportunity to begin to explore and gain insight into subconscious or conscious assumptions and stereotypes that may influence their behavior. CEPs should participate in campus-sponsored workshops designed to promote intercultural humility and cultural competence. Although there are curricula, materials, and workshops available for academics, a critical component of intercultural humility involves building trust through face-to-face interactions and conversations.

Another expectation for CEPs is to establish and maintain meaningful partnerships with various offices and groups across campus that serve marginalized students. Effective CEPs regularly schedule meetings and conversations with their professional counterparts from these offices to explore ways of working together that advance civic learning. For example, CEPs have approached student leaders in Black student unions and staff of intercultural centers to coordinate and support activities of the Black Lives Matter movement. As such, it is incumbent on CEPs to do research about resources on campus that effectively work with the diversity of the student body and then establish contact with colleagues and the students they serve on a regular basis for ongoing dialogue and collaborative efforts.

Able to Facilitate Peer-to-Peer Discussions

Research suggests that discussions on civic issues present information, resources, and motivation that influence civic behaviors (Klofstad, 2010). Specifically, peers play an important role in sharing and exchanging political ideas that influence civic competence and civic engagement (McClurg, 2003). Mitchell, Gillon, Reason, and Ryder (2016) conducted a study at Iowa State University on how peer-to-peer discussions affects two civic dimensions of the Personal and Social Responsibility Inventory developed by the Research Institute for Studies in Education at Iowa State University and the Association of American Colleges & Universities as part of the university's Core Commitments Initiative. The results of that study suggested peer-to-peer discussion enhanced the experience of community-based learning on two essential civic learning outcomes: the importance students place on contributing to a larger community and students' development of personal and social responsibility. Similar outcomes on the impact of peer-to-peer discussion in learning contexts outside civic engagement were found in a review of the literature by Smith and colleagues (2009), suggesting that peer-mediated conversations enhance student performance on cognitive measures.

CEPs must be able to facilitate dialogue between and among students to promote civic engagement. Baker, Jensen, and Kolb (2002) developed a model for dialogue based on experiential learning theory (Kolb, 1984) that consists of five concurrent dialectical dimensions that offer "a space where conversation can occur" (Baker, Jensen, & Kolb, 2002, p. 64). Through discussion, students construct meaning through the cycle of experiencing, reflecting, abstracting, and acting. In this model learning occurs through the integration of concrete experience and abstract thought, the integration of reflection and action, the spiral nature of reflection and action, the relationship between separate and connected knowing, and the balance between collaboration and leadership.

Brookfield and Preskill (2005) developed the following procedure for creating basic guidelines for peer-to-peer group discussions.

- Invite students to think about and describe the best group discussions in which they have been involved, and then ask them to describe what happened to make them so effective.
- Next ask the students to recall poor group discussions in which they have participated and describe what made them so unsatisfactory.
- Have the students suggest three things the group could do to make discussions more productive for each of the positive characteristics.

- Use the suggestions to draft a set of ground rules by which the group will agree to abide.
- Record the guidelines and post them or bring them to discussion group sessions.
- Periodically, evaluate whether the guidelines are being followed and whether they work.[1]

Able to Construct Solid Learning Outcome Goals

Educators, in general, go into teaching and learning with well-intentioned and grand aspirations that students will be transformed and emerge from the experience as different people with new insights, knowledge, and skills. Those aspirations are often articulated in lofty goals such as improve student attitudes, develop and apply skills, and demonstrate understanding. The challenge comes when we attempt to ascertain what and how these achievements manifest themselves. Where, when, and how can we know a student's attitude has improved? What does understanding look like? The traditional approach has been to use exams, when in reality it is possible that exams really only assess students' prowess at taking tests and their short-term memory rather than determine the degree to which meaningful assimilation of cognitive information has taken place.

To address this, learning objectives must be observable and measurable to help us determine whether or not we have actually accomplished what we set out to do. An effective learning goal generally includes, in no particular order, a behavior, a condition for the behavior, a criterion, and sometimes a duration or time frame (Welch, 2007; Welch & Sheridan, 1995). A behavior is an action or application of newly assimilated information or skill that manifests itself in some kind of product such as a score on a performance test, conducting an event, or creating a tangible artifact. A condition is a setting, location, context, or circumstance in which the behavior occurs. This could be over the course of a semester in a class or at a community partner site. An important aspect of articulating a condition is the authenticity of where, when, and how the knowledge or skill is applied and generalized as opposed to a temporary and somewhat artificial circumstance such as an exam. A criterion is a standard of quality that serves as a target or goal. This is often quantifiable in the form of percentages or actual numbers, such as increasing voter registration by 20%. Finally, a solid learning outcome goal often includes either a duration or a window of time in which the behavior is to occur.

These four components create a robust rubric for determining to what extent learning outcomes were actually achieved. These can be used with groups other than students, including faculty or community partners. Instructional activities, curricula, and action plans are incorporated to meet these learning outcome goals. The following are some examples of well-constructed learning goals in the context of civic learning and engagement for courses and civic action.

Example 1: Students will correctly name or list (behavior) key historical figures of the civil rights movement in their proper chronological order from memory (condition) with a minimum of 80% accuracy (criterion) on the final exam at the end of the semester (duration or timeline).

Example 2: By the end of the weekend retreat (duration or timeline), student leaders will practice and apply (behavior) effective interpersonal verbal and nonverbal communication skills presented in weekly training workshops during mock interviews or small-group problem-solving teams (condition) with 100% proficiency (criterion) as collectively assessed by peers and the staff leader using an observation rating form.

Example 3: Students will demonstrate their understanding of key community organizing strategies discussed in class by applying them (behavior) in a team of peers during the semester (condition) to implement and coordinate an information fair on behalf of their community partner on the first Saturday of May (duration or time frame) to educate and advise the organization's constituencies in the neighborhood on available program services to the agency's satisfaction (criterion).

Example 4: Students' self-reported attitudes toward civic participation will improve (behavior) as demonstrated in a statistically significant difference (criterion) in the pre- and postmeasurement of responses on a validated survey instrument in an undergraduate civic leadership development course (condition) at the end of the semester (duration or timeline).

Example 5: Demographic and contact information on Hispanic and Latino residents will be collected and entered into a computer database (behavior) from a 20-square-block area by three trained neighborhood ambassador volunteers for the next 3 weeks (condition) representing a minimum of 75% of the residents based on census data (criteria) by month's end (duration) to be used in the voter registration efforts.

Example 6: In keeping with the institution's strategic plan to advance engaged teaching and scholarship, we (center staff) will develop and implement (behavior) a year-long learning community consisting of at least 10 faculty from various departments (condition) to assimilate best practice in conceptualizing service-learning courses resulting in course proposals and draft syllabi at the conclusion of learning community at the end of spring semester (duration or time frame) to be reviewed by the curriculum committee using the institutionally approved benchmarks to obtain official designation as a service-learning course to be taught next academic year (criteria).

We recommend you try your hand at developing a strong learning objective by completing the assignment in Box 7.3.

Embrace an Asset-Based Mind-Set That Guides Students

An asset-based perspective is a significant shift from a deficit-based approach. Traditionally, educators have often viewed some students and their background experience in terms of problems or challenges. This approach can and does manifest itself not only in explicit actions and behaviors but also through language of power and privilege as well (Mitchell et al., 2012). For example, a deficit-based approach emphasizes and focuses on words such as *needs* or *wants* and camouflages terms such as *inner city* versus a subtle yet affirming word choice like *goals* and *aspirations* of its *citizens*. Embracing an asset-based mind-set involves two dimensions and contexts. First, a CEP must recognize the assets students bring to this work as well as shepherd students toward their own self-discovery and celebration of their strengths. Second, CEPs need to incorporate an asset-based approach to the work students, faculty, and community partners do in the classroom and community. We suggest that

BOX 7.3
Compass Point: Civic Learning–C

Educators often use verbs such as *improve* or *demonstrate* in learning objectives. What do improve and demonstrate mean, and how would you assess whether or not these outcomes have been achieved? What are the challenges of using this type of terminology?

Likewise, educators tend to use nebulous dependent variables such as *attitudes* or *knowledge* as targets for learning. What do these mean, and how would a CEP assess them in effective and authentic ways?

Think about and identify a learning goal you might have for students or faculty you work with. Develop a learning goal that incorporates a behavior, condition, criteria, and duration, not necessarily in that order.

after reading the following sections concerned with student and community assets, complete the reflection prompts in Box 7.4.

Student Assets

Students typically enter into community engagement with a fairly narrow view of how this work can manifest itself. Based on their prior experience in high school, youth groups, or scouting, many students equate community engagement with direct service, which is indeed a common and legitimate approach. There are, however, other approaches that can tap into students' interests and skills. The Haas Center for Public Service (2018) at Stanford University has developed a robust framework called pathways to service and justice, consisting of six forms of civic and public service: activism, community engaged scholarship, direct service, philanthropy, policy/politics, and social entrepreneurship. The approach includes a personal inventory in which students consider and identify examples of service that in turn reveals an approach commensurate with their skills and interests. Although the inventory was initially intended to offer students pathways to a potential civic professionalism, the process is also useful in that it helps students self-discover their own assets and predispositions. CEPs are invited to join a working group collectively focused on implementation, analysis, use, and refinement of the pathways of public service and a civic engagement diagnostic tool (Haas Center Pathways of Public Service and Civic Engagement International Working Group, 2018).

BOX 7.4

Compass Point: Civic Learning–D

Imagine your role as a CEP in working with a group of students and a faculty member preparing to embark on a community engagement project.

How would you frame the geographical setting and activity at hand using an asset-based approach? What language or terms would you use?

How would you assist students in identifying their own personal and collective assets and strengths that could be used in the work?

To what extent do you already incorporate and practice the operational principles for asset-based community development created by the Collaborative for Neighborhood Transformation? How might you explicitly use or state them when developing students' civic learning? Which ones resonate with you the most and why?

CEPs must also help students become aware of their own personal attributes that will empower them to be civic leaders and members of teams. An asset-based approach allows students to identify traits and contexts in which they excel. A simple and informal teamwork style inventory (Welch, 2008) allows students to determine their preferred thinking and interaction styles when working with others in a group (see Figure 7.1). In Part I, students identify one description that best portrays their thinking style. Students then choose one characterization that reflects how they typically interact with others in a team. Students individually chart the location of their thinking and interaction styles on a matrix and then review the scatter of their collective individual assets and styles to consider the positive (as well as weaker) attributes of the group (see Figure 7.2). Rather than a formal validated personality inventory, response patterns allow an individual student and a group of students working together to become aware of and informally discuss their assets in ways that will promote constructive work and interactions. In this way, individuals and a group come to recognize and use strengths in terms of thinking and interaction styles when conducting civic work.

Finally, it is important to recognize and use a unique set of assets that first-generation students bring to their civic learning. A qualitative study by Garrison and Gardner (2012) identified proactivity, goal direction and optimism, and reflexivity as three key assets of this growing student demographic. These three key assets were strengthened with 13 identified characteristics or virtues: resourcefulness, strategic thinking, self-reliance, practical realism, flexibility, persistence, positivity, hopefulness, self-confidence, insightfulness, compassion, gratitude, and balance. The researchers recommended students must be aware of and use these assets. Likewise, CEPs must incorporate these characteristics into their curricular design and civic learning activities when working with students.

Community Assets

CEPs must also model and demonstrate an asset-based approach when working in community settings. This can be done by following basic operating principles for effective asset-based community development as described by the Collaborative for Neighborhood Transformation (2018).

- Everyone Has Gifts. With rare exception, people can contribute and want to contribute. Gifts must be discovered.
- Relationships Build a Community. See them, make them, and utilize them. An intentional effort to build and nourish relationships is

Figure 7.1 Interaction style inventory.

Part I—Thinking Style

Read each descriptor. Place an "X" on the line next to the one that best describes your usual thinking style and approach to working on a group task.

__ [6] I like to create something from nothing. I tend to be a visionary and can see the "big picture" in a project or task. However, I'm not particularly good with or interested in details.

__ [5] I generally do not come up with new ideas but I can work with ideas and improve them. I tend to be able to look at many ways of doing things. I usually place some importance on details but I'm not "obsessed" by them or worry about them.

__ [4] I generally follow direction and ideas. I like to be involved when directions and ideas are establishing. I am comfortable working within the status quo. I generally like thinking about projects that have already been developed and then improve upon them. I don't need or like to "re-invent the wheel."

__ [3] I like to think about the "big picture" but I also need to know how something is going to get done. I will "chime in" with ideas but I also want to discuss the logistics of completing a task. I like policy and procedures to guide actions but I'm flexible and realize there are times when a team must be creative and "make it up" as needed.

__ [2] I like to pay attention to the areas that need details filled in. I'm not particularly interested in the concepts of the "why's" of a project. I tend to notice things that others miss because I like to finish a task to completion. I like closure. I like policies, procedures, rules, regulations, and flowcharts because they provide structure to my thinking.

__ [1] I'm detailed and methodical. I dot the "I's" and cross the "T's." I would describe myself as being very analytical. I am a concrete thinker. I tend to be very linear in the way I think about getting things done. I don't like making it up as I go. I consider what comes first, then next, and so on.

Part II—Interaction Style

__ [A] I'm a "take charge" kind of person. I am a talker and a delegator. However, I am aware that I sometimes run the risk of dominating a group. I tend to have my own agenda and ideas about things.

__ [B] I'm an active participant with others on projects. I can and will take delegated assignments. I'm open to other ideas but I also like to share some of my own ideas from time to time.

(*Continues*)

Figure 7.1 (*Continued*)

__ [C] I'm somewhat active in a group but I don't like to take charge of things. I tend to sit back and listen to what others have to say, especially before I volunteer or share information and ideas. I don't have to be asked to participate, but I usually wait to "chime in" until the timing is just right and I'm feeling comfortable.

__ [D] I'm usually involved in a group . . . especially as a "good listener" to others in the group. I will speak up when I have to. I'm good at summarizing or clarifying what others have said.

__ [E] I'm basically a listener, an observer, and a follower. I'm not necessarily shy . . . it's just that I rarely contribute to a working conversation; I am willing to but only when asked. I prefer receiving direction and I'll contribute/participate when asked or invited. Many people would think I'm shy, but I'm not really . . . just quiet.

__ [F] I'm extremely shy. I'm quiet and prefer solitary work over group work. I usually do not initiate things in a group. I will, however, do assignments on my own.

Figure 7.2 Thinking and interaction inventory matrix.

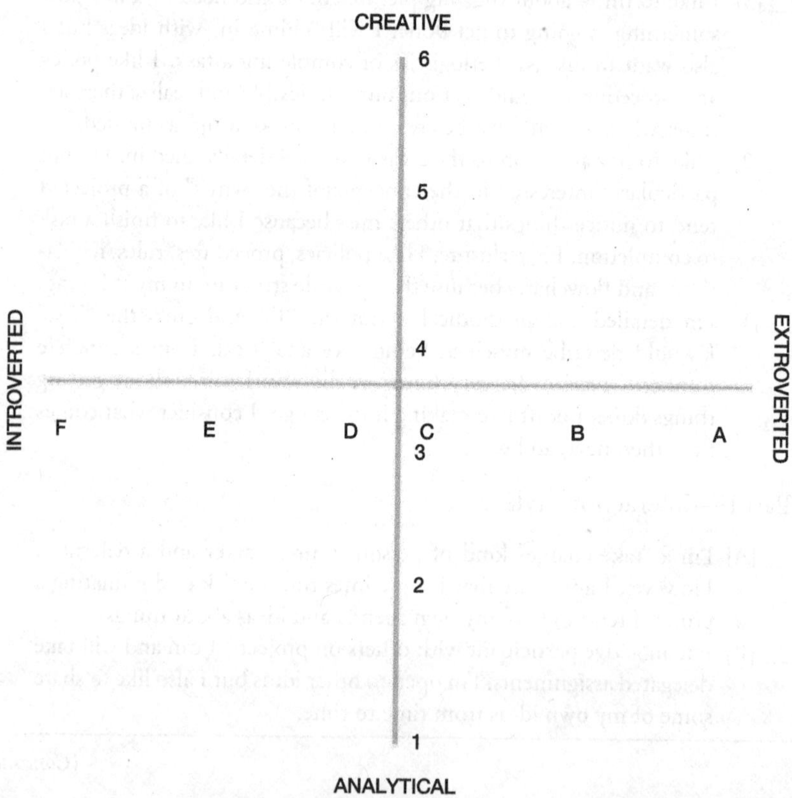

the core of Asset-Based Community Development and of all community building.

- Citizens at the Center. It is essential to engage the wider community as actors (citizens) not just as recipients of services (clients).
- Leaders Involve Others as Active Members of the Community. Leaders from the wider community of voluntary associations, congregations, neighborhoods, and local business can engage others from their sector. This "following" is based on trust, influence, and relationship.
- People Care About Something. Agencies and neighborhood groups often complain about apathy. Apathy is a sign of bad listening. People in communities are motivated to act. The challenge is to discover what their motivation is.
- Motivation to Act. Motivations must be identified. People act on certain themes they feel strongly about, such as concerns to address, dreams to realize, and personal talents to contribute. Every community is filled with invisible "motivation for action." Listen for it.
- Listening Conversation. One-on-one dialogue or small-group conversations are ways of discovering motivation and invite participation. Forms, surveys, and asset maps can be useful to guide intentional listening and relationship building.
- Ask, Ask, Ask. Asking and inviting are key community-building actions. "Join us. We need you." This is the song of community.
- Asking Questions Rather Than Giving Answers Invites Stronger Participation. People in communities are usually asked to follow outside experts' answers for their community problems. A more powerful way to engage people is to invite communities to address "questions" and find their own answer—with agencies following up to help.
- A Citizen-Centered "Inside-Out" Organization is the Key to Community Engagement. A "citizen-centered" organization is one where local people control the organization and set the organization's agenda.
- Institutions Have Reached Their Limits in Problem-Solving. All institutions such as government, non profits, and businesses are stretched thin in their ability to solve community problems. They cannot be successful without engaging the rest of the community in solutions.
- Institutions as Servants. People are better than programs in engaging the wider community. Leaders in institutions have an essential role in community-building as they lead by "stepping back," creating opportunities for citizenship, care, and real democracy.

Embrace the Value of Contributing to the Larger Community

Historically, the esteem and value we hold for educators and scholars in higher education are directly tied to the quality and contributions of their skill and knowledge in the confines of learning environments and discipline on campus. A competent teacher may have a tremendous impact on student learning, and his or her research may provide important new information to a particular field. Although these attributes are important, they are constrained to the academy. A civic-minded professional, whether a CEP, student, staff member, instructor, or administrator, transcends the parochial expectations of merely serving the classroom, residential hall, and discipline to extend his or her talent, knowledge, and commitment to serve the community at large (Hatcher, 2008; see Figure 7.3). Boyer (1997), envisioned the "academy as citizen," arguing that

> The scholarship of engagement means connecting the rich resources of the university to our most pressing social, civic, and ethic problems. . . . Campuses should be viewed by both students and professors not as isolated islands, but as staging grounds for action. (p. 92)

In this way, a CEP, as well as other key players on campus, must embrace and embody the virtues and characteristics of a civic-minded professional as a role model for students, faculty, administrators, and community partners through word and deed. But what does that look like?

The Indiana University Purdue University Indianapolis Center for Service Learning developed a paradigm of the civic-minded professional (Hatcher, 2008), who integrates personal identity with vocation and role as a citizen.

At the intersection of these three dimensions, the CEP embodies three broad characteristics, knowledge, skills, and dispositions, that can manifest themselves in a variety of ways:

- Knowledge
  - Volunteer and pro bono service opportunities
  - Contemporary social issues, community issues
- Skills
  - Competency with diversity
  - Consensus building across diverse opinions
  - Participatory civic skills

Figure 7.3 The civic-minded professional.

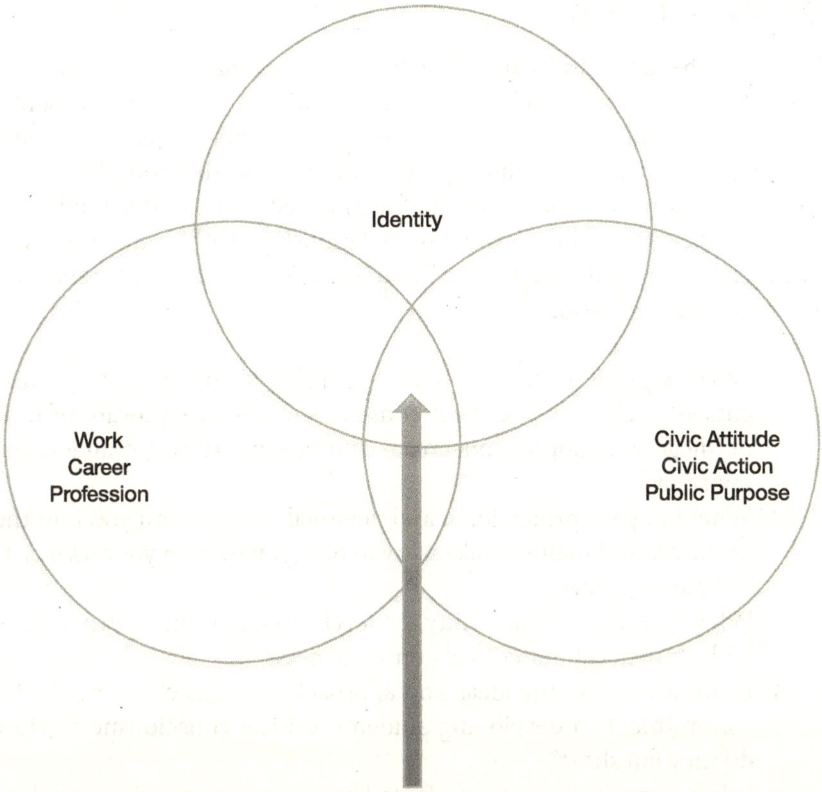

Note: Adapted from *Civic Minded Professional* by J. Hatcher, 2008, Center for Service and Learning, Indiana University Purdue University at Indianapolis, https://csl.iupui.edu/teaching-research/tools-instruments/graduate/index.html. Used with permission.

- Dispositions
  - Values, voluntary and pro bono service
  - Motivated to serve others
  - Sense of gratitude
  - Social trustee of knowledge
  - Passionate about work
  - Sense of calling, either civic or religious
  - Democratic values

We recommend reflecting further on the civic minded professional by reviewing the case study in Box 7.5 and responding to the reflective prompts offered there.

Deepening Our Critical Commitments: Questions to Ask

Above and beyond assimilating the competencies that advance students' civic skills, CEPs must also make a commitment to cultivating authentic relationships with students while developing students' critical consciousness, which we examined in chapter 2. Building on that foundation, we can begin to generalize our foundational knowledge and understanding of critical consciousness in our work and relationships with students to facilitate their own civic development. To do so, CEPs must critically reflect on some important questions.

1. What is *privilege*? How would you define or describe it? As discussed in chapter 2, critical consciousness is being aware of how privilege and oppression create and sustain systemic and social injustices.
2. Where in your professional and personal contexts can you find the resources and mentors necessary to help you deepen your own critical consciousness?
3. What is your current ability, or level of skill, to have discussions with students about critical consciousness?
4. In what ways do the ideas and approaches in this chapter reflect a commitment to developing students' critical consciousness? How do they fall short?
5. What opportunities do students have on your campus to explore the ideas of power, privilege, and oppression? What opportunities exist in the community?

In what ways do the ideas and approaches presented in this chapter reflect a commitment to cultivating authentic relationships with students? Give specific examples.

Students have an innate and internal authenticity meter they use to assess the authenticity of instructors and others. What does an authentic relationship look like? How can and does a CEP exude and demonstrate authenticity?

In what ways do the ideas and approaches presented in this chapter reflect a commitment to developing students' critical consciousness? To what extent do students understand and practice critical consciousness? How is it different from the toxic and vitriolic discourse present in the popular media, news, and political arenas?

BOX 7.5

Compass Point: Civic Learning–E

Review this case study and determine whether or not specific examples from each of the three characteristics of a civic-minded professional were evident.

Stevens is a chemistry professor at a small private, faith-based liberal arts college. She infuses community engagement into her courses by having her students conduct chemical analyses of water and soil at school playgrounds and community gardens in various locations. Students provide the results to community partners. Through the course of the activity, students come to recognize a significant difference in the accumulation of toxins in soil samples from underresourced, inner-city settings prominently populated by poorer families, typically of color, whereas samples from suburban areas with higher socioeconomic demographics were generally pristine. Through critical reflection tied directly to the instructional objectives of learning how to conduct, analyze, interpret, and report chemical analyses, students began to explore and grapple with complex issues associated with environmental racism. Class discussions went beyond merely reporting scientific data to include exploring the moral and ethical implications of their work. This included students' personal reflections on their role and responsibilities as a future chemist, a moral person in a faith tradition, and a citizen in the context of the risk and virtues of addressing social issues in a corporate setting for the benefit of the common good. The critical reflection generated significant cognitive dissonance as students grappled and wrestled with the potential ramifications for their job and conscience if they would be employed in settings focused on profit and did not necessarily address the ethical implications of the chemical industry.

Reflect on how you might introduce the concept and practice of the civic-minded professional to your student leaders in your center. How might you approach an instructor to share and explore this with his or her students in courses doing community engagement? Is this even feasible? Why or why not? What are some strategic ways you might advance the concept of the civic-minded professional to faculty and career service staff on your campus? Finally, review the civic-minded professional inventory to reflect on and examine your own actions and commitments.

Note

1. For other resources for facilitating small-group discussions, see the Harriet W. Sheridan Center for Teaching and Learning at Brown University website (www.brown.edu/about/administration/sheridan-center/teaching-learning/effective-classroom-practices/discussions-seminars/facilitating) and the Eberly Center for Teaching Excellence at Carnegie Mellon University website (www.cmu.edu/teaching/solveproblem/strat-dontparticipate/groundrules.pdf).

Chapter Eight

PROVIDING FACULTY DEVELOPMENT

Tell me and I forget, teach me and I may remember, involve me and I'll learn.

—Benjamin Franklin

Surveys by Welch and Saltmarsh (2013) and Campus Compact (2014) reveal that nearly all institutions and centers for community engagement provide some form of faculty development. However, the scope, depth, and formats of those efforts vary considerably (Welch & Plaxton-Moore, 2017). Therefore, the practice of faculty development remains a particular challenge as most current approaches lack theoretical foundations and contain a hodgepodge of formats and strategies (Van Note Chism, Palmer, & Price, 2013). Additionally, community engagement professionals (CEPs) must have not only the technical skills but also the credibility to effectively work with faculty in the highly autonomous culture of academia. This chapter presents competencies associated with conceptualizing and implementing effective faculty development. It includes a description of content, logistical coordination, and format of professional development programs as well as a discussion on the dynamics and cultural factors that can either promote or impede effective faculty development to advance community engagement initiatives. After completing this chapter, the reader should be able to demonstrate an understanding of the competencies presented in Table 8.1.

TABLE 8.1
Competencies and Critical Commitments Associated With Providing Faculty Development

8.1 Knowledge of how to approach differently motivated faculty using different strategies 8.2 Knowledge of how various departments or disciplines place value on categories of faculty work—teaching, research, and service 8.3 Knowledge of institutional constraints and possibilities that prevent or support faculty engagement 8.4 Knowledge of the logistic support needed to implement engaged teaching and research 8.5 Knowledge of the needs, research interests, and areas of expertise of faculty engaging in community engaged scholarship	8.6 Knowledge of various faculty career stages and ranks 8.7 Able to articulate the pressures or existential unease of engagement without alienating or discouraging faculty 8.8 Able to customize developmental training and support to fit each faculty member's needs and interests 8.9 Able to empathize with faculty and understand possibly conflicting demands on faculty time 8.10 Able to facilitate critical reflection wherein faculty encounter the limits of their own experience and value of taking advantage of community expertise	8.11 Able to facilitate faculty members' learning from one another 8.12 Able to help faculty brainstorm how to incorporate community engagement into teaching and research 8.13 Embrace innovation and designing and implementing new programs 8.14 Able to help faculty synergize their teaching, research, and community engagement 8.15 Embrace multidisciplinary and interdisciplinary collaborations 8.16 Able to model how to construct solid student learning outcome goals 8.17 Embrace persuasion 8.18 Embrace humility 8.19 Embrace patience
Critical commitments • Able to model effective communication to enhance coconstruction of courses, research, and other collaborative enterprises between community partners and faculty • Understanding dynamics of power and privilege in faculty roles in moving toward emancipatory and democratic practices		

Knowledge of How to Approach Differently Motivated Faculty

CEPs need to know what motivates faculty to become involved in various forms of engaged teaching and scholarship. It is likely that many of the motivational factors to pursue one form can be generalized to other approaches. Mundy (2004) conducted a comprehensive study of faculty predispositions to teaching service-learning involving more than 300 respondents at 15 institutions of various types. Multiple regression analysis revealed only one significant factor to predict faculty motivation and interest, which was related to their perception of service-learning. However, the findings of that study also revealed that faculty who participate in service-learning are generally concerned with student learning in courses related to social and personal values, personally oriented to community service, perceive support for this work from administrators and colleagues, perceive less institutional support in terms of promotion and tenure, perceive adequate resources and support on campus to assist them in teaching service-learning, and perceive service-learning as an effective pedagogy (Mundy, 2004). Demb and Wade (2012) identified four dimensions that influence faculty involvement in engaged teaching and scholarship and appear to validate as well as consolidate some of Mundy's findings. The communal dimension is characterized by an association with and socialization from like-minded individuals or groups. The institutional dimension reflects the mission, priorities, and systemic structure of the institution. The personal dimension is composed of factors such as race, ethnicity, gender, personal values, and previous experience. Finally, the professional dimension is characterized by a drive toward tenure status, rank, and professional ambition.

In a qualitative study of faculty members, Snyder-Hall (2015) explored their motivation for reconnecting their professional and public lives through engaged teaching and scholarship. Similarly, this study also revealed that many are continuing their interest and prior activities directly associated with social justice they experienced as youths and even college students at the undergraduate and graduate levels. Interviewees also reported they appreciated seeing the impact the work had on their students. Despite increased workloads, these faculty found this work to be meaningful and to have created a sense of community with like-minded colleagues, students, and community partners.

These findings are important for CEPs as they are indicators of how to approach the various motivations, interests, and concerns faculty may have related to engaged teaching and scholarship. CEPs must determine and then tap into a variety of factors that influence faculty decisions to explore community engagement. They must be equipped with a quiver of reasons and rationales to offer to potentially interested faculty. This requires documentation of institutional mission statements supporting engagement as well as written transcriptions of statements from high-level administrators advocating this work. Providing testimonials from colleagues documenting the support they received from the community engagement center on campus also assures prospective professors. Offering abstracts and summaries of research documenting the efficacy of engaged teaching and learning and a catalog or library of readily available resources, including one-on-one consultation for technical support, is also potentially appealing. Perhaps the most important motivational factor is demonstrating how engaged teaching and scholarship can be a catalyst rather than an impediment to attaining promotion and tenure when carried out intentionally and strategically. Research has shown that fears associated with risk to promotion and tenure tend to be the greatest barrier to implementation (O'Meara, 2010). Some faculty members will respond to a one-on-one conversation over coffee in the student union. Others may tentatively explore the idea of engaged teaching and scholarship by attending an informal brown bag lunch discussion that articulates reasons for this type of teaching and scholarship, coupled with ample evidence of support services and testimonials from well-respected colleagues.

Reflecting on her decision to leave a tenure-track position, Snyder-Hall (2015) explored whether or not faculty experience "public happiness" (Arendt, 2006, p. 114) through interviews with 40 faculty from various types of institutions. The interviews revealed that despite additional workloads and limited recognition, faculty found that this type of engaged scholarship produced feelings of professional, personal, and civic fulfillment that appear to play a significant role in motivating faculty to be involved with civic engagement on their campuses and in their communities. To further reflect on faculty motivations for community-engaged work, respond to the prompts offered in Box 8.1.

Knowledge of How Categories of Faculty Work Are Valued

Administrators of academic departments approach the academic trilogy of research, teaching, and service in their own way. Likewise, those in

BOX 8.1

Compass Point: Faculty Development–A

Where and how would you find out what motivates faculty to do this work? What type of information would you provide to faculty that may garner greater interest?

How might you determine an instructor's affinity for community service, social justice, or activism that might be considered as motivation?

Where and when might you host an informal informational meeting? Who might serve as advocates with testimonials? What specific information and resources might you offer?

some disciplines may view one aspect of the trilogy as more important than does another department. For example, history departments tend to place value on publishing books more than other types of scholarship such as journal articles. Those in applied professional disciplines such as education, psychology, nursing, and social work generally regard teaching as very important and assume that faculty will write about the scholarship of teaching and learning. Knowing how different disciplines value scholarship is important as it provides a perspective that can help generate ideas and help explore how engaged faculty can integrate and apply their work in ways that will assist them in the promotion and tenure review process. Consequently, a CEP must gain insight on how departments and disciplines value each component of the academic trilogy. The most effective way is through a one-on-one conversation with a department chair, which also helps build important social capital through the gesture of showing your interest and support. Consider asking for a copy of the department's promotion and tenure criteria if your institution has a decentralized approach that allows staff of individual departments to determine these important benchmarks. Another approach is to ask a faculty representative who may serve on your center's faculty advisory board to provide this information.

Knowledge of Institutional Constraints and Possibilities of Faculty Engagement

Institutional factors that can either constrain or support the work of engaged faculty (Welch, 2016) can be intangible cultural values as well as physical factors. A good place to start is to become knowledgeable of your institution's mission and goals from strategic planning. In this way, you and the faculty you work with can frame and justify the value of engaged teaching and scholarship as foundational to the core purpose of the institution. In essence, this type of foundational knowledge supports this work. Administrators of some institutions, especially research universities, highly regard research activities that may even result in patents or other types of intellectual property that can be commodified. Faculty at this type of institution may be dissuaded to partake in any teaching or research activity that does not reflect these priorities. Many institutions, especially teaching institutions, put a higher value on teaching many courses. The amount of time and energy required to prepare for these courses, in addition to grading papers, can significantly hinder the additional challenges associated with engaged teaching and learning. Finally, instructors are also expected to take on service roles and responsibilities by serving on or chairing various committees on campus, some of which require an exorbitant amount of time and energy.

Conversely, institutional resources and support can actually catalyze faculty engagement. Departments or other units on campus may provide mini-grants that can be used to support innovative engaged teaching or research projects. Other faculty development opportunities may be available from other offices and units on campus. Departments or colleges may offer financial support to attend conferences. Consider a conversation with engaged faculty to learn about the various constraints they are dealing with to convey empathic support as well as to gain insight as to how you and your office might support them. Similarly, conduct some campuswide reconnaissance to identify other possible resources. Once identified,

BOX 8.2

Compass Point: Faculty Development–B

Two important competencies address departmental and institutional variables that can promote or impede engaged teaching and scholarship.

What are some examples of these factors at your institution? How can this work be framed in the institutional mission and strategic plan goals?

How did or will you go about gaining information regarding these factors?

consider forging a partnership with those offices. Take a moment to reflect further on these ideas by responding to the prompts in Box 8.2.

Knowledge of Logistic Support Teaching and Research

A CEP and center staff must be prepared to provide logistical support to faculty. In addition to lofty, macrolevel support in the form of mission statements, you and center staff must be able to readily provide the nuts and bolts of this work, which encompasses conceptualization, development, implementation, and assessment of engaged scholarship. Logistical support extends beyond immediate and direct implementation of courses and research to postinstruction and research work that includes how to disseminate new knowledge and how to prepare for promotion and tenure review. Faculty are experts in their disciplinary field and are generally unaware of how to go about incorporating best practices. Therefore, a CEP and center staff must be ready and have in place a variety of policies, procedures, and resources that efficiently and effectively empower faculty available at the campus center and on its website. Sample syllabi to serve as models are very useful. Collect exemplary samples from your institution to have on file and refer faculty to the extensive sample syllabi database at Campus Compact (https://compact.org/resource-type/syllabi/). We recommend completing the assignment in Box 8.3 as a way to consider

BOX 8.3
Compass Point: Faculty Development–C

Conduct a task analysis of all the steps and resources that are necessary to conceptualize, implement, and assess an engaged course or engaged research project, and create a flowchart, timeline, or checklist of the scope and sequence of the process. Consider using this tool for each faculty member. Develop or collect the necessary documents and include them in a list to chart and monitor the process. See that these documents are put in a digital format that can be easily accessed by faculty from your center's website. Include ideas and resources that will assist faculty in disseminating new knowledge through peer-reviewed journals and conferences. Obtain the institutional or departmental promotion and tenure guidelines that can be used to help faculty prepare how to describe this work in their review portfolio.

and organize the support necessary to offer faculty who are engaging their teaching or research with a community.

Knowledge of Needs, Research Interests, and Areas of Expertise

There really is only one effective way to know the needs, interests, and expertise of faculty doing this work and that is to meet and talk with them. This personal touch is important as it begins to establish a meaningful relationship. A simple meeting for a cup of coffee on or off campus is an inviting setting and a good approach to this professional reconnaissance. This process reflects the art of being an effective CEP. People like to talk about themselves, so begin the conversation by asking how they got to their position and institution. Invite them to share what excites them. Consider asking for a copy of their curriculum vita to see their scholarly record and how you could support that work. Keep a file or notes on each individual faculty member because you will not be able to remember everything. Build into your week's calendar one or two touching-base conversations with faculty. Follow up with an e-mail message thanking them for taking time from their busy schedule and consider offering some kind of resource related to their interests and needs as a gesture of support. Another approach is to host a small gathering of faculty for a brown bag lunch or after-work gathering in a popular nearby watering hole for networking. In this social setting, they get to know each other as well as you.

Knowledge of Faculty Career Stages and Ranks

Tenure-track faculty go through various stages in their career to achieve a certain rank (Welch, 2010b). New tenure-track faculty enter academia as assistant professors under a probationary period of usually two or three years. During this time they must demonstrate adequate and satisfactory performance in teaching, research, and service according to official criteria. Assuming they successfully pass this probationary period, they are retained," which is where the term *retention* comes in. Over the next two to three years, the faculty member must continue to meet performance criteria to move up to the rank of associate professor. Faculty members in these stages are deeply preoccupied and concerned with satisfactory performance in teaching, research, and service. Consequently, they and their department chair are dubious of any activity that might divert them

BOX 8.4
Compass Point: Faculty Development–D

> How would you determine the rank of faculty currently doing engaged teaching and scholarship at your institution?
>
> Where, when, and how you would determine the rank and stage of faculty?

from this important professional goal. Therefore, many instructors view service-learning and engaged scholarship as potential deterrents to attaining promotion and tenure. Finally, an instructor earns the rank of full professor or professor after demonstrating a consistent satisfactory or stellar record of teaching, research, and service.

Not all faculty are on the tenure track. Some are adjunct or clinical faculty who are not under the same performance expectations. These faculty may be more inclined to take risks by teaching service-learning or conducting engaged scholarship. This trend appears to be supported by research conducted by the Higher Education Research Institute at the University of California, Los Angeles, which reveals an increase in the number of adjunct faculty doing this work (Eagan et al., 2014). CEPs should consider mapping and tracking the type and rank of instructors doing this work across campus (see Box 8.4).

Able to Articulate Pressures or Existential Unease

Faculty may encounter at least two forms of unease or tension as they do this work. First, there usually is an inherent risk when beginning a new endeavor or incorporating something that may be perceived as radical or countercultural. Each of us has had this experience when applying a new skill, even as basic and familiar as learning how to drive a car. CEPs must remind their colleagues of this fact while at the same time not minimizing or dismissing their anxieties. Faculty must be given permission to feel uneasy about this work while being assured of support from the CEP, staff from campus centers for engagement, and colleagues with previous experience. Remind them that their experienced colleagues and mentors were subject to similar feelings of discomfort.

Second, as faculty enter this democratic, cocreated educational experience, many discover they are not necessarily the sole expert and driving force in this work (Butin, 2007). They often encounter and gradually come to recognize community partners as what Ramaley (2010) described as "public scholars" with their own valid knowledge and expertise (p. 355). Similarly, applying complex theoretical constructs presented in the benign confines of a classroom may be tested or even called into question by students and community partners in authentic settings (Butin, 2007). Initially, this can appear threatening or disconcerting to a faculty member. However, CEPs must be prepared to point out that this tension can also provide a unique opportunity for profound teaching and learning moments by exposing students to multiple areas of expertise (Sandy & Holland, 2006) while incorporating the process of reciprocal validity (Welch et al., 2005) that may in fact enhance or strengthen a scholar's theoretical framework.

Able to Empathize With Faculty and Understand Demands

An effective CEP knows, understands, and appreciates the array of demands of teaching, research, and service faculty must juggle. Initial discussions should begin by asking instructors to describe all their current roles and responsibilities in the context of their teaching, research, and service. Overtly discussing and exploring ways to juggle as well as integrate these responsibilities conveys empathy and lays the foundation for a strong relationship based on trust and respect. This suggests a sincere interest in their professional and personal well-being as part of the art of this work. It also provides a glimpse into possibilities of how to integrate and consolidate their efforts, which may actually be an efficient approach to academic productivity. A CEP might invite instructors to explore possible ways of integrating their work and double dipping by writing an article on their engaged course or making a presentation at a professional conference. However, an instructor's overwhelming array of demands may mean this is not the best time to pursue or initiate any forms of engaged teaching and scholarship. Instead, it may be advantageous to wait for another semester or possibly another academic year. This honest and realistic assessment will ultimately be appreciated and interpreted that you have their best interests at heart.

Able to Facilitate Faculty's Critical Reflection

As noted earlier, another role of an effective CEP is to facilitate colleagues' critical reflection of their limits in terms of their time and energy as well as

BOX 8.5

Compass Point: Faculty Development–E

The previous three competencies involve potentially emotional experiences of a faculty member. A CEP's interaction and relationship with instructors often take detours into these uncharted territories. This requires and entails sensitivity and respect, which again reflects the art of being a CEP. Reflect on experiences in your own personal or professional life in which another person (e.g., family member, employer, colleague) engaged in sensitive discussions in an attempt to support you in difficult circumstances. What was effective and ineffective in his or her approach? Where, when, and how did these sensitive conversations take place, and how might you incorporate these insights into ways you can engage in supportive conversation with a faculty member? Is this type of conversation common in academia? Why or why not?

their knowledge of complex realities in authentic settings of the community. In regard to authentic settings, a CEP reemphasizes the notion and practice of community partners as coeducators rather than merely placement sites. This reframes the relationship so that an instructor can recognize, appreciate, and actually use the public expertise of a community partner. A simple approach to facilitating this type of critical reflection is to frame it using the What? So what? Now what? reflection rubric often used with students (Eyler, Giles, & Schmiede, 1996). Instructors reflect on and identify what they know and don't know about the context and the implications of their knowledge or limitations (So what?) followed by exploring the next steps to take (Now what?), which may include consulting with and incorporating the public expertise of their community partner or other resources. Take a moment to reflect further on your approach to working with faculty by responding to the prompts in Box 8.5.

Able to Customize Developmental Training and Support

Faculty development requires CEPs to meet individual faculty at various entry points of experience and understanding. In this way, a CEP embodies the spirit of the epigraph that opens this chapter by involving them and meeting them where they are on their pathway to engaged teaching and scholarship. Lawler (2003) characterized effective faculty development as creating a climate of respect, encouraging active participation, building on experience, employing collaborative inquiry, learning for action, and empowering the participants. Chism, Palmer, and Price (2013) synthesized the following developmental components common to most theoretical foundations for faculty professional development:

1. An entry point based on need. Faculty enter continued professional education because of an exterior trigger such as an organizational mandate or an interior motivation based on personal experience.
2. Formulating a plan to change practice. Participants explicitly or implicitly contemplate how to revise their professional practice based on new information.
3. Active experimentation. Faculty will incorporate new knowledge or skills on a trial basis rather than entirely adopt and assimilate them on a permanent basis.
4. Observation of impact. Faculty will observe the impact of the experimental implementation of new knowledge or skills.
5. Reflection and implications. Based on the observation, a faculty member reflects on the impact the trial application has and determines whether to adopt or reject the new knowledge or skill.

Blanchard and colleagues (2009) developed a comprehensive scope and sequence of 14 competencies of an engaged scholar. They categorized each competency across three levels of experience and expertise ranging from novice to intermediate to advanced.

Able to Facilitate Faculty Learning From One Another

According to the literature, a common approach to facilitate learning with and from each other is through a faculty learning community (Welch & Plaxton-Moore, 2017). We hope you are part of a professional learning community as you work through this book with colleagues either in person or virtually using various forms of technology. In other words, the learning process can be enhanced when it involves and includes others. Cox (2004) characterized a faculty learning community as a cross-disciplinary group of 6 to 15 faculty and staff members participating in an active, collaborative, sustained (often consisting of one academic year) program with a curriculum designed to enhance teaching and learning through regularly scheduled seminars and activities to advance learning, development, the scholarship of teaching, and community building. Faculty learning communities consist of 9 essential components and 10 fundamental qualities. Components include mission and purpose, a curriculum, administration and coordination, connections, affiliated participants, meetings and activities, a scholarly process, assessment, and enablers and rewards (Cox, 2004). Effective learning communities have the following qualities: safety and trust, openness, respect, responsiveness, collaboration, relevance, challenge, enjoyment, esprit de corps, and empowerment (Cox, 2014). The questions in Box 8.6 can help you to consider important factors in developing a faculty learning community.

Able to Help Faculty Brainstorm How to Incorporate Engagement

Welch (2010) developed a metacognitive strategy incorporating a mnemonic device (OPERA) to help faculty conceptualize ways to incorporate community engagement into their teaching and research. This heuristic framework allows faculty to break the broader, macro task of course development into five manageable components. This is not to suggest or imply that course development is a simple process of a mere five steps. On the contrary, critical consideration of each of the five components invites instructors to intentionally examine an array of dynamics and factors that often do not initially manifest themselves. The first letter, *O*, represents objectives for the course and the community partner. The letter *P* represents partnership, in which faculty must identify potential partners and agree on mutually beneficial objectives that could be met through engaged teaching and research. This is a significant paradigm shift from a placement model to establishing a mutually beneficial relationship with professionals

BOX 8.6

Compass Point: Faculty Development–F

Consider how you might organize a faculty learning community. How would you announce it and invite participants? When and where would the group meet? How often would you meet? What materials would you use or share? Aside from the logistics of putting together a faculty learning community, how would you go about incorporating the essential components and qualities? What challenges might you encounter?

in the community. The next step for the partnership is to explore the activities students will engage (the letter *E*) in for the service component of the course or the collaborative research efforts, which includes deeper examination and exploration of critical behaviors and activities related to cultural competency as instructors contemplate how and why students work with community partners in authentic settings to promote an ethos of mutual benefit and doing no harm. Consideration of when and how reflection will be conducted is presented by the letter *R*. This helps instructors discern how to incorporate reflection before, during, and after the engagement experience. This is typically an area of need for faculty as they do not necessarily know what reflection is or how to effectively incorporate it into their engaged teaching and research. Consider developing and hosting a series of workshops on reflection. Finally, the instructor and community partner move to the last letter, *A*, which is assessment of the extent to which course objectives and partner objectives were met and assessment of whether the research questions were adequately answered. At first glance, these five components may seem like a simple, straightforward process. In reality, each requires intentional consideration and support.

The CEP must also be prepared to help faculty explore ways to integrate their engaged teaching into their research and scholarship. This includes considering possible publications, identifying appropriate journals, and making scholarly presentations of their work at refereed professional conferences. A CEP must be knowledgeable of and have access to a list of publications and conferences, which can be found on the websites of Campus Compact (https://compact.org/events/) and the Engagement Scholarship Consortium (https://engagementscholarship.org).

Embrace Innovation and Designing and Implementing New Programs

Network with CEPs in your area; learn how they go about doing things. Meet informally for lunch once a semester (see the case study in Box 8.7). Attend professional conferences to hear about new best practices and innovative programs. Read the professional literature. Remember, this work and field are not static, they change often and quickly. Another straightforward approach that nurtures trust in your professional relationship with faculty is to simply ask them to share and describe their own positive faculty development experiences. This attunes the CEP to the personal learning style of your colleague, which can help shape aspects of faculty development and one-on-one technical support.

BOX 8.7
Compass Point: Faculty Development–G

CEPs from three institutions in a large metropolitan area periodically met for lunch in a central location of the city. This was an informal gathering they referred to as their Mental Health Club. In addition to exchanging ideas and updating each other on activities at their campuses, the gathering provided a safe space to discuss an array of topics such as professional aspiration, institutional politics, and frustrations with staff.

Consider and identify colleagues in your geographical area. Invite them to meet off campus to catch up.

In what ways does or could this type of informal networking provide professional personal self-care?

Able to Help Faculty Synergize Teaching, Research, and Community Engagement

Faculty enter this work with excitement and a certain level of trepidation. Part of the CEP role is to provide resources and support in various ways that stimulate their work. This includes being ready to provide or suggest materials or information ranging from websites, articles, ideas for publications and presentations, and strategies that will help them earn promotion and tenure. Refer them to other colleagues on your campus. Ask to visit their class or if you can take them to visit a potential community partner. Your excitement and enthusiasm will be contagious.

Embrace Multi- and Interdisciplinary Collaborations

Diverse ideas and perspectives enhance this work. Consider implementing an advisory committee or a course approval or designation committee with faculty from various disciplines to provide a rich variety of perspective and ideas. This promotes cross-pollination of ideas, strategies, and perspectives. Invite and accompany faculty to explore possible partnerships with colleagues from other disciplines. CEPs can reduce the pressure placed on individual service-learning courses, and by association the faculty who teach them, in the following ways: (a) connecting service-learning courses focused on the same civic issue or geographic community to one another, and (b) weaving a common thread of engaged teaching and learning into the fabric of institution committed to civic engagement (Dostilio & McReynolds,

2015). For example, a faculty member teaching a sociology class might collaborate with a colleague teaching a nursing course if both are using the same agency as a community partner. Shared, cofacilitated reflection sessions that bring perspectives from each discipline broaden the educational experience. Likewise, a shared experience might lend itself to collaborating on articles for journals in their disciplines. Consider the experience of one professor in the case study in Box 8.8.

Able to Construct Solid Outcome Goals

As noted in the discussion of the OPERA mnemonic, learning outcomes or objectives should drive the engaged learning activities in ways that benefit the student and community partner. Many instructors are comfortable

BOX 8.8
Compass Point: Faculty Development–H

Read the following case study. Identify ways the faculty member effectively integrated her teaching, research, and service as an engaged scholar. To what extent were multidisciplinary and interdisciplinary collaborations implemented?

Rogers is a tenure-track faculty member in the Department of Botany at a large research-based land-grant university. She teaches a course in agricultural studies as well as one liberal arts course for nonmajors in environmental studies. Her research interests are in drought-tolerant hybrid corn and maize as a food source and efficient irrigation procedures. She is in her fifth year as a faculty member and is coming up for review for promotion and tenure.

As part of the liberal arts course, Rogers created a service-learning class in which students created an ecocurriculum for an inner-city school. University students worked with junior high students to develop the instructional materials and then spent at least one hour a week in the school working with small groups of students. As part of the course, Rogers conducted pre- and posttests to assess the university students' cognitive skills for the course's objectives in basic introductory environmental studies. Using another section of the course taught by a colleague for a comparison group for her analysis, she eventually published an article on the class in a refereed journal. As part of the service-learning course, Rogers also conducted

(*Continues*)

BOX 8.8 (*Continued*)

reflection sessions using a rubric to assess students' affective, behavioral, and cognitive processes in written journal entries and presented the results at a refereed conference on service-learning.

Rogers was also awarded a grant from the United Nations and teamed up with colleagues in the School of Business and School of Engineering to create an interdisciplinary study and service trip on creating irrigation infrastructure to support a maize program in Africa. Students in the botany, business, and engineering programs and the faculty members spent three weeks during the summer working with local farmers and government officials. Their study examined the long-term impact of the project. Likewise, each instructor conducted pre- and posttests on cognitition and attitude of their students in each program. Each instructor published the results and shared authorship in each disciplinary journal. Part of the three-week project included student reflection sessions in which students discussed their impression of their experience and how they planned on using this experience in the future in their careers.

Rogers's service activities include serving as a consultant and adviser to the state extension agency. In that capacity, she helped develop a needs assessment with the agency and conducted workshops. Extension agents and the farmers they served identified specific issues. Following the workshops, Rogers helped local farmers learn how to collect productivity data to assess the impact of the irrigation methods that were introduced. The project results were published in refereed journals.

She also used the project's activities and results in her course work and brought her class to one site for a field trip. Other service activities included serving on the botany department's admissions committee, the college curriculum committee, and the library periodicals advisory board. Finally, Rogers serves as a reviewer on an editorial review board of a national refereed journal. In preparing her personal statement for the promotion and tenure review, she referred to the university's mission statement and departmental criteria, both of which emphasized the institution's commitment to integrate teaching with research to serve the community. Rogers also described her service-learning as a form of pedagogy, citing Kolb's (1984) model as the theoretical foundation for the course, and demonstrated effectiveness through the data she had collected.

and familiar with articulating their instructional objectives by describing what they teach (e.g., This class will examine . . .). However, many instructors have difficulty shifting to a paradigm of learning objectives that describes what they hope students will learn (e.g., Students will apply assimilated skills to . . .). Complicating this even more is the nebulous nature of assessing student learning to determine whether or not learning objectives were achieved. For example, an academic learning goal might state, "The student will gain an understanding of key concepts and terms." Traditionally, a passing grade on an exam would suggest the student met the academic objective of the course. But this may actually only assess a student's prowess at test taking rather than meaningful assimilation of knowledge.

As discussed in chapter 6, a more robust outcome is observable or measurable in a context or setting and ideally includes some kind of duration and criterion. Learning outcomes and objectives typically incorporate an academic or cognitive dimension that manifests itself in an action verb; for example: "Students will demonstrate [as opposed to gain] their understanding of key concepts by correctly delineating specific historical events in their correct chronology with the individuals involved with at least 80% accuracy" [the criterion]. Other possible student learning objectives might involve pre- and postmeasures of cognition or attitudinal assessment instruments; for example: "Enhance or improve students' personal attitudes regarding cultural factors related to diverse groups as measured by the pre- and posttest scores on a validated attitudinal survey instrument." In this case, movement in a positive direction as measured by a validated instrument serves as the criterion to determine whether or not the learning outcome has been met. Finally, and most applicable to engaged teaching and learning, creation of actual products that a community partner adopts or incorporates into a program represents a form of authentic assessment or social validation that students were able to apply new knowledge, information, and skills from a course into creating tangible evidence of their learning; for example: "Students will demonstrate their mastery of marketing strategies by developing a marketing plan for a nonprofit agency incorporating benchmarks discussed in class that will be adopted by the community partner agency."

Embrace Persuasion, Humility, and Patience

An effective CEP takes on the concomitant roles of marketing specialist, evangelist, and cheerleader for multiple audiences or stakeholders to advance this work. Embracing persuasion, humility, and patience transcends the technical skills of this work to manifest the relational aspects in the art of this work. Therefore, a CEP must know the values, interests, and concerns of a particular audience to respond to them. One study revealed that faculty and administrators hold very different views and priorities of this type of work (Welch, Leise, & Bergerson, 2004). Faculty tend to focus their interests on pedagogical, civic, and logistical issues, whereas administrators such as deans and department chairs look at institutional factors such as resources and budgetary constraints. Achieving promotion and tenure are priorities for both constituencies. This requires CEPs to present compelling facts and arguments as well as available resources to support engaged teaching and scholarship. This includes being able to cite or provide empirical evidence from the professional literature as well as marketing arguments in which this work is valued and validated by the Carnegie Foundation and professional and disciplinary accreditation organizations.

A CEP must practice humility and patience as well as promote those qualities in faculty and students who work with diverse groups in an array of settings. Although CEPs are experts in their field of engaged teaching and scholarship, they must maintain an accommodating demeanor when working with students, faculty, and community partners that will nurture trust and meaningful partnerships. The CEP must also remind faculty and students to embrace and practice humility and patience in the community, as presented in Box 8.9. Unlike carefully controlled settings such as traditional classrooms or labs, this work is often unpredictable and complicated, which requires being comfortable with ambiguity. We offer some prompts in Box 8.10 to help you reflect further on how you approach, support, and persuade faculty to take up community-engaged work.

Deepening Our Critical Commitments: Questions to Ask

CEPs often serve as bridges between faculty and community partners. Consequently, CEPs must be able to articulate principles and procedures in ways that are accessible to stakeholders. This includes avoiding jargon or acronyms common to academic settings. Community partners are unaware of and do not necessarily understand academic culture, policies, or calendars. Partners often operate on a day-to-day basis, whereas faculty and academic culture move at a much slower, even glacierlike pace, involving an array of bureaucratic procedures that may seem strange and inefficient. The CEP must serve as an ambassador of sorts to help community partners

BOX 8.9
Compass Point: Faculty Development–I

Read the following brief scenario. Reflect on and discuss your thoughts regarding town-and-gown issues and cultural competency. What went well, and what didn't go well? What might have been done differently? How could this be addressed through faculty development?

Smith, a brilliant scholar in health and nutrition, was asked by the administration of an urban inner-city school with low-income families primarily of African American heritage to come to discuss nutrition. She was thrilled to be invited and prepared her materials and PowerPoint presentation. On arrival, she immediately described her background and educational degrees from Ivy League schools and presented a list of her publications and awards. She did not ask families to introduce themselves or ask what they hoped to gain from the workshop. Instead, she turned to her PowerPoint and began lecturing on the importance of whole grains in breads, buns, brown rice, and fresh fruit and vegetables that could be bought at any supermarket or farmer's market, even though the school is located in a food desert. Smith then distributed a take-home how-to sheet instructing families on how to eat properly. She also indicated her college students would be coming to the school to tutor and provide technical assistance to anyone who wanted more information.

BOX 8.10
Compass Point: Faculty Development–J

Think of a department or discipline, or on a smaller scale, think of a faculty member with whom you would like to discuss and explore engaged teaching and scholarship. Consider how you would persuasively explain and promote this work in this context. What's in it for this faculty member? Why should he or she be interested? What are the costs and risks as well as benefits? What kind of support will be available?

navigate the language as well as the complexities of policies and procedures. Likewise, most community partners are not aware of the difference between students engaged in voluntary service and those in service-learning courses or preprofessional practicum experiences. CEPs might consider creating and hosting a workshop on the basics of higher education for a group of community partners to introduce academic culture and common terms or issues such as promotion and tenure. Conversely, CEPs should explore ways to educate faculty on the realities facing community partners through workshops. Cultural understanding and a common lexicon will promote effective partnerships. How might you consider creating and implementing professional development for community partners? Where and when would it be scheduled and delivered? What topics might be included?

A critical commitment of a CEP is the ability to model effective communication to enhance coconstruction of courses, research, and other collaborative enterprises between community partners and faculty. This is typically done through faculty development. Despite the apparent agreement for the need, importance, and implementation of faculty development to advance community engagement, most programs lack theoretical foundations for adult learning as well as robust assessment procedures to determine the impact on actual implementation and practice (Welch & Plaxton-Moore, 2017). Given that one of the major roles of a CEP is to develop and implement faculty development, a few questions are offered here for your consideration.

1. Does your institution have a formal office or program for faculty development? If so, does it have the expertise and resources to support instructors in developing and implementing engaged teaching or research? If you were providing faculty development, could this be a potential political land mine or turf issue? If not, how might you consider proposing and providing faculty development through your center? Could or would you consider working with an office of faculty development?
2. Why do most faculty development programs lack theoretical foundations for adult learning and assessment of implementation and impact? What would you do to counter this trend and practice?
3. What is the format of faculty development at your institution? Is it primarily a didactic experience that is a passive accumulation of new ideas, or does it actively involve and engage faculty in ways that reflect the epigraph at the beginning of this chapter? How would you involve faculty to promote meaningful engagement in their professional growth?
4. What is the nature and general attitude toward faculty development at your institution? Is this form of continued professional education actively promoted? Why or why not? Are there adequate infrastructures, resources, and programs at your institution to advance faculty development in general? What incentives are available?
5. How would you articulate the value and importance of faculty

development?
6. Because time is a major barrier to faculty development, how might you address this issue as you design a faculty development program?

Thanks to academic freedom, faculty are able to pursue their teaching and scholarship with a great deal of autonomy in a culture that embraces disciplinary expertise. Traditionally, higher education has approached educational experiences in the community for students and scholarly pursuit by faculty in a very unilateral, academically centered way in which students and faculty are the prime beneficiaries of authentic experiences in the community. At times, these benefits are unintentionally at the expense of, and sometimes to the detriment of, members of the community who may receive little or no benefit from the experience. Engaged teaching and scholarship represents a significant paradigm shift from unilateral scholarly expertise and benefit to include public expertise and benefit through what Saltmarsh (2010) characterizes as democratic-centered engaged epistemology. CEPs must carefully and diplomatically introduce and promote the mutual benefits of the public purpose of higher education. Although community engagement is potentially transformative, CEPs must work with faculty to create an intentional awareness of the inherent power and privilege in higher education through self-reflection and self-critique to recognize unintentional and intentional racism and classism that may influence their behavior (Ross, 2010).

CEPs assist faculty and students in forming community partnerships, especially those located in diverse and underresourced geographical locations, with an appreciation of and respect toward those who have invited them as guests into their communities (Mattar, 2011, 2014). This promotes democratic, nonauthoritarian trust and collaborative relationships. It is critical for a CEP to have an understanding of the dynamics of power and privilege in faculty roles in moving toward emancipatory and democratic practices.

1. Given the autonomous culture and expert model in academia, how would you articulate the nature and importance of the countercultural democratic-centered framework (Saltmarsh, 2010) for engaged pedagogy and scholarship to faculty? How would this be integrated into faculty development efforts?
2. How might you use faculty development to broach the subject and issue of power and privilege?
3. What materials, if any, might you consider incorporating? Who might be guest speakers?

Chapter Nine

CULTIVATING HIGH-QUALITY PARTNERSHIPS

> *Partnership is both the norm and an aspiration within higher education civic engagement practice today. Books, journal articles, organizational mission statements, and student learning outcomes routinely feature the language of partnership, collaboration, and co-creation in descriptions and discussions of civic work. . . . Notwithstanding the best intentions, the smartest program design, the most committed collaborators (among faculty, staff, and community colleagues), the best institutional support, and so forth, partnership is an essentially elusive thing. Why? Because rather than being primarily an exchange or an agreement, partnership within the context of civic engagement is fundamentally relational, and a relationship is always a work in progress. (Ray, 2016, p. 8)*

The language of partnership is threaded throughout the work of community or civic engagement. In our experience, the word *partnership* becomes a blanket term, sometimes inappropriately. We have observed many instances in which community engagement professionals (CEPs), faculty, and students refer to any sort of relationship or interaction between on- and off-campus stakeholders as a partnership. For example, placements and partnerships are different things. There is an operational difference between placements and partnerships and a difference in the ends that are served by placements and partnerships. Amid an array of relationships and interactions, the concept of partnership means something very specific, and CEPs need to differentiate among the various kinds of relationships and interactions. We feel there is a pressure in our field and on our campuses to use the language of partnership. We encourage you to call things by their right names; sometimes stakeholders simply want or need an interaction or a transaction and aren't looking for a partnership. Other times, a partnership is the right vehicle. In Bringle and colleagues' (2009) work to promote a "richer, more nuanced, more precise, and more useful conceptual framework for the analysis of relationships and partnerships" (p. 3), the authors suggest characterizing partnerships as having three qualities: closeness, equity, and integrity.

Bringle and colleagues (2009) also advance the SOFAR framework of engagement relationships, which identifies five key constituencies—*S* (students), *O* (organizations), *F* (faculty), *A* (administration), and *R* (residents)—and shows that partnerships happen among different configurations of stakeholders. A campus-community partnership between the institution, centrally, and a community, across organizations, has a different complexity from a CEP-organization partnership, in which a CEP and a community organization staff member form a partnership that students and faculty plug into. Partnerships can be informal, in which two or more people (such as a faculty member and community agency staff) choose to work together independently of their organizations and in typically informal ways. Partnerships can also be formal with goals, responsibilities, and financial commitments in accordance with some kind of organizational policy (Eddy, 2010). Again, we feel it is helpful to be specific about the kind of partnership a CEP is talking about.

As part of its Community Engagement Classification, the Carnegie Foundation defined *partnerships* as, "ongoing, long-term relationships in which each partner brings individual goals, needs, assets and strategies, and through collaborative processes blends them into common goals and outcomes" (as cited by Northern Illinois University Office of Outreach, Engagement, and Regional Development, 2018, para 2). A number of professional associations (e.g., Community-Campus Partnerships for Health, Campus Compact, and the Council of Independent Colleges) have explored the qualities of effective partnerships and offer various frameworks whose characteristics overlap considerably. Mutual authority for decision making, aligning partnership efforts with community goals and assets, and balancing benefits with costs are hallmarks across frameworks (Community Campus Partnerships for Health, 2006; Leiderman, Furco, Zapf, & Goss, 2003; Torres & Schaffer, 2000).

After completing this chapter, those working in the field of community engagement or currently working as a CEP will be able to reflect on the areas in which they are competent (see Table 9.1) and identify areas they would like to develop further. Those who are new to supporting community engagement or who aspire to enter the community engagement

TABLE 9.1
Competencies and Critical Commitments Associated With Cultivating High-Quality Partnerships

9.1. Knowledge of self: self-awareness 9.2. Knowledge of local community, history, strengths, assets, agendas, goals 9.3. Able to initiate and maintain effective partnerships 9.4. Able to connect campus and community assets	9.5. Able to communicate across boundaries and roles, between internal and external stakeholders 9.6. Able to involve partnership members in reflection on and assessment of partnerships 9.7. Able to resolve conflict	9.8. Embrace passion for and commitment to community engagement 9.9. Desire to participate in the ongoing life of the community, participating in community-building events, serving on boards, being aware of and invested in community concerns
Critical Commitments • Conscious of power relations inherent in partnerships • Committed to cultivating authentic relationships with communities		

profession will demonstrate awareness and emerging understanding of these areas of competence.

Knowledge of Self: Self-Awareness

Walking into partnership work without a sense of who you are and what assumptions and needs you are bringing with you, seen and unseen, is problematic. Further, if you are not from the community your partner is from, walking into partnership work without familiarity about that community or the intention to learn about it is arrogant. If CEPs choose to do partnership work without critically considering themselves, the partner, and the communities that surround the potential partnership, this suggests the CEPs assume the relationship will unfold according to their own ways of partnering, their own cultural contexts, and in accordance with their assumptions about the community. The relationships might proceed, but we believe the CEPs are primed to misstep and will likely encounter many surprises that may derail the engagement.

As Bringle and Hatcher (2002) stated, "Campus-community partnerships are complex, in part, because of the cultural differences that exist between higher education and the community in terms of how each generates knowledge and solves problems" (pp. 505–506). To effectively navigate, appreciate, and honor the cultural crossings in partnership work, CEPs need to begin by knowing themselves as cultural beings. This requires being aware of your cultural contexts, personal and professional, and their inherent orientations, pressures, and goals. Opportunities to learn about your potential partner's specific orientations to partnership, pressures, and goals are critical.

Knowledge of Local Community

Many of us come from the communities where our partners are located. Some of us do not. A CEP must also have knowledge about the broader community where the partnership is situated. It is vital for you to become familiar with the community's cultures and histories, its past experiences with your institution, the network of assets that exist to promote the community's strength and functioning as well as your particular focus area (e.g., assets that support entrepreneurship or assets that support food security), and the short- and long-term agendas and goals of the community. We offer one strategy we particularly enjoy, visiting with community elders, for learning about a community in Box 9.1.

Able to Initiate and Maintain Effective Partnerships

Torres and Schaffer (2000) describe the stages of partnerships as designing the partnership, building collaborative relationships based on trust and mutual respect, and sustaining partnerships over time. The role of the CEP can vary in these stages from being the campus stakeholder who initiates or is the primary university partner in the partnership to being supportive of campus stakeholders who occupy these roles. Knowing the role of the CEP in the partnership and the stages of partnership work is important for CEPs. The stages described next assume the CEP is the leader or holder of the partnership, but the material will also help a CEP to be an effective coach to others doing partnership work.

Eddy's (2010) change model for forming a partnership lays out the tasks when initiating and maintaining a partnership:

- Verbalize motivation and context for partnering
- Align the social capital of the champion and organizational capital of partners

- Establish partnership goals and team governance
- Frame the partnership to stakeholders
- Negotiate conflicts
- Frame outcomes
- Evaluate the process
- Institutionalize the partnership (p. 25)

In Eddy's (2010) model, potential partners should discuss whether the motivation for partnering is intrinsic (a shared concern) or extrinsic (opportunity to garner funding or a mandated collaboration). They should also discuss the context and ask if the environment surrounding the partnership is stable and predictable or shifting. Motivation and context influence each partner's goals for the collaboration.

A champion advocates for a partnership to happen and brings together the people who should be involved. That champion needs to take advantage of his or her social capital, that is, the people who know and trust the champion who will help the partnership. The partners involved need to use their organizational capital, that is, the resources such as space, funding, technology, information, and human resources available to the partnership through members' organizations.

BOX 9.1

Compass Point: Cultivating Partnerships–A

We have found it particularly helpful to learn about a community from respected community members. Some of the communities where we work have elders or trustees who have been a part of the community for a very long time. Many of them have helped their community grow and change over a period of many years. Having kitchen table conversations with these elders or trustees can be invaluable. We recommend doing as much footwork as you can to learn about the community in advance of meeting with these elders. We find it encouraging to share our knowledge and perspectives when we know the other person is truly interested and has taken initiative to learn a thing or two. Simple questions, such as the following, can elicit rich information: What was this community like when you first moved here or when you were younger? How has it changed? What have been some of the most important events? What do you like most about this community? What do you think surprises outsiders about your community? Who are some of your community's most important leaders? Whom do you consider to be the glue of your community?

Partnership members develop the shared goals for the partnership as well as their individual goals and discuss how the partnership will be governed, including how power, authority, resources, and decision-making will be shared. Depending on the formality of the partnership and the context of your institution, sometimes a memorandum of understanding is used to specify the goals, governance, the roles of each stakeholder, and how outcomes will be assessed.

Once the partnership's work is under way, maintenance of the partnership becomes important. Ongoing communication and evaluation of the collaboration is important to keep the partnership on track, and when conflicts arise, partners need to work together to resolve them. Maintenance functions are discussed later.

Regardless of whether the CEP is the leader or champion of the partnership or whether or not he or she is consulting with a campus stakeholder who wants to develop a partnership, familiarity with the tasks of initiating and maintaining a partnership is very important. Helping those we support to know there are discernable stages of partnership development and the tasks involved reduces anxiety of the faculty, staff, and community partner about collaborating and can help their efforts go more smoothly. Keith's (2015) book helps democratic civic professionals navigate partnerships using a critical lens, democratic commitments, and authentic relationships.

Able to Connect Campus and Community Assets

Before we move into the sections concerned with partnership maintenance, we feel it is important to stress an asset-based approach to partnership development, which differs from a needs-based approach or deficit-thinking model. It assumes that communities are asset rich and rejects the idea that communities must rely on outside assistance for their development (Garoutte & McCarthy-Gilmore, 2014; Kretzmann & McKnight, 1993). The asset-based approach to community development was formalized by McKnight and Kretzmann (1993) and promoted through the work of the Asset-Based Community Development Institute, now headquartered at DePaul University. It promotes a process of community development that embraces a place-based approach, usually a community or neighborhood, where residents identify or map the assets (local knowledge, skills, resources, organizations, and networks) of their community and their history of cooperative problem-solving (Coghlan & Brydon-Miller, 2014). An asset-based approach also includes seemingly subtle and nuanced language, requiring a shift from deficit-based terms such as *needs*, *issues*, *problems*, and *challenges* to affirmative ones such as *goals*, *aspirations*, and *vision*.

Increasingly, campus leaders are turning to asset-based community development to inform their approaches to community-campus engagement and also their approaches to partnership development. There are two lessons here. First, the assets in a community are identified before the role of outside supportive resources is determined (McKnight, 2017). This fundamentally reorients a conversation about community engagement partnerships from, What do you need and how can we help? to What is this community already doing that we might learn from and then may we join you in these efforts? Second, we can't separate the action of identifying and connecting assets from developing asset-based thinking (Snow, 2014). Because the act of identifying assets leads to asset-based thinking, we feel it is very important to involve the many stakeholders of a partnership in the exercise of identifying the assets that can be connected to reach the partnership's goals.

The result is a constellation of stakeholders who see communities as asset rich rather than need based, who notice resources that could be potentially overlooked (Kretzmann & McKnight, 1993) and who recognize the assets of stakeholders (Donaldson & Daughtery, 2011) such as community residents or students, in addition to those of employees of organizational partners such as faculty or community-based organization staff. Hamerlinck and Plaut's (2014) work illustrates the principles and practices of asset-based community engagement, providing an invaluable resource that should be on a CEP's bookshelf and used as source material when coaching others in community engagement.

Able to Communicate Across Boundaries and Roles

Communication is bidirectional: giving and receiving information. When hiring staff, two of the more desirable qualities we look for in candidates are the ability to listen and accurately hear what is being expressed and the ability to clearly convey information in a way that is honest and authentic. When a candidate can do this, we feel he or she will likely do the same in partnership communication, which is so central to this work.

Listening is a critical component of communication among boundary spanners (Williams, 2002). Actively listening allows the CEP to understand what another person is really saying and be open to valuing and being influenced by the views of other people. A CEP needs to model the ability to listen and how to be open to the views and voices of others as they steward campus and community stakeholders in partnership work. Martin and Crossland (2017) suggest that two-way partnership communication is largely concerned with CEPs developing a commitment to include community stakeholder voices in partnership development. Because community engagement activities are often initiated by campus stakeholders as a means to enhance students' education or faculty research or as tools of economic development, there has been a tendency for campus stakeholders to drive the conversation rather than prioritize community partners as equal voices in determining the activities, qualities of interactions, and benefits in partnerships. At times community stakeholders are unfamiliar with the capacities and constraints of faculty and students they wish to work with as partners. Helping to facilitate and model deep listening between campus and community stakeholders is key in helping to build mutual understanding (Furco, 2010) as well as consensus building (Martin & Crossland, 2017) in partnership development.

In addition to listening, inclusive sharing of information consistently and continually is key to partnerships. Effectiveness in oral, written, and presentational communications is foundational to how boundary spanners share information (Williams, 2002) but must be accompanied by transparency, inclusion, and forthrightness. Helping people to communicate openly and transparently share their motivations, expectations, and limitations allows stakeholders to mutually determine the nature of the partnership (Leiderman et al., 2002). Being aware of who receives information, who does not, and who is included in communication efforts is one way CEPs can practice inclusive communication. Finally, being forthright in partnership communications means CEPs are consistent in what they tell to whom, do not shy away from delivering disappointing or negative feedback (but do so with compassion and tact), and build credibility with those involved (see Box 9.2). Direct, clear communication is central to this work. We offer a variety of scenarios in Box 9.3 for your consideration. Take some time to reflect on your approach to communication by responding to the scenarios and prompts offered there.

Able to Involve Partners in Reflection and Assessment

Throughout a partnership, it is important for members to have the opportunity to check in with each other periodically about how the partnership is working and what needs to happen differently. This strengthens the relationship among partners and facilitates a healthy way of working

BOX 9.2
Compass Point: Cultivating Partnerships–B

Communicating clearly and consistently is a fundamental skill for a CEP. Being able to deliver disappointing news or negative feedback is key to partnership communication. Becoming aware of your tolerance to do so is an important aspect of self-awareness.

Can you communicate the rationale for a partnership in three lines of text or less? If you are communicating it orally, can you do so in one minute or less, and if you are using a presentation, in three bullets or less?

In your role as a CEP, do you tend to explain your institution's intentions or the purpose of an initiative two different ways depending on the audience? Is the difference in delivery a matter of style, or are you trying to avoid raising someone's concern?

BOX 9.3
Compass Point: Cultivating Partnerships–C

Consider these cases with a peer or mentor and then discuss the questions at the end.

- The executive director of an organization who works with three of your first-year-experience classes leaves a message for you one day in October saying, "Please give me a call. I have some bad news. The staff person who has been working with your first-year students has gone on medical leave and there's no way we'll be able to continue the projects." You realize that (a) this will affect about 80 students; (b) it's the middle of the semester; (c) it will affect 3 faculty members' teaching plans; and (d) without the students' work, the organization's clients will be impacted.
- A faculty member sends you an e-mail asking to meet with you to discuss plans to organize a service component to an upcoming study abroad trip to Tanzania. She describes plans for bringing a water purification technology to the community her group will be working in. She has a close colleague who has done a similar project using the technology in Latin America. In the e-mail, the faculty member says she has brought students to Tanzania once before but will be going to a new region and needs help making contacts. You realize that the faculty member (a) is proposing to

(*Continues*)

BOX 9.3 (*Continued*)

bring a technology to a community without knowing whether or not it's needed, appropriate, or wanted, and (b) will be looking to you for assistance.

- Your college president announced that the campus will be undertaking a place-based approach to engagement that will help those on campus work more intentionally with one of its nearby neighborhoods. You begin fielding questions and comments from community partners and faculty, for example, (a) Does this mean our partnerships in X neighborhood need to be shifted to Y neighborhood? (b) No one talked with us and now you are publicly announcing that you're going to be doing work in my neighborhood? (c) Does this mean we no longer value global engagement? (d) The recent funding climate has been tough on our organization, and we are so excited for the partnerships that are now possible with your campus. I'd like to discuss how we can arrange a community benefits fund.[1] We can see all the ways this place-based strategy will benefit the campus, and we just want to ensure that the neighborhood will benefit equally.

Questions for Discussion: How does this initially make you feel (emotions)? What stories about the other person's rationale or future reactions are you telling yourself (assumptions)? What more information will you need to clearly understand the situation (clarity)? What information can you supply to help the other person understand the situation (clarity)? What is the best way to have this conversation (mode)? What key messages do you need to convey (goals)? What outcome do you hope for (goals)? What would you say or do in response?

Note

1. A community benefit fund is a monetary fund set up to support activities or programs that will benefit a neighborhood or its residents. Such a fund is often created when a large entity (e.g., a casino or sports arena) wants to locate in a particular neighborhood. The neighborhood's stakeholders agree to support the location and property development if the entity creates a system to financially support community-benefitting activities that are developed and owned by the community.

together that hopefully produces the benefits desired by all as well as ensures members feel respected and valued. Although this is common sense, CEPs need to be able to guide others in actively planning for and managing these processes. In the absence of ongoing partnership reflection and assessment, which both of us have witnessed, some members can end up feeling exploited, or a lack of trust or regard among partners emerges, or the partnership gets off track and members feel it is too late to fix it. Partnership reflection can be used for fostering partnerships or to restore and strengthen a partnership (Catholic Relief Services, 2015).

Reflection during the stage of fostering or forming partnerships typically leads to a shared understanding of the purposes the partnership serves and how it will be conducted. This can be done in a variety of ways, but at its most formal a memorandum of understanding or agreement will be issued, which is becoming increasingly common among boards of nonprofit organizations. These memoranda may include topics such as the following:

- Purpose of the partnership
- Proposed activities
- Benefits or outcomes that are expected for each party
- Resource commitments from each partner
- Roles and responsibilities of those involved
- Acknowledgment that risks associated with partnership activities have been mitigated or will be managed following the included outline
- Time frame of the partnership and its subsidiary activities
- Cocreated ground rules to ensure considerate behavior among partners
- Decision-making procedures to determine who is responsible for what
- Agreed-on partnership check-ins
- Outcome evaluation procedures

Some institutions have standardized expectations for partnership agreements or memoranda. In some instances, partners reject the formality of memoranda, and when this occurs we feel that developing an artifact that reflects the understanding and agreements that shape a partnership is very important, but its format should reflect the context and comfort of those involved.

Reflection used to strengthen a partnership could also be considered assessment of the partnership, which offers a "structured framework for self-appraisal" and "legitimizes inquiry" (Gelmon, 2003, p. 42). Despite getting the partnership off to a good start, without the ability to reconvene periodically, the mutuality we so prize in our work can quickly slip away and with it the desired outcomes and regard partnership members have for one another. Such restorative reflection requires "authentic give-and-take discussion beyond campus efforts where the inclusivity appears contrived or staged" (Beere, 2009, p. 61). If periodic check-ins were included as part of the partnership formation stage, these kinds of conversations should be more comfortable because they are expected and may allow partners to avoid irrevocable difficulties. CEPs must also prioritize community partner participation in the assessment of partnership outcomes and have the ability to guide others to do so. In addition to being considerate of a community partner's capacity and desire to participate in assessment activities, CEPs must also be (or become) adept at creating the conditions in which partnership members can share candid, sometimes critical feedback. CEPs can provide assurance to community partners that sharing negative feedback will not preclude them from other collaborations with the institution, facilitate ground rules for conversations that give participants ample listening and speaking time, and validate the importance of honest feedback. Some examples of frameworks or instruments for assessing partnerships that expressly include community partners in the process include the PAIR (Partnership Assessment in Community-Based Research) measure (Arora, Krumholtz, Guerra, & Leff, 2015) for community-engaged participatory research, which examines elements such as communication, collaboration, partnership values, benefits, and evaluation, and the community-level assessment matrix (Gelmon, 2001, 2003), a framework for assessing variables in service-learning partnerships such as the nature of the partnership, nature of interactions, satisfaction, and sustainability.

Able to Resolve Conflict

When we do partnership work, conflicts will arise and how they are dealt with can either sustain the partnership or destroy it. By nature, partnerships bring together people from different organizational and personal cultures, norms, interests, and operating practices (Bringle, Games, & Malloy, 1999). These differences, if not acknowledged and mediated, can produce differing expectations of the partnership and behaviors among members. Often, the disagreement isn't about the actual behavior and events but rather what those behaviors and events signify about the way the partnership works, that is, the value and benefit of the partnership to the organizations, the quality of the relationships among partners, and the level of input and authority of each partner. Although conflict is natural in relationships, there are some oversights in partnership development that can increase the likelihood of disagreements. Confusion and disagreement are more likely to occur when partners do not sufficiently define the partnership's purpose or who is considered a member of the partnership or how decisions will be made (Prins, 2005).

Bracken (2008) also suggests we need to acknowledge and deal with the "hard stuff" (p. 9) embedded in community-university partnerships. Specifically, she calls attention to the authority norms associated with being a faculty person: Faculty are professionally positioned as being authoritative toward students and as experts in their fields and may unintentionally transfer that expectation of authority into partnership work with others. Many faculty are also under pressure associated with the campus merit system of review, promotion, and tenure. The obligation to produce scholarly work in alignment with a department's expectations may influence the purposes that lead faculty to seek partnerships and outcomes they value. Also, Bracken suggests we need to attend to how differences of gender, race, class, ethnicity, and sexual orientation influence our "approaches, strategies, understandings, and experience of community-university partnerships" (p. 10).

We also feel that efficiency can be the enemy of harmony. Even when partnership conversations have adequately addressed the qualities mentioned earlier, members can sometimes disregard what has been agreed on because it is faster or easier to make a decision by oneself, do the work by oneself, or confine an aspect of the partnership's work to one's own organization because it's easier to navigate one set of organizational rules and norms rather than two or more.

Ignoring conflict is not helpful; it undermines the partnership's chances of success and is associated with lower partnership satisfaction (Mohr & Spekman, 1994). When seeking to resolve partnership conflicts, Prins (2005) provides five lessons she and other members of a school-university-family support center learned:

> First, the case demonstrates how ambiguous purposes and membership can lead to confusion about authority, communication, and decision making. . . . Second, to reduce the possibility of unintentionally misinforming, manipulating, or otherwise creating inequitable relationships, partners should discuss their expectations of each other early on. . . . Third, partners need to discover and acknowledge what matters to others while advocating sensitively for their own concerns. . . . Fourth, members of planning partnerships should balance the individual and the group, recognizing that they exist in "productive tension.". . . Finally, planners should recognize how institutional contexts (organizational

> roles and responsibilities) shape how they and others frame problems and define legitimate goals and practices, and how others perceive them. University partners should first examine the basis and consequences of their own actions. (pp. 70–71)

CEPs help faculty, staff, and students develop partnerships with others. CEPs also support partnership members as they navigate conflicts. It is important to help partnership members understand that conflict is natural in partnership work, but it can also be mitigated. Assisting stakeholders to address conflict when it arises is equally important. CEPs can be a supportive, but frank, thought partner to help partnership members see where their expression of cultural and organizational differences, or expectations of authority, are getting in the way of productive collaboration. We offer a series of case studies in Box 9.4. Take a few moments to reflect on the nature of conflict present within each scenario. There are guiding questions at the conclusion of the scenarios for your consideration.

Embrace Passion and Commitment

Just as in the beginning of this chapter we recommend CEPs not call every kind of relationship a partnership, we also recommend that CEPs know the difference between engagement and other forms of involvement. CEPs ought to understand that when we are passionate about and committed to community engagement, we are committed to helping our campuses do work that involves sharing decision-making and power and embracing higher education's civic purposes.

This might be stating the obvious, but community engagement isn't solely a postsecondary education practice. Rather, the higher education sector adopted the terminology from community development and community organizing efforts. In fact, readers who have always worked in postsecondary education might be surprised that some people in community-based organizations are confused by what college folks mean when they talk about community engagement. Typically, it refers to engaging the members of a community in the advancement of their own community. It later becomes used by organizations (government, business, social service systems) that were not part of a particular community to describe their efforts to attract members of that community to work with the outside entity. As you might intuit, when outside organizations seek to engage communities, the nature of community involvement and whether the benefits are truly mutual involve some compromise and power sharing. Also,

BOX 9.4

Compass Point: Cultivating Partnerships–D

Read the following case studies and reflect on the discussion questions provided at the end.

- A marketing faculty member and a program manager from a nearby community organization form a partnership in which marketing students learn about the organization, its mission and clients, and develop a suite of marketing materials for a new program the organization will be launching. The students are scheduled to present their projects at the last 3 class meetings of the semester with the program manager in attendance. These sessions are from 2:00 to 2:50 p.m. Monday, Wednesday, and Friday. The program manager sits in the front row and is invited to ask questions and give comments for about 5 to 10 minutes at the conclusion of each presentation. The faculty sits toward the back of the room and grades each presentation. Unexpectedly, the program manager e-mails the faculty member after the second day of presentations explaining he isn't able to return for the third day. When the CEP convened the community and faculty partners at a coffee meeting for a debriefing, both parties expressed frustration with each other. The faculty partner was disappointed that the program manager didn't attend the final set of presentations and felt this was a letdown for the students who had worked so hard all semester. The faculty member was also personally offended that the program manager wasn't able to attend on all three dates even though they were scheduled at the beginning of the semester. The program manager was disappointed that the projects were being presented at the end of the semester with no time left for revisions or additions that would have made the marketing materials more usable for the community agency. The program manager also felt the presentations were difficult to attend given they were in the middle of the day and fell at the same time the organization was preparing a large grant proposal.
- A campus and local middle school are interested in pursuing a federal grant to create a full-service community school.[1] The campus is a comprehensive research university, predominantly White, and the middle school serves a racially diverse student population that the district describes as 53% African American, 26% Latino, 9% Asian or Pacific Islander, 8% nonspecified, and 2% White. School leaders request that university students who will work in the school be reflective of the

(*Continues*)

BOX 9.4 (*Continued*)

racial diversity of the student population. University partners feel unable to fully meet this request because the faculty and students who will be working in the school will be doing so as part of academic programs. As a result, the university staff feel they cannot provide the community-based learning experience to some students while denying it to others based on race. As they begin to outline various disciplinary contributions in academic, social, and health services, university leaders are eager to tie their contributions to a series of research grants to financially support their involvement. As a result, among other services, they identify three grant-funded university initiatives that will supply tutoring, positive behavior support interventions, and dental services to the middle school students and their families. As part of offering these services, the university makes plans to (a) track how the tutoring affects academic performance of Latino students (a priority of their education research grant), (b) involve caregivers in parenting workshops on the topics of managing disruptive behavior and follow up with behavior modification surveys each quarter, and (c) develop a dental intake process that asks for household information including income level, number of dependents, patient citizenship status or Medicaid eligibility, and residential address. School leaders are nervous about what they perceive as overly restrictive and invasive conditions on the services the university will provide. They are also very concerned that the students and faculty who will be working in the school will not reflect the racial diversity of the student body. Very quickly, the budding partnership begins to flounder. The school indicates it is rethinking pursuing the grant with the university.

Questions for discussion: What disagreements are present in these cases? What do these disagreements suggest about the way each organization perceives the value and benefit of the partnership, the quality of the relationships among partners, and the level of input and authority of each partner? What hard stuff (Bracken, 2008) is at the heart of the conflicts? What would you do as a CEP who is supportive to the partners to acknowledge and help resolve these conflicts?

Note

1. For more information about community schools, including the full-service community schools model, see the Coalition for Community Schools, U.S. Department of Education, or the Netter Center's University-Assisted Community Schools initiative.

in those communities where previous community engagement processes used by outside organizations have been exploitative, your school's efforts may be met with skepticism.

We believe CEPs who are responsible for cultivating high-quality community partnerships need to have a passion for community engagement. Those of us who have this passion see community participation in our work and that of higher education as vital, not just nice to have but necessary. And this passion needs to be accompanied by commitment because cultivating engagement with the community and true collaboration means changing the power dynamics of how we configure teaching, research, and institutional business operations. Figure 9.1 shows two different schemas of participation and their associated power dynamics. In the table, the stages in each framework aren't positioned as equal to each other, but they do indicate a separation point when shared decision making starts to happen between Biggs' consultative participation and collaborative participation and between Arnstein's placation and partnership. Apply these frameworks to your work using the prompts offered in Box 9.5.

Desire to Participate in the Ongoing Life of the Community

Can you imagine trying to cultivate partnerships with members of a community you know little to nothing about? It's hard, very hard. In part it's hard because you won't know who is interested in working with you and has the capacity to do so. It's also hard because the approach is one sided. Without knowing the community and its agendas and desires, you come with only the agendas and desires of the campus. If you continue to operate like that, without consideration of the community's assets and agendas, conversations will more likely end with "No, thanks." And yet, some CEPs do their work like this. We feel the field is partially responsible. Much of the early service-learning literature instructed us to use service-learning to meet community-identified needs. Much of the volunteerism literature instructed us to find ways our students or staff volunteers could meet the greatest need. As a result, some CEPs spend their days figuratively knocking on community doors asking people what they need. We say this knowing that a good number of CEPs are from the communities they seek to engage but cede participation in the community to their professional work.

Figure 9.1 Conceptions of participation.

<table>
<tr><th colspan="2">Biggs' Modes of Participation (Cornwall & Jewkes, 1995, p. 1669)</th><th colspan="2">Arnstein's Ladder of Citizen Participation (Arnstein, 1969)</th></tr>
<tr><td rowspan="2">Collegiate Participation</td><td rowspan="2">Researchers and local people work together as colleagues with different skills to offer, in a process of mutual learning where local people have control over the process.</td><td>8. Citizen Control</td><td rowspan="3">Citizen Power: Ranging from the ability to negotiate (within the partnership rung) to citizen's having full decision-making control (within the citizen control rung). This set of modes indicates the sharing or transfer of power between citizen and traditional power-holders.</td></tr>
<tr><td>7. Delegated Power</td></tr>
<tr><td>Collaborative Participation</td><td>Researchers and local people work together on projects designed, initiated, and managed by researchers.</td><td>6. Partnership</td></tr>
<tr><td rowspan="3">Consultative Participation</td><td rowspan="3">People are asked for their opinions and consulted by researchers before interventions are made.</td><td>5. Placation</td><td rowspan="3">Tokenism: Participants are invited to hear from power-holders and be heard by power-holders, but there is no guarantee that participants' views will be incorporated into change efforts; power-holders retain decision-making power.</td></tr>
<tr><td>4. Consultation</td></tr>
<tr><td>3. Informing</td></tr>
<tr><td>Contractual Participation</td><td>People are contracted into the projects of researchers to take part in their enquiries or experiments.</td><td>2. Therapy</td><td>Nonparticipation: Power-holders desire to educate or cure participants.</td></tr>
</table>

BOX 9.5

Compass Point: Cultivating Partnerships–E

Review Figure 9.1 and the portfolio of engagements you are responsible for facilitating. Where do they fall in these frameworks? Can you identify when and how decision-making and power have been shared in each activity?

What strategies do you use to persuade campus and community stakeholders that such decision-making or power-sharing is important to community-engaged work?

We recommend for CEPs to take a much different approach. CEPs are invested in the communities they seek to engage. When appropriate, they attend community meetings, frequent businesses, participate in events and festivals, serve on organizational boards, and are plugged into community-planning processes. Of course, this is all assuming that they do so in ways that are appropriate to what the community perceives as authentic participation. In other words, they don't push their way in despite community frustration.

And so, the desire to participate in the ongoing life of the community and the ability to do so require sensitivity and judgment. For many of us, we come from the communities our institutions seek to engage, and we must balance the needs of the organization that employs us with our commitments to our community. Others work with communities they are not from and need to carefully enter the community as a learner, listener, and guest before assuming they can participate. Boyle, Ross, and Stephens (2011) provide a comparative analysis of three community-university partnerships that illustrates how power, legitimacy, and urgency differ among partnership stakeholders and wonderfully describe how they affect partnership sustainability. We recommend for CEPs to take the time to read their work.

Deepening Our Critical Commitments: Questions to Ask

CEPs must be conscious of power relations inherent in partnerships. Likewise, they must be committed to cultivating authentic relationships with communities. In addition to the description of power sharing approaches discussed in this chapter, we also think it is important for CEPs to be familiar with three specific kinds of power: visible power (observable structure, rules, authority, procedures of decision-making), hidden power (who has access to where, when decisions are made, and what is on the agenda), and invisible power (who shapes meaning and whom that meaning favors through socialization, culture, and ideology; Donaldson & Daughtery, 2011). Each type of power can be used to exclude or marginalize, or it can be used to include and enable others' full participation.

1. Think of a community-campus partnership. Describe how each form of power is expressed, who it includes, and who it excludes. How can you work to make that partnership more inclusive?

The concept of cultivating authentic relationships pervades the work of a CEP and is also addressed in chapter 6, which we recommend you review. The ability to develop authentic relationships between campus and community, between CEPs and community leaders, or CEPs and community members depends on the ability to do a number of things covered in this chapter: approach others with an asset-based mind-set, be open to sharing decision making and power, know about yourself and care to know about others (their experiences, histories, realities), and to this we would add, be open to being changed by the other.

2. Think of the most authentic relationships in your life. In what ways has being in that relationship changed you? How does the other person in that relationship offer you feedback, and why are you willing to change as a result of hearing that feedback?
3. Think of a community-campus partnership you've experienced. In what ways did community stakeholders offer feedback? Was it heard by the campus partners? What about the feedback from the campus partners? Was it heard by community partners? Did anything change as a result? Why was change possible? Name the reasons. How can you create the conditions for feedback to be heard and considered?

Chapter Ten

IMPLEMENTING ANCHOR INSTITUTION STRATEGIES

To act is to anchor in an imminent future, so imminent it becomes almost tangible; to act is to feel you are consubstantial with that future. (Cloran, 1960)

The previous chapters of this guidebook describe various roles and responsibilities that generally entail fairly autonomous coordination and oversight by a CEP in collaboration with center staff and other stakeholders on and off campus. Anchor institutions, however, represent a complex, hybrid approach to community engagement that requires considerable commitment and investment of resources by high-level administrators and perhaps trustees and regents on behalf of the institution as a whole. Therefore, the role of the CEP in this context is that of a team member who generally has his or her finger on the pulse of various forms of engagement on and off campus as well as an understanding of the structures and dynamics of anchor programs. The CEP is, in many ways, a consultant for the administration and a liaison with community agencies in the conceptualization, development, and implementation of anchor programs. The CEP is also a potential member of a coordinating committee for shared governance of anchor programs. After completing this chapter, the reader should be able to demonstrate the competencies in Table 10.1 related to establishing anchor programs.

TABLE 10.1
Competencies and Critical Commitments Associated With Carrying Out Anchor Institution Strategies

10.1 Knowledge of anchor institution concept 10.2 Knowledge of key components to anchor programs 10.3 Able to articulate a rationale for adopting an anchor institution commitment 10.4 Able to conceptualize a proposal for developing anchor programs	10.5 Knowledge and understanding of strategies for establishing anchor programs 10.6 Able to articulate a rationale for adopting an anchor institution commitment 10.7 Knowledge and understanding of collective impact	10.8 Able to articulate and enumerate key components of asset mapping and readiness assessment

In contrast to short-term, course-based partnerships traditionally used in curricular and cocurricular engagement programs that essentially come and go, often in the time frame of a semester, an anchor approach is a sustainable, long-term partnership in a specific geographic location that "cannot move" (Axelroth Hodges & Dubb, 2010, p. 2), hence the use of the term *anchor*. Howard (2014) refers to anchor institutions as "sticky capital" (p. 1), which has an economic self-interest in capacity building to promote safe, vibrant, and healthy communities.

This in turn requires significant effort in articulating what it is to administrators and faculty who may only have a vague, fundamental understanding of community engagement in general, as well as considerable effort in actual implementation. Consequently, an effective CEP must be able to articulate not only what an anchor approach is but also how to develop and implement it as well.

Knowledge of the Anchor Institution Concept

Anchor programs typically target and address economic development, education, and health issues in the community, whereby participating institutions of higher education usually make a major financial commitment in partnership with local foundations through providing capital or low-income loans to initiatives and various forms of engaged teaching and scholarship by students and faculty (Welch, 2016). Many anchor programs focus on education and health, hence the common euphemism "eds and meds" (Harkavy & Zuckerman, 1999, p. 1) to describe this type of community engagement. Axelroth Hodges and Dubb (2010) suggested a number of strategic contexts in addition to education and health partnerships that anchor programs can take, including neighborhood revitalization, community economic development through corporate innovation, local capacity building, and scholarly engagement.

According to Dubb, McKinley, and Howard (2013),

> Anchor institutions are place-based entities such as universities and hospitals that are tied to their surroundings by mission, invested capital, or relationships to customers, employees, and vendors. These local human and economic relationships link institution well-being to that of the community in which it is anchored. (p. v)

Axelroth Hodges and Dubb (2010) describe three expressions or formats of the institution's role in anchor programs: facilitator, leader, and convener.

Knowledge of Key Components of Anchor Programs

The Annie E. Casey Foundation has made a significant investment in supporting anchor programs, stating the foundation for these efforts is based on the following anchor mission:

> a commitment to consciously apply the long-term, place-based economic power of the institution, in combination with its human and intellectual resources, to better the long-term welfare of the communities in which the institution is anchored. (Dubb, McKinely, & Howard, 2013, p. 1)

Anchor programs can consist of at least seven key components: a primary focus on capacity building in the community coupled with a closely related secondary emphasis on academic scholarship, quantifiable and observable indicators of impact, physical location of long-standing sustained programs with agencies off campus (e.g., hospitals, schools), shared goals, shared coordination and ongoing communication through shared governance bodies, shared resources including students and faculty, and financial investment from the institution and other participating organizations and businesses in the community.

Figure 10.1a Categories of anchor partnerships, outcomes, and indicators.

ECONOMIC DEVELOPMENT

OUTCOME	INDICATORS	DATA SOURCE
EQUITABLE LOCAL AND MINORITY HIRING	• Percent of local and minority hires in staff positions • Percent employed at living wage or above	Institutional data
EQUITABLE LOCAL AND MINORITY BUSINESS PROCUREMENT	• Percent of procurement dollars directed to local, minority-owned, and woman-owned businesses	Institutional data
AFFORDABLE HOUSING	• Dollars invested in creating affordable housing • Dollars invested in community land trusts • Percent of households below 200 percent of poverty line that spend <30 percent of income on housing	Institutional data, official records (census)
THRIVING BUSINESS INCUBATION	• Jobs and businesses created and retained (1 year, 5 years) • Percent of incubated businesses serving low-income and minority populations • Dollars directed toward seed funding for community-owned business	Institutional data
VIBRANT ARTS AND CULTURAL DEVELOPMENT	• Dollars spent on arts and culture-based economic development • Number of arts and cultural jobs and businesses created and retained	Institutional data
SOUND COMMUNITY INVESTMENT	• Percent of endowment and operating dollars directed toward community impact investments (e.g., support of community development financial institutions)	Institutional data

Note. From *The Road Half Traveled: University Engagement at a Crossroads*, p. 15, by R. Axelroth Hodges & S. Dubb, 2010, College Park, MD: Democracy Collaborative, University of Maryland. Copyright 2013 by the Democracy Collaborative. Reprinted with permission.

First and foremost, a significant feature of anchor programs is the primary focus on outcomes for the community, reflecting a fundamental shift in emphasis and purpose from the student-centric and academically based programs described elsewhere in this guidebook. This is not to suggest that students, faculty, or the campus do not benefit from participating in anchor programs. On the contrary, students and faculty make an important contribution to these efforts and derive their own rewards through teaching, learning, and research. However, the foundation of anchor institution programs is capacity building for communities.

Figure 10.1b Categories of anchor partnerships, outcomes, and indicators.

	OUTCOME	INDICATORS	DATA SOURCE
COMMUNITY BUILDING	STABLE AND EFFECTIVE LOCAL PARTNERS	• Existence of partnership center or community advisory board • Positive feedback from survey of service-learning/capstone partners • Civic health index rating	Institutional and survey data
	FINANCIALLY SECURE HOUSEHOLDS	• Percent of households in asset poverty • Dollars spent on community financial education • Dollars and human resources directed to income tax filing assistance	Official records; institutional data
EDUCATION	EDUCATED YOUTH	• High school graduation rate • Percent of students advancing to college or apprenticeship programs • Math and reading proficiency	Public school reported data
HEALTH, SAFETY & ENVIRONMENT	SAFE STREETS AND CAMPUSES	• Dollars spent on streetscape improvements • Rates of violent crime • Rates of property crime	Institutional data, survey data, official records
	HEALTHY COMMUNITY RESIDENTS	• Dollars spent on public health initiatives (e.g., clinics) • Number of grocery stores per zip code	Institutional data, official records
	HEALTHY ENVIRONMENT	• Percent of carbon emissions • STARS index rating • Greenhealth index rating	Institutional data

Note. From *The Road Half Traveled: University Engagement at a Crossroads*, p. 17, by R. Axelroth Hodges & S. Dubb, 2010, College Park, MD: Democracy Collaborative, University of Maryland. Copyright 2013 by the Democracy Collaborative. Reprinted with permission.

A study by CEOs for Cities and the Institute for a Competitive Inner City (2002) presents a framework of six areas where institutions of higher education can work with community partners and government agencies to promote capacity building for communities: sale of goods and services, employment, property development, establishing business incubators, advising businesses, and workforce development.

Similarly, the Democracy Collaborative at the University of Maryland focused on four broad areas when creating its Anchor Dashboard (Dubb, McKinley, & Howard, 2013) to help identify specific goals and measures for community-university anchor partnerships. The dashboard is not a guide or tool for implementing anchor programs. Instead, it serves as a framework or rubric to assess the impact the collaborative partnership has on the community rather than on students. The dashboard evolved from a comprehensive series of 75 interviews with academic and community leaders, representatives from professional organizations associated with academic institutions to identify key performance or outcome indicators for dashboard to measure outcomes. The following broad categories emerged: economic development consisting of six outcomes, educational partnerships consisting of one outcome, health and safety consisting of three outcomes, and community building consisting of two outcomes (see Figure 10.1a and Figure 10.1b).

A second distinctive characteristic of anchor institutions is the development and use of quantifiable measures for key performance indicators designed to assess impact on the community rather than exclusively on assessing college students' cognitive development. In establishing the anchor program of the Democracy Collaborative, five goals or guiding principles for assessing impact emerged to help guide the process: make the indicators relevant to low-income communities, develop measures that correspond with what communities care about, build in flexibility, identify outcomes that are important yet not overly burdensome to measure, and develop indicators in areas where there is institutional capacity and interest (Dubb, McKinely, & Howard, 2013, pp. 13–14). For example, one of the goals of the Central Corridor Anchor Partnership (n.d.) in Minneapolis-St. Paul, Minnesota is to "achieve a workforce among our anchor institutions that is more representative of local communities along the Central Corridor in order to contribute to better local health outcomes, improved educational achievement, and increased household incomes" (para. 1). To achieve that goal, the consortium of partners enumerated the following three quantifiable objectives: increase anchor institution employment from Central Corridor zip codes from 13% to 18 % in 5 years, achieve racial diversity goals across all job categories among Central Corridor anchor institutions in five years, and reduce the racial employment gap in the Central Corridor zip codes from 14% to 10% in 5 years. These objectives will be accomplished through various curricular and cocurricular programs developed and delivered by Augsburg College (Central Corridor Anchor Project, n.d.).

A third, more obvious feature of anchor programs is that the work is conducted off campus in a long-standing physical location such as a hospital, school, community organization, or specific neighborhood. This often necessitates allocation of some physical space for administrative staff and classroom space. In this way, the community organization serves almost as an annex for the college or university, allowing the institution to literally become a part of the community. This clearly requires formal agreements and coordination. This relates to a forth component of key characteristics of anchor programs, in which the academic and scholarship goals of students and faculty are embedded in and commensurate with the mission and operation of the agency as well as the goals of the community. A significant prerequisite is clearly identifying goals that are mutually beneficial. Shared coordination and ongoing communication in governance reflects the fifth key component, typically an oversight committee of representatives from community and government agencies, the community members, and the university. Shared coordination is in sharp contrast to traditional approaches in academia in which faculty or academic administrators administer programs primarily designed to meet academic or scholarly agendas. Agency staff and instructional representatives from the institution of higher education typically have a portion or all of their job description devoted to work in this community setting rather than as a periodic sidebar role or activity that traditionally would fall under service in the academic trilogy. Thus, resources in terms of equipment, knowledge, and people are shared.

Finally, the institution makes a significant financial investment to sustain operational programming on and off campus. This requires manipulating funding and financial resources from various sources in addition to the institutional investment. One example is LeMoyn-Owen College, which received seven grants for historically Black colleges and universities from the Office of University Partnerships at the U.S. Department of Housing and Urban Development. These grants, averaging $550,000 each year, were used as operating funds for the college's anchor initiative in neighborhood revitalization efforts that received millions of dollars in additional public and private funds (Axelroth Hodges & Dubb, 2010). Two anchor programs are briefly described in Compass Point Box 10.1.

To learn more about anchor programs, see the Netter Center for Community Partnerships (www.nettercenter.upenn.edu/what-we-do/anchor-institution-strategy), download and review the Anchor Tool Kit published by the Netter Center (www.nettercenter.upenn.edu/sites/default/files/Anchor_Toolkit6_09.pdf), and consider using it to help you formulate a proposal and plan for an anchor program. Share it with your administrators and representatives of community organizations.

Able to Articulate a Rationale for Creating an Anchor Institution

Maurrasse (2001) provided the following rationale for establishing anchor partnerships: It is good business, it promotes the socioeconomic health of the geographic area near the institution, healthy neighborhoods attract

BOX 10.1

Compass Point: Anchor Programs–A

Read the following descriptions of two anchor programs and then address the discussion questions provided at the end.

Augsburg College is a participant in the Central Corridor Anchor Partnership (www.centralcorridoranchorpartnership.org) of businesses, government agencies, nine medical facilities, and seven colleges along the light-rail line between downtown Minneapolis and St. Paul (Walljasper, 2013). The project grew from a living cities symposium and funding from the McKnight Foundation and the Central Corridor Funders Collaborative. The goal of the anchor program is to invest in physical infrastructure to serve the families, students, patients, and employees of the neighborhood. The president of the college chairs the coordinating committee, which meets quarterly, composed of a chief executive officer or representative of participating businesses and organizations participating in the project. The program has established the following goals:

1. Procurement: A study by Central Corridor Funders Collaborative determined 16 major anchor institutions had already spent more than $300 million in goods and services from neighborhood businesses.
2. Workforce development: The project targets hiring local residents at each of the participating businesses and organizations. The nursing and physician assistant programs at Augsburg College are actively involved in preparing and recruiting neighborhood youths for employment at the nine participating medical clinics. Similarly, the Urban Scrubs Camp hosted by Augsburg College is designed to develop interest in youths to become future health care professionals.
3. Engaged learning: The college has a long history of coordinating service-learning courses in the corridor. Preprofessional nursing students work at drop-in health centers at Riverside Plaza and Central Lutheran Church. Other students have provided in-kind assistance through service-learning at area schools, homeless shelters, youth programs, and senior and community centers.
4. Placemaking: The college is committed to maintaining the character and gifts of the neighborhood with efforts to control and minimize gentrification.

(*Continues*)

BOX 10.1 (*Continued*)

Syracuse University is an active partner in the Syracuse Art, Literacy, Technology District initiative that is designed to promote economic development, cultivate the arts while celebrating culture, foster employment opportunities, and provide teaching and learning opportunities for students and faculty. The program is coordinated by a nonprofit organization, the Near Westside Initiative, established by a grant from the Gifford Foundation in partnerships with Syracuse University, Home HeadQuarters, the city of Syracuse, the Syracuse Center of Excellence, and the National Grid. Since its inception, 26 organizations and businesses have participated (Lundborg, 2009). The Near Westside Initiative has been housed in the Office of Community Engagement and Economic Development at the university since 2007. The district contained abandoned single-family houses, older warehouses, and commercial buildings. In partnership with the city, the Syracuse University School of Architecture has been renovating these properties for a variety of uses, including art galleries. The master plan includes developing pedestrian corridors, improved transit service, multiple new parks, protection of the neighborhood's creek and floodplain, and housing with a range of affordability (Benfield, 2011). Many of the programs have been designed to address health issues. Syracuse University's Lerner Center for Public Health Promotion has worked with the Maxwell School, Nojaim's Brother's Supermarket, and St. Joseph's Primary Care to establish health clinics and nutrition education programs. The initiative also focuses on neighborhood safety by providing space for recreation and cultivating the arts. More than 70 faculty and 1,200 students have participated in various programs since its inception.

Questions for discussion: Based on the information from these two examples and the six characteristics of anchor programs, what might an anchor program consist of at your institution? What existing community organizations or specific neighborhoods might serve as an anchor location and partner? What departments, educational programs, and schools in your institution might serve as potential resources?

visitors and retain residents as well as businesses and students, benefits are mutual for the community and institution, it is in the enlightened self-interest of the institution to invest in and support its surrounding community, and it is the ethical and moral responsibility of the institution.

As Augsburg College committed to the Central Corridor Anchor Partnership in the Twin Cities, its president, Paul Pribbenow, stated,

> This is not do-gooderism. This is moving beyond the charity model. We have real interests that are at play with the neighborhood. For us, this is about our students. It contributes to their education, their safety, and a vital urban environment where they live. This is not just what we give to the community, it's about our shared interests and mutual benefits. (Walljasper, 2013, para. 11)

Able to Conceptualize a Proposal for an Anchor Program

Conceptualizing a proposal for developing an anchor program is very much like the proverbial chicken and egg conundrum: Does the process begin with the institution or the community? A CEP cannot first approach community organizations without discussion with and approval from the institution's administration. At the same time, an effective and strategic CEP has taken the pulse out in the community with existing partners to determine whether or not such a proposal would even be considered.

It is important to explain what anchor programs are along with the benefits for stakeholders. Given the busy schedules of administrators and community leaders, anchor programs should be described and presented in a two- to three-page brief, which should include a description and rationale for anchor programs and examples of mutual benefit. This document should include, in bullet form, a short list of proposed steps and phases of development and implementation such as conducting a readiness assessment and asset mapping of the community and institution. The brief should conclude with a list of references or resources for further information.

Next, early and separate informal conversations should take place with community partners and institutional administration. Based on these initial conversations, a CEP should suggest convening a formal joint meeting of representatives from the potential participants. If there is support for this, the conversation shifts to identifying mutual goals and objectives followed by planning and coordination of asset mapping and readiness assessment that will help guide implementation of the plan.

Knowledge and Understanding of Anchor Programs

Axelroth Hodges and Dubb (2010) listed the following issues and challenges that can affect establishing anchor programs:

1. Creating a community. Traditionally, institutions of higher education are seen as a community within the boundaries of the campus. An alternative perspective in community engagement and anchor institutions is to see the institution as a part of the surrounding community and neighborhoods. Many campuses are located in urban settings in which students and faculty can literally step across the street and be physically located in a geographically and culturally defined neighborhood. Students at other institutions cannot but are in less tangible ways linked to their community at large. Similarly, some campuses have a relationship with a community agency in specific neighborhoods that can serve as annex facilities.
2. Establishing partnerships and goals. An anchor approach typically incorporates the aspirations of the community as the driving force behind achieving specific goals. Keeping in mind that colleges and universities are not social service agencies, they can take on the role of a convener that brings various groups together. Likewise, because they are academic institutions, they can readily provide students and faculty as assets.
3. Instituting an anchor vision. A commitment to anchor programs is not merely an external commitment to the community. It also requires an internal commitment from the institution to do this work. An ethos and commitment to community engagement is a combination of top-down administrative and bottom-up faculty support. Axelroth Hodges and Dubb (2010) emphasize the absolute prerequisite need for support by high-level administration to set an agenda and commit resources. Likewise, faculty must agree to invest time, energy, and resources to go beyond the four walls of a classroom to work with partners, a concept and practice that is counterculture to traditional autonomy.
4. Securing and leveraging funding. Anchor programs require money. Universities and colleges can use internal budgets, dollars from federal sources and philanthropic foundations, and targeted fundraising campaigns with alumni and friends of the institution. Funds from one of these sources can be used as leverage to obtain other fiscal resources. This also requires the institution to revisit and reallocate internal funds in new and creative ways.
5. Building a culture of shared economic inclusion. Directly providing funds is one, and often somewhat unfeasible, way of nurturing the economic health of a neighborhood. Institutions can indirectly support economic development through other ways such as providing open-door access to enrollment through credit- and

noncredit-bearing courses to students from underresourced backgrounds and neighborhoods at no or limited cost. Traditionally, the practice of service-learning and other forms of engaged teaching and scholarship indirectly contribute to the economic well-being of the community in the form of volunteer dollars. Institutions can also provide economic support by establishing contracts with local vendors of goods and services that help keep money in the area. Finally, and at a more complex degree, institutions can purchase property in nearby communities to establish university-based programs such as health clinics, business incubators, and art centers.

6. Sustaining participant planning and community relationships. Anchor programs take time and transparency to overcome long-held tension and distrust that often occur through a clash of town-and-gown cultures. There must be visibility of high-level administrators to convey legitimacy and commitment on the part of the institution. This can only be accomplished through a series of conversations on and off campus.
7. Meeting the needs of low-income neighborhoods. As stated previously, a key component to anchor programs is when activities and goals are driven by the aspirations and goals of the community members. This is in direct contrast to traditional approaches of faculty researchers that involve coming into communities to complete projects that serve their own teaching and research agendas.

Able to Articulate Key Components of Asset Mapping and Readiness Assessment

Asset mapping and readiness assessment are two strategies that can be applied as part of any new initiative, not just when proposing an anchor institution program. Asset mapping is taken from community organizing and, unlike deficit-based programs reacting to problems, takes a positive and constructive approach to identifying existing assets in an array of domains like people, physical locations, tools, information, and traditions in a specific geographic area to achieve goals. This often involves thinking creatively to use nontraditional resources such as neighborhood elders with a vast life experience. It includes identifying resources that are often underused and right under the nose of the community, such as classrooms or fellowship halls in churches that are generally used only on Sundays.

Readiness assessment can range from a complex, formal process to a fairly simple and straightforward one. The systems framework checklist presented in chapter 4 (see Figure 4.2) of this guidebook could be adapted and used as a readiness assessment inventory. Succinctly summarized, a readiness assessment is composed of four steps and components: need + have + obtain + allocate. The first step is identifying the resources necessary to meet a goal or objective, followed by determining if they are readily available. This essentially asks the questions, What do we need to achieve this goal? followed by, What do we already have? If the resources are not accessible, the third step is to brainstorm where and how to obtain them or modify existing resources followed by the final step of allocating them in an action plan to meet the goal. The true scenario in in Box 10.2 illustrates the readiness assessment process in a smaller, modest context involving one school.

Knowledge and Understanding of Collective Impact

Collective impact is an approach of community capacity building that emerged from the work of Kania and Mak Kramer (2011) and can be incorporated as an operational template when establishing and maintaining robust community partnerships and anchor programs. Collective impact incorporates five operational principles: Equity is a priority in the design and implementation of the initiative's efforts; community members are actively involved and given a voice; data are gathered and used to continuously learn, adapt, and improve the initiative; trust and respect are fostered among and between participants; and the local context customizes efforts (Collective Impact Forum, 2014). Five essential conditions are necessary in collective impact: a common agenda in which all participants and stakeholders have a shared vision and goals, establishment of consistently gathered and shared measurements to assess impact and hold everyone accountable, mutually reinforcing activities coordinated through a shared plan of action, continuous communication for monitoring efforts while building trust and promoting shared motivation, and a backbone team orchestrating the work of the organizations (Hanleybrown, Kania, & Kramer, 2012).

Implementation of collective impact consists of three phases—initiate action, organize for impact, and sustain action and impact—each of which contains four broad components for success: governance and infrastructure, strategic planning, community involvement, and evaluation and improvement (Hanleybrown et al., 2012). The Collective Impact Forum (2014) provides an almost overwhelming amount of information and resources ranging from reading materials and webinars on topics and issues such as equity and cultural competency to case studies and training

BOX 10.2

Compass Point: Anchor Programs–B

The teachers and families of a Title I elementary school in a low-income neighborhood in Boston wanted to establish a family resource center in the school where parents could socialize as well as meet as a group and learn parenting skills. The physical layout and financial limitations of the school simply could not accommodate the construction of a new center. The school conducted an asset map of the school and determined the library was not used during a part of the morning on specific days of the week because of academic scheduling across all grades. Likewise, they observed an underused space in the library that could be used as a center. They also realized most parents worked during the day, so they decided they needed to allocate one night a week for workshops and social events in the center or school gym. They brainstormed what items would be needed for the center and conducted a readiness assessment. A used refrigerator, coffee pot, shelves, table, chairs, and sofa were located in the community and donated to the school for use in the center. Two parent volunteers offered to coordinate the use of the center and maintain its appearance. In partnership with a nearby college, faculty and students in education and psychology courses provided information and resources during a parent education class every Wednesday night. Students in a living-learning community from the nearby college provided child care in the kindergarten room while parents attended workshops. Local restaurants donated food to provide dinner for the participants. The creation of this anchor program was accomplished with little to no financial investment by creatively incorporating existing and underused resources.

1. What elements or components of anchor programs were evident in this modest context and example?
2. Does your institution have a similar existing and modest partnership that might serve as an anchor program? What might that be and what could an anchor program consist of?

videos. Especially useful are the tool kits for backbone organizations, working groups, and steering committees. Even with these useful results, effectively implementing the collective impact approach is fraught with challenges as illustrated in Box 10.3.

BOX 10.3

Compass Point: Anchor Programs–C

The pathway to develop, implement, and institutionalize anchor programs takes many twists and turns, sometimes taking a major detour or arriving at a momentary roadblock. This case study depicts many successful and effective steps as well as instances where the initiative tripped along the way. After reading this, note examples of following specific steps and principles as well as unanticipated road bumps along the way. An awareness of what can go wrong as well as right can help campuses effectively develop anchor programs.

A CEP at a small faith-based, liberal arts college with a robust service-learning program met with her vice president of academic affairs and a faculty committee to discuss expansion of the college's curricular community engagement. During the meeting, the CEP described the collective impact model as a way to establish long-term, sustained community partnerships that would accommodate community engagement courses as well as reflect the institution's faith-based mission of social justice. The CEP also introduced the idea of having a physical presence in specific neighborhoods where well-established partnerships with community organizations already existed. The CEP explained the concept of obtaining brick and mortar at community agencies to provide space for program delivery and on-site classrooms where students and faculty could carry out course-related service and community-based research that meet the partner organization's programmatic goals and build capacity in the area. The concept was well received, and the CEP was encouraged to work with the university development office to obtain a seed grant from a local foundation to undertake the planning process. Permission to apply for the grant was granted by the CEP's vice president of academic affairs and the college's provost. The grant provided funds to convene a planning team consisting of community organization representatives and faculty representatives from each of the schools in the college.

The team read articles, viewed short videos obtained from the collective impact website to learn about the process, and visited four anchor institutions across the country to learn about their programs. The team also made site visits to each of the participating centers and their surrounding neighborhoods, which included meeting with residents and clients to hear their aspirations for possible partnerships. These local visits and monthly meetings helped establish a

(*Continues*)

BOX 10.3 (*Continued*)

relationship among planning team members and trust while learning about the mission and goals of each community partner. Meanwhile, the community partners learned more about the mission of the college and gained insight into its role as the backbone organization in the project.

Six months into the project, the team began to create its own mission statement, goals, and objectives primarily focusing on families and education. Specifically, the direction of the project turned to creating family resource centers where educational support programs could be delivered. One of the community agencies offered to lease an entire building to the college for $1 a year as dedicated space for programming. The CEP took her vice president to visit the community partner's building. During the drive back to campus, the vice president expressed surprise at the offer of physical space. It was clear the vice president hadn't anticipated a brick-and-mortar presence for the project and indicated it would also be a surprise to the provost. The CEP reminded her vice president that the planning grant proposal had been approved and signed off by administration. Despite the vice president's surprise, the CEP began meeting with the deans of each school to identify potential faculty who might be willing to incorporate their courses or research agendas into the emerging program.

The deans were generally supportive of the concept but confessed they knew little about it and were unaware of the progress that had been made over the past nine months. The CEP was taken aback by this, assuming that the faculty representatives from each school had been reporting to their dean on the progress and status of the initiative. In turn, subsequent discussion of the project took place during the dean's council meeting with the provost. Significant concern was expressed on two important issues: the degree of potential commitment and investment on the part of the college while a major capital campaign for a new building was in progress, and many deans questioned the mission alignment of the emerging project, arguing the college was not a social service agency to help community agencies. The deans supported the idea of community engagement and practice of service-learning. However, they felt this project seemed to take the college off its academic course with already limited resources and competing priorities on campus.

(*Continues*)

BOX 10.3 (*Continued*)

As a result, the initial effort of establishing a place-based anchor program was tabled.

1. Which, if any, of the five guiding principles from the Democracy Collaborative were evident in this case?
2. Which expression of anchor institutions did this institution appear to take: facilitator, leader, or convener?
3. Which, if any, of the five operational principles and five essential conditions inherent in the collective impact model were apparent?
4. What issues and challenges described by Axelroth Hodges and Dubb (2010) do you see in this scenario? How and to what extent were they addressed?

Deepening Our Critical Commitments: Questions to Ask

Anchor institutions present a radically different approach to community engagement. It requires a significant financial investment as well as formal contractual agreements regarding property in the community.

1. To what extent is this model attainable at your institution? How would such an approach be received in the culture and mission of your institution?

   Furthermore, institutions of higher education have a history of going into the community for short periods of time to impose initiatives or programs that are often short lived or unilaterally beneficial to the academy with little or no benefit to the community. Funds allocated for this type of partnership are often institutional funds, and therefore the institution is essentially in control of the fiscal resources, which perpetuates an elitist almost colonial paradigm in which the community is merely a recipient of funds rather than a full-fledged partner with a voice and hand in how those funds might be used. Without a long-term written agreement and collaborative governance structure, communities and their agencies are rightfully dubious of well-intentioned academics. They have seen firsthand what could be derived from drive-by service in which short-term, poorly conceptualized and implemented programs unilaterally administered by educators who are unlikely to know the context and culture of the community come and go. The intentional term and concept of *anchor* is an attempt to counter the fleeting nature of traditional town-and-gown partnerships by ensuring the resources are anchored in the community. It connotes a long-term presence and commitment to the community.

2. To what extent has your institution implemented a drive-by service model? How do you think community partners and their stakeholders would view and receive a proposal for an anchor program?

At the same time, it is important to remember that institutions of higher education are not social service agencies. Their primary mission is education through creating and disseminating new knowledge. However, as discussed elsewhere, engaged scholarship and engaged epistemology reflect a democratic process of cocreating new knowledge in which the community plays an important role.

3. How then can or does an institution maintain its primary public purpose without becoming a social service agency or a foundation that is perceived by community organizations as providing grants or donations? How can a CEP disarm critical statements from administrators or colleagues that anchor programs are nothing more than providing social services to the community?

Review your responses to the questions in Compass Point: Anchor Programs–A. Conceptualize a preliminary draft of a proposal for establishing an anchor program at your institution.

4. What rationale would you present? What aspect of your institutional mission would reflect and support the proposal? What questions and concerns do you anticipate emerging from the proposal?

REFERENCES

Angelo, T., & Cross, K. P. (1993). *Classroom assessment techniques: A handbook for college teachers.* San Francisco, CA: Jossey-Bass.

Arbnor, I., & Bjerke, B. (2009). *Methodology for creating business knowledge.* Thousand Oaks, CA: Sage.

Arendt, H. (2006). *On revolution.* New York, NY: Penguin Classics.

Arnstein, S. R. (1969). A ladder of citizen participation. *Journal of the American Institute of Planners, 35*, 216–224.

Arora, P. G., Krumholz, L. S., Guerra, T., & Leff, S. S. (2015). Measuring community-based participatory research partnerships: The initial development of an assessment instrument. *Progress in Community Health partnerships Research, Education, and Action, 9*, 549–560.

Asset-Based Community Development Institute. (2016). *ABCD toolkit: What is asset based community development?* Evanston, IL: Northwestern University, School of Education and Social Policy

Association of American Colleges & Universities. (2010). *Civic engagement VALUE rubric.* Retrieved from https://www.aacu.org/civic-engagement-value-rubric.

Association to Advance Collegiate Schools of Business. (2016). *Eligibility and accreditation standards for business accreditation: Engagement, innovation, and impact.* Retrieved from https://www.aacsb.edu/-/media/aacsb/docs/accreditation/standards/business-accreditation-2017-update.ashx?la=en

Astin, A. W., Astin, H. S., & Lindholm, J. A. (2011). Assessing students' spiritual and religious qualities. *Journal of College Student Development, 52*, 39–61.

Astin, H. S., Astin, H., Boatsman, K., Bonous-Hammarth, M., Chambers, T., & Goldberg, S. (1996). *A social change model of leadership development: Guidebook.* Retrieved from http://www.heri.ucla.edu/PDFs/pubs/ASocialChangeModelofLeadershipDevelopment.pdf

Axelroth Hodges, R., & Dubb, S. (2010). *The road half traveled: University engagement at a crossroads.* College Park, MD: Democracy Collaborative, University of Maryland.

Baartman, L. K., & de Bruijn, E. (2011). Integrating knowledge, skills and attitudes: Conceptualising learning processes towards vocational competence. *Educational Research Review, 6*, 125–134.

Baker, A., Jensen, P. J., & Kolb, D. A. (2002). *Conversational learning: An experiential approach to knowledge creation.* Westport, CT: Quorum Books.

Bartunek, J. M., & Moch, M. K. (1987). First-order, second-order, and third-order change and organization development interventions: A cognitive approach. *Journal of Applied Behavioral Science*, 23, 483–500.

Battistoni, R. M. (2002). *Civic engagement across the curriculum*. Providence, RI: Campus Compact.

Beere, C. (2009). Understanding and enhancing the opportunities of community-campus partnerships. *New Directions for Higher Education*, 147, 55–63.

Bender, T. (1993). *Intellect and public life*. Baltimore, MD: Johns Hopkins University Press.

Benfield, K. (2011). *Salt of rebirth: An arts district brings life to Syracuse—and it's green, too.* Retrieved from http://grist.org/urbanism/2011-02-09-ambitious-revitalizing-arts-district-goes-green-in-syracuse/

Benson, L., Harkavy, I., & Hartley, M. (2005). Integrating a commitment to the public good into the institutional fabric. In J. Burkhardt, T. Chambers, & A. Kezar (Eds.), *Higher education for the public good: Emerging voices from a national movement* (pp. 185–216). San Francisco, CA: Jossey Bass.

Benson, L., Harkavy, I. R., & Puckett, J. L. (2007). *Dewey's dream: Universities and democracies in an age of education reform: Civil society, public schools, and democratic citizenship*. Philadelphia, PA: Temple University Press.

Blanchard, L. W., Hanssmann, C., Strauss, R. P., Belliard, J. C., Krichbaum, K., Waters, E., & Seifer, S. D. (2009). Models for faculty development: What does it take to be a community-engaged scholar? *Metropolitan Universities*, 20(2), 47–65.

Bloome, D., Power Carter, S., Christian, B. M., Otto, S., & Stuart-Fairs, N. (2005). *Discourse analysis and the study of classroom literacy and literacy events: A microethnographic perspective*. Mahwah, NJ: Erlbaum.

Bolman, L. G., & Deal, T. E. (2008). *Reframing organizations: Artistry, choice, and leadership*. San Francisco, CA: Jossey-Bass.

Bolman, L. G., & Gallos, J. V. (2011). Leading from the middle. *Reframing academic leadership [electronic resource]*, 143-162.

Bonner Foundation. (2018a). *The Bonner Program*. Retrieved from http://www.bonner.org/the-bonner-program

Bonner Foundation. (2018b). *The Bonner Program*. Retrieved from http://bonner-network.pbworks.com/w/page/13112067/Bonner%20Program

Bowman, J. S., West, J. P., Berman, E. M., & van Wart, M. (2004). *The professional edge: Competencies in public service*. Armonk, NY: M. E. Sharpe.

Boyer, E. (1990). *Scholarship reconsidered: Priorities of the professoriate*. Princeton, NJ: Carnegie Foundation for the Advancement of Teaching.

Boyer, E. (1997). *Selected speeches: 1979–1995*. Princeton, NJ: Carnegie Foundation for the Advancement of Teaching.

Boyle, M. E., Ross, L., & Stephens, J. C. (2011). Who has a stake? How stakeholder processes influence partnership sustainability. *Gateways*, 4, 100–118.

Boyte, H. (2018). *Public achievement*. Retrieved from http://inside.augsburg.edu/publicachievement/

Boyte, H., & Fretz, E. (2011). Civic professionalism. In J. Saltmarsh & M. Hartley (Eds.), *To a larger purpose: Engagement for democracy and the transformation of higher education* (pp. 82–101). Philadelphia, PA: Temple University Press.

Bracken, S. J. (2008). Changing times? Past, present, and future discussions of community-university partnerships. *PAACE Journal of Lifelong Learning, 17*, 1–17.

Bringle, R. G., Clayton, P. H., & Price, M. (2009). Partnerships in service learning and civic engagement. *Partnerships: A Journal of Service Learning & Civic Engagement, 1*(1), 1–20.

Bringle, R. G., Battistoni, R. M., & Hatcher, J. A. (2010). *International service learning: Conceptual frameworks and research*. Sterling, VA: Stylus.

Bringle, R. G., Games, R., & Malloy, E. A. (1999). *Colleges and universities as citizens*. Needham Heights, MA: Allyn & Bacon.

Bringle, R. G., & Hatcher, J. A. (2002). Campus–community partnerships: The terms of engagement. *Journal of Social Issues, 58*, 503–516.

Bringle, R. G., Hatcher, J. A., & Muthiah, R. N. (2010). The role of service-learning on the retention of first-year students to second year. *Michigan Journal of Community Service Learning, 16*(2) 38–49.

Brook, J., Catlin, S., DeLuca, C., Doe, C., Huntly, A., & Searle, M. (2010). Conceptions of doctoral education: The PhD as pathmaking. *Reflective Practice, 11*, 657–668.

Brookfield, S., & Preskill, S. (2005). *Discussion as a way of teaching: Tools and techniques for democratic classrooms* (2nd ed.). San Francisco, CA: Jossey-Bass.

Butin, D. (2007). Focusing our aim: Strengthening faculty commitment to community engagement. *Change, 39*(6), 34–39.

Campus Compact. (2014). *Campus Compact membership survey*. Boston, MA: Author.

Carnegie Foundation for the Advancement of Teaching. (2007). Elective classification: Community engagement—2008 documentation framework preview (Vol. 2009).

Catholic Relief Services. (2015). *Partnership reflection: A guide for facilitators. Catholic Relief Services Training Manual*. Baltimore, MD: Author.

Central Corridor Anchor Partnership. (n.d.). *Workforce*. Retrieved from http://www.centralcorridoranchorpartnership.org/workforce/

CEOs for Cities and Institute for a Competitive Inner City. (2002). *Leveraging colleges and universities for urban economic revitalization: An action agenda*. Boston, MA: Author.

Cioran, E. (1960). *History and utopia*. New York, NY: Skyhorse.

Clayton, P. H., Bringle, R. G., & Hatcher, J. A. (2013a). *Research on service-learning: Conceptual frameworks and assessment* (Vol. 2A). Sterling, VA: Stylus.

Clayton, P. H., Bringle, R. G., & Hatcher, J. A. (2013b). *Research on service-learning: Conceptual frameworks and assessment* (Vol. B). Sterling, VA: Stylus.

Coghlan, D., & Brydon-Miller, M. (Eds.). (2014). *The Sage encyclopedia of action research*. Thousand Oaks, CA: Sage.

Collaborative for Neighborhood Transformation. (2018). *Principles for effective asset-based community development*. Retrieved from https://www.neighborhoodtransformation.net/pdfs/What_%20is_Asset_Based_Community_Development.pdf

Collective Impact Forum. (2014). *Collective impact principles of practice*. Retrieved from http://collectiveimpactforum.org/resources/collective-impact-principles-practice

Collins, J. C. (2001). *Good to great: Why some companies make the leap . . . and others don't*. New York, NY: Random House.

Community Campus Partnerships for Health. (2006). *Guiding principles of partnerships*. Retrieved from https://www.ccphealth.org/guiding-principles-ofpartnerships/

Cornwall, A., & Jewkes, R. (1995). What is participatory research? *Social Science & Medicine, 41*, 1667–1676.

Council for the Advancement of Standards in Higher Education. (2015). *CAS professional standards for higher education: Civic engagement and service-learning programs* (9th ed.). Washington, DC: Author.

Cox, M. D. (2004). Introduction to faculty learning communities. *New Directions for Teaching and Learning, 97*, 5–23.

Crawford, M. (2009). *Shop class as soulcraft: An inquiry into the value of work*. New York, NY: Penguin.

Deans, T. (1999). Service-learning in two keys: Paulo Freire's critical pedagogy in relation to John Dewey's pragmatism. *Michigan Journal of Community Service Learning, 6*, 15–29.

Dee, J. R., & Leišytė, L. (2016). Organizational learning in higher education institutions: Theories, frameworks, and a potential research agenda. In M. B. Paulsen (Ed.), *Higher education: Handbook of theory and research* (pp. 275–348). Cham, Switzerland: Springer International.

Demb, A., & Wade, A. (2012). Reality check: Faculty involvement in outreach and engagement. *Journal of Higher Education, 83*, 337–366.

Dempsey, S. E. (2010). Critiquing community engagement. *Management Communication Quarterly, 24*(3), 1–32.

Dewey, J. (1938). *Experience and education*. Indianapolis, IN: Kappa Delta Pi.

Diener, M. L., & Liese, H. (2009). *Finding meaning in civically engaged scholarship: Personal journeys/professional experiences*. Charlotte, NC: Information Age.

Dingwall, R. (2008). *Essays on professions*. Burlington, VT: Aldershot.

Donaldson, L. P., & Daughtery, L. (2011). Introducing asset-based models of social justice into service learning: A social work approach. *Journal of Community Practice, 19*(1), 80–99.

Dostilio, L. D. (2012). *Democratically engaged community-university partnerships: Reciprocal determinants of democratically oriented roles and processes*. Unpublished doctoral dissertation, Duquesne University, Pittsburgh, PA.

Dostilio, L. D. (2017a). Planning a path forward: Identifying the knowledge, skill, and dispositions of second generation Community Engagement Professionals. In L. D. Dostilio (Ed.), *The community engagement professional in higher education: A competency model for an emerging field* (pp. 27–55). Boston: MA, Campus Compact.

Dostilio, L. D. (Ed.). (2017b). *The community engagement professional in higher education: A competency model for an emerging field.* Boston: MA, Campus Compact.

Dostilio, L. D. (2017c). The professionalization of community engagement: Associations and professional staff. In T. D. Mitchell, T. Eatman, & C. Dolgan (Eds.), *Cambridge handbook for service learning and community engagement* (pp. 370–384). Cambridge, UK: Cambridge University Press.

Dostilio, L. D., & McReynolds, M. (2015). Community engagement professionals in the circle of service-learning and the greater civic enterprise. *Michigan Journal of Community Service Learning,* 22(1), 113–117.

Dostilio L. D., & Molchan, K. A. (2015). Relational approach to co-constructed risk management. In O. Delano-Oriaran, M. W. Penick-Parks, & S. Fondrie, S. (Eds.), *The SAGE sourcebook of service-learning and civic engagement* (pp. 435–442). Thousand Oaks, CA: Sage.

Dostilio, L. D., & Perry, L. G. (2017). An explanation of community engagement professionals as professionals and leaders. In L. D. Dostilio (Ed.), *The community engagement professional in higher education: A competency model for an emerging field* (pp. 1–26). Boston, MA: Campus Compact.

Driscoll, A. (2009). Carnegie's new community engagement classification: Affirming higher education's role in community. In L. R. Sandmann, C. H. Thornton, & A. J. Jaeger (Eds.), *Institutionalizing community engagement in higher education: The first wave of Carnegie classified institutions* (pp. 2–12). San Francisco, CA: Jossey-Bass.

Dubb, S., McKinley, S., & Howard, T. (2013). *The anchor dashboard: Aligning institutional practices to meet low-income community needs.* Retrieved from http://www.aecf.org/resources/the-anchor-dashboard-1/

Duke University. (2018). *Office of Assessment: Assessment.* Retrieved from https://assessment.trinity.duke.edu/assessment

Eagan, M. K., Stolzenberg, E. B., Berdan Lozano, J., Aragon, M. C., Suchard, M. R., & Hurtado, S. (2014). *Undergraduate teaching faculty: The 2013–2014 faculty survey.* Los Angeles: Higher Education Research Institute, University of California.

Eckel, P., Hill, B., & Green, M. F. (1998). *En route to transformation.* Washington, DC: American Council on Education Fulfillment Services.

Eddy, P. L. (2010). *Partnerships and collaboration in higher education: AEHE.* Hoboken, NJ: Wiley.

Eraut, M. (1994). *Developing professional knowledge and competence.* London, UK: Routledge.

Etienne, H. F. (2012). *Pushing back the gates: Neighborhood perspectives on university-driven revitalization in west Philadelphia*. Philadelphia, PA: Temple University Press.

Evetts, J. (2006) Introduction: Trust and professionalism: Challenges and occupational changes. *Current Sociology, 54*, 515–531.

Eyler, J., Giles, D. E., & Schmiede, A. (1996). *A practitioner's guide to reflection in service-learning: Student voices and reflections*. Nashville, TN: Vanderbilt University.

Fals-Borda, O. (1987). The application of participatory action-research in Latin America. *International Sociology, 2*, 329–347.

Fisher, I. (1998). We make the road by walking: Building service-learning in and out of the curriculum at the University of Utah. In E. Zlotkowski (Ed.), *Successful service-learning programs: New models of excellence in higher education* (pp. 210–231). Bolton, MA: Anker.

Fitzgerald, H., Burack, C., Seifer, S. D., & Votruba, J. (2010). *Handbook of engaged scholarship* (Vol. 1). East Lansing, MI: Michigan State University Press.

Freire, P. (1970). *Pedagogy of the oppressed* (M. B. Ramos, Trans.). New York, NY: Continuum.

Furco, A. (1996). *Service-learning: A balanced approach to experiential education*. In Corporation for National Service (Ed.), *Expanding boundaries: Serving and learning* (pp. 2–6). Columbia, MD: Author.

Furco, A. (1999). *Self-assessment rubric for the institutionalization of service-learning in higher education*. Berkeley, CA: Service-Learning Research and Development Center, University of California, Berkeley.

Furco, A. (2002). *Self-assessment rubric for the institutionalization of service-learning in higher education* (rev. ed.). Berkeley, CA: Service-Learning Research and Development Center, University of California, Berkeley.

Furco, A. (2003). Issues of definition and program diversity in the study of service-learning. In S. H. Billig & A. S. Waterman (Eds.), *Studying service-learning: Innovations in education research methodology* (pp. 13–33). Mahwah, NJ: Erlbaum.

Furco, A. (2005). *Promoting civic engagement at the University of California*. Berkeley, CA: Center for Studies in Higher Education, University of California, Berkeley.

Furco, A. (2010). The engaged campus: Toward a comprehensive approach to public engagement. *British Journal of Educational Studies, 58*, 375–390.

Garoutte, L., & McCarthy-Gilmore, K. (2014). Preparing students for community-based learning using an asset-based approach. *Journal of the Scholarship of Teaching and Learning, 14*(5), 48–61.

Garrison, N. J., & Gardner, D. S. (2012, November). *Assets first generation college students bring to the higher education setting*. Paper presented at annual conference of the Association for the Study of Higher Education, Las Vegas, NV.

Gelmon, S. (2001). *Assessing service-learning and civic engagement: Principles and techniques*. Providence, RI: Campus Compact, Brown University.

Gelmon, S. B. (2003). Assessment as a means of building service-learning partnerships. In B. Jacoby & Associates (Eds.), *Building partnerships for service-learning* (pp. 42–63). San Francisco, CA: Jossey-Bass.

Glover, R. (2016). Principles of great design: Craftsmanship. Retrieved from https://www.smashingmagazine.com/2010/01/principles-of-great-design-craftsmanship/

Gottlieb, K., & Robinson, G. (2006). *A practical guide for integrating civic responsibility into the curriculum.* Washington, DC: Community College Press.

Guba, E. G., & Lincoln, Y. S. (1993). Competing paradigms in qualitative research. In N. K. Denzin & Y. S. Lincoln (Eds.), *Handbook of qualitative research* (pp. 105–117). Thousand Oaks, CA: Sage.

Guthrie, J. (2003). *He can see clearly now: Third Eye Blind's Stephan Jenkins looks at success, love, and creativity.* Retrieved from http://www.sfgate.com/entertainment/article/He-can-see-clearly-now-Third-Eye-Blind-s-2653924.php

Haas Center for Public Service. (2018). *Pathways of public service and engagement.* Retrieved from https://haas.stanford.edu/about/about-our-work/pathways-public-service

Hackett, R. (2016). *Civic professionalism resources.* Retrieved from http://bonnernetwork.pbworks.com/w/page/67376434/Civic%20Professionalism%20Resources

Hackett, R. (2018). *Bonner student development: Goals and framework.* Retrieved from http://bonner.pbworks.com/w/page/105850659/Student%20Development%20-%20%20Goals%20and%20Framework

Hamerlinck, J., & Plaut, J. (2014). *Asset-based community engagement in higher education.* Minneapolis, MN: Minnesota Campus Compact.

Hanleybrown, F., Kania, J., & Kramer, M. (2012). *Channeling change: Making collective impact work.* Retrieved from http://www.ssireview.org/blog/entry/channeling_change_making_collective_impact_work?cpgn=WP%20DL%20-%20Channeling%20Change

Harkavy, I. (2004). Service-learning and the development of democratic universities, democratic schools, and democratic good societies in the 21st century. In S. Billig & M. Welch (Eds.), *New perspectives in service-learning: Research to advance the field* (pp. 3–22). Greenwich, CT: Information Age.

Harkavy, I. (2006). The role of universities in advancing citizenship and social justice in the 21st century. *Education, Citizenship and Social Justice, 1*(1), 5–37.

Harkavy, I., & Zuckerman, H. (1999, August). *Eds and meds: Cities' hidden assets.* The Brookings Institution Survey Series. The Brookings Institution, Center on Urban and Metropolitan Policy. Washington, DC: The Brookings Institution.

Harper, S. R. (2011). Strategy and intentionality in practice. In J. H. Schuh, S. R. Jones, S. R. Harper, & S. R. Komives (Eds.), *Student services: A handbook for the profession* (pp. 287–302). San Francisco, CA: Jossey-Bass.

Harriger, K. J., McMilan, J. J., Buchanan, C., & Gusler, S. (2017). *The long-term impact of learning to deliberate: A follow-up study of democracy fellows and a class cohort.* Washington, DC: Kettering Foundation.

Hart, T. (2009). *From information to transformation: Education for the evolution of consciousness*. New York, NY: Peter Lang.

Hartley, M., Harkavy, I., & Benson, L. (2005). Putting down roots in the groves of academe: The challenges of institutionalizing service-learning. In D. W. Butin (Ed.), *Service-learning in higher education* (pp. 205–222). New York, NY: Palgrave Macmillan.

Harwood Group (1999). *Community rhythms: Five stages of community life*. Flint, MI: The Charles Stewart Mott Foundation.

Hatcher, J. A. (2008). *The public role of professionals: Developing and evaluating the Civic-Minded Professional scale* (Doctoral dissertation). Retrieved from ProQuest Dissertation and Theses database. (UMI No. 3331248)

Hatcher, J. A., Bringle, R. G., & Hahn, T. W. (2016). *Research on student civic outcomes in service-learning: Conceptual frameworks and methods*. Sterling, VA: Stylus.

Hernandez, K., & Pasquesi, K. (2017). Critical perspectives and commitments deserving attention from community engagement professionals. In L. D. Dostilio (Ed.), *The community engagement professional in higher education: A competency model for an emerging field* (pp. 56–78). Boston, MA: Campus Compact.

Hickman, C. R., & Silva, M. (1984). *Creating excellence: Managing corporate culture, strategy and change in the new age*. New York, NY: New American Library.

Hinton, K. E. (2012). *A practical guide to strategic planning in higher education*. Ann Arbor, MI: Society for College and University Planning.

Holland, B. (1997). Analyzing institutional commitment to service: A model of key organizational factors. *Michigan Journal of Community Service-Learning, 4*(1), 30–41.

Holland, B. A. (2005). Institutional differences in pursuing the public good. In A. Kezar, T. C. Chambers, & J. C. Burkhardt (Eds.), *Higher education for the public good: Emerging voices from a national movement* (pp. 235–259). San Francisco, CA: Jossey-Bass.

Holland, B. (2009). Will it last? Evidence of institutionalization at Carnegie classified community engagement institutions. In L. R. Sandmann, C. H. Thornton, & A. J. Jaeger (Eds.), *Institutionalizing community engagement in higher education: The first wave of Carnegie Classified institutions* (pp. 85–98). San Francisco, CA: Jossey-Bass.

Holland, B., & Langseth, M. (2010). Leveraging financial support for service-learning: Relevance, relationships, results, resources is a valuable resource. In B. Jacoby & P. Mustascio (Eds.), *Looking in reaching out: A reflective guide for community service-learning professional* (pp. 185–210). Boston, MA: Campus Compact.

Hollander, E., Saltmarsh, J., & Zlotkowski, E. (2001). Indicators of engagement. In L. A. Simon, M. Kenny, K. Brabeck, & R. M. Lerner (Eds.), *Learning to serve: Promoting civil society through service-learning* (pp. 31–49). Norwell, MA: Kluwer.

Horton, V. L., Early, J. L., Resler, M., Trussell, A., & Howard, C. (2016). The university next door: Developing a centralized unit that strategically cultivates community engagement at a urban university. *Metropolitan Universities, 27*(1), 97–121.

Howard, T. (2014, January). How communities can make the most of their anchor institutions. *Governing Magazine.* Retrieved from http://www.governing.com/gov-institute/voices/col-communities-local-government-anchor-institutions-democracy-collaborative-dashboard.html

Hoy, A., & Meisel, W. (2008). *Civic engagement at the center: Building democracy through integrated co-curricular and curricular experiences.* Washington, DC: Association of American Colleges & Universities.

Hübler, R., & Quan, M. (2017). The role of community engagement professionals. In L. D. Dostilio (Ed.), *The community engagement professional in higher education: A competency model for an emerging field* (pp. 98–117). Boston, MA: Campus Compact.

Independent Sector. (2018). *Hourly value of volunteer service.* Retrieved from https://independentsector.org/resource/the-value-of-volunteer-time/

Indiana University Purdue University at Indianapolis. (2018). *Civic minded graduate survey.* Retrieved from http://csl.iupui.edu/teaching-research/opportunities/civic-learning/graduate.shtml

Israel, B. A., Eng, E., Schulz, A. J., & Parker, E. A. (Eds.). (2013). *Methods for community-based participatory research for health* (2nd ed.). San Francisco, CA: Jossey-Bass.

Jacoby, B. (2010). *Service-learning course design: What faculty need to know.* Madison, WI: Magna.

Jacoby, B. (2015). *Service-learning essentials: Questions, answers, and lessons learned.* San Francisco, CA: Jossey-Bass.

Jacoby, B., & Mutascio, P. (Eds.). (2010). *Looking in reaching out: A reflective guide for community service-learning professionals.* Boston, MA: Campus Compact.

James, J. H., & Van Deventer Iverson, S. (2014). Conclusions: Re-visioning community engagement as feminist praxis. In S. Van Deventer Iverson & J. H. James (Eds.), Feminist community engagement: Community engagement in higher education (pp. 193–203). New York, NY: Palgrave Macmillan.

Johnson, M., Levy, D., Cichetti, P., & Zinkiewicz, C. (2013). An untapped reservoir for student community engagement: What we are learning from the NASCE. In A. Hoy & M. Johnson (Eds.), *Deeping community engagement in higher education: Forging new pathways* (pp. 65–79). New York, NY: Palgrave Macmillan.

Kajner, T., Chovanec, D., Underwood, M., & Mian, A. (2014). Critical community service-learning: Combining critical classroom pedagogy with activist community placements. *Michigan Journal Community Service Learning, 19*(2), 36–48.

Kania, J., & Kramer, M. (2011, Winter). Collective impact. *Stanford Social Innovation Review.* Retrieved from https://ssir.org/articles/entry/collective_impact

Kecskes, K. (2006). *Engaging departments: Moving faculty culture from private to public, individual to collective focus for the common good.* Boston, MA: Anker.

Keith, N. Z. (2015). *Engaging in social partnerships: Democratic practices for campus-community partnerships*. New York, NY: Routledge.

Kellogg Foundation. (2004). *Logic model development guide*. Battle Creek, MI: Author.

Kezar, A. (2014). Higher education change and social networks: A review of research. *Journal of Higher Education, 85*, 91–125.

Kinefuchi, E. (2010). Critical consciousness and critical service-learning at the intersection of the personal and the structural. *Journal of Applied Learning in Higher Education, 2*, 77–93.

Klofstad, C. A. (2010). The lasting effect of civic talk on civic participation: Evidence from a panel study. *Social Forces, 88*, 2353–2376.

Kolb, D. A. (1984). *Experiential learning: Experience as the source of learning and development*. Englewood Cliffs, NJ: Prentice-Hall.

Kotter, J. P. (1995). Leading change: Why transformation efforts fail. *Harvard Business Review, 73*(2), 59–67.

Kretzmann, J., & McKnight, J. (1993). *Building community from the inside out*. Evanston, IL: Center for Urban Affairs and Policy Research.

Kuh, G. D. (2008). *Excerpt from high-impact educational practices: What they are, who has access to them, and why they matter*. Washington, DC: Association of American Colleges & Universities.

Lawler, P. (2003). Teachers as adult learners: A new perspective. *New Directions for Adult and Continuing Education, 98*, 15–22.

Leiderman, S., Furco, A., Zapf, J., & Goss, M. (2002). *Building partnerships with college campuses: Community perspectives*. Washington, DC: Council of Independent Colleges.

Levine, P. (2007). *The future of democracy: Developing the next generation of American citizens*. Medford, MA: Tufts University Press.

Levy, D., & Johnson, M. (2009). *National assessment of service and community engagement*. Retrieved from https://www.siena.edu/centers-institutes/siena-research-institute/national/about-nasce/

Lewin, K. (1946). Action research and minority problems. *Journal of Social Issues, 2*(4), 34–46.

Lindsay Wildlife Museum. (2015, Winter). *Wildlife wonders*, p. 5.

Lundborg, P. (2009). *Syracuse's Near West Side neighborhood looks for future in SALT*. Retrieved from http://www.syracuse.com/news/index.ssf/2009/10/syracuses_near_west_side_finds.html

Maher, C., & Bennett, R. E. (1984). *Planning and evaluating special education services*. Englewood Cliffs, NJ: Prentice-Hall.

Martin, L., & Crossland, S. (2017). High quality community-campus partnerships: Approaches and competencies. In L. D. Dostilio (Ed.), *The community engagement professional in higher education: A competency model for an emerging field* (pp. 161–178). Boston, MA: Campus Compact.

Masterson, K. (2016, December 16). How to court a foundation: Go big, build relations, and think long term. *Chronicle of Higher Education*, p. A8.

Mattar, S. (2011). Educating and training the next generations of traumatologists: Development of cultural competencies. *Psychological Trauma, 3*, 258–265.

Mattar, S. (2014). *Waiting to be invited: Developing cultural competencies.* Moraga, CA: Saint Mary's College of California.

Maurrasse, D. J. (2001). *Beyond the campus: How colleges and universities form partnerships with their communities.* New York, NY: Routledge.

McChesney, C., Covey, S., & Huling, J. (2012). *The 4 disciplines of execution: Achieving your wildly important goals.* New York, NY: Simon & Schuster.

McClurg, S, D. (2003). Social networks and political participation: The role of social interaction in explaining political participation. *Political Research Quarterly, 56*, 449–464.

McKnight, J. (2017). *Asset-based community development: The essentials.* Chicago, IL: Asset-Based Community Development Institute.

McRae, H. (2015). Situating engagement in Canadian higher education. In O. Delano-Oriaran, M. Penick-Parks, & S. Fondrie (Eds.), *The Sage sourcebook of service-learning and community engagement* (pp. 401–408). Thousand Oaks, CA: Sage.

McReynolds, M. (2015). The practice of engagement: Developing as a practitioner-scholar. In O. Delano-Oriaran, M. Parks, & S. Fondrie (Eds.). *Service-learning and civic engagement: A sourcebook.* Thousand Oaks, CA: Sage.

McTighe Musil, C. (2002). Educating for citizenship. *Peer Review, 5*(3), 4–8.

McTighe Musil, C. (2009). Educating students for personal and social responsibility: The civic learning spiral. In B. Jacoby (Ed.), *Civic engagement in higher education* (pp. 49–69). San Francisco, CA: Jossey-Bass.

McTighe Musil, C. (2015). *Civic prompts: Making civic learning routine across the disciplines.* Washington, DC: Association of American Colleges & Universities.

Meyerson, D. E. (2001). *Tempered radicals.* Boston, MA: Harvard Business School.

Meyerson, D. E. (2004). The tempered radicals: How employees push their companies little by little to be more socially responsible. *Stanford Social Innovation Review, 2*(2), 14–22.

Meyerson, D. E. & Scully, M. A (1995). Tempered radicalism and the politics of ambivalence and change. *Organization Science, 6*, 585–600.

Minkler, M., & Wallerstein, N. (Eds.). (2002). *Community-based participatory research for health.* San Francisco, CA: Jossey-Bass.

Mitchell, J. J., Gillon, K. E., Reason, R. D., & Ryder, A. J. (2016). Improving student outcomes of community-based programs through peer-to-peer conversation. *Journal of College Student Development, 57*, 316–320.

Mitchell, T. D. (2008). Traditional vs. critical service-learning: Engaging the literature to differentiate two models. *Michigan Journal of Community Service Learning, 14*(2), 50–65.

Mitchell, T. D. (2013). Critical service-learning as a philosophy for deepening community engagement. In A. Hoy & M. Johnson (Eds.), *Deepening community engagement in higher education: Forging new pathways* (pp. 263–269). New York, NY: Palgrave Macmillan.

Mitchell, T. D., Donahue, D. M., & Young-Law, C. (2012). Service-learning as a pedagogy of whiteness. *Equity and Excellence in Education, 45*, 612–629.

Moely, B. E., Mercer, S. H., Ilustre, V., Miron, D., & McFarland, M. (2002). Psychometric properties and correlates of the Civic Attitudes and Skills Questionnaire (CASQ): A measure of students' attitudes related to service-learning. *Michigan Journal of Community Service Learning, 8*(2), 15–26.

Mohr, J., & Spekman, R. (1994). Characteristics of partnership success: Partnership attributes, communication behavior, and conflict resolution techniques. *Strategic Management Journal, 15*, 135–152.

Morphew, C. C., & Hartley, M. (2006). Mission statements: A thematic analysis of rhetoric across institutional type. *Journal of Higher Education, 77*, 456–471.

Morrison, E. (2013, December). *"Strategic doing": A new discipline for developing and implementing strategy within loose regional networks.* Paper presented at the annual conference of the Australian-New Zealand Regional Science Association International, Hervey Bay, Queensland, University of Southern Queensland, Australia.

Morton, K. (1995). The irony of service: Charity, project, and social change in service-learning. *Michigan Journal of Community Service Learning,* 2(1), 19–32.

Mundy, M. E. (2004). Faculty engagement in service-learning: Individual and organizational factors at distinct institutional types. In M. Welch & S. H. Billig (Eds.), *New perspectives in service-learning: Research to advance the field* (pp. 169–194). Greenwich, CT: Information Age.

National Commission on Civic Renewal. (1998). *A nation of spectators: How civic disengagement weakens America and what we can do about it.* College Park, MD: University of Maryland.

National Survey of Student Engagement. (2018). *National Survey of Student Engagement; About NSSE.* Retrieved from http://nsse.indiana.edu/html/about.cfm

National Task Force on Civic Learning and Democratic Engagement. (2012). *A crucible moment: College learning and democracy's future.* Washington, DC: Association of American Colleges & Universities.

Northern Illinois University Office of Outreach, Engagement, and Regional Development. (2018). *Tools for engagement: Carnegie Foundation definitions of engagement and partnership.* Retrieved from https://www.niu.edu/outreach/documents/Definitions%20of%20Engagement/Carnegie%20-%20Definitions%20of%20Engagement%20and%20Partneships.pdf

O'Meara, K. A. (2010). Rewarding multiple forms of scholarship and tenure. In H. E. Fitzgerald, C. Burack, & S. D. Seifer (Eds.), *Handbook of engaged scholarship: Contemporary landscapes, future directions* (pp. 271–293). East Lansing, MI: Michigan State University Press.

Palonen, T., Boshuizen, H. P. A., & Lehtinen, E. (2014). How expertise is created in emerging professional fields. In S. Billett, T. Halttunen, & M. Koivisto (Eds.), *Promoting, assessing, recognizing and certifying lifelong learning: International perspectives and practices* (pp. 131–150). New York, NY: Springer.

Pariser, E. (n.d.). *Eli Pariser quotes.* Retrieved from http://www.brainyquote.com/quotes/quotes/e/elipariser550953.html

Paton, V. O., Fitzgerald, H. E., Green, B. L., Raymond, M., & Borchardt, M. P. (2014). U.S. Higher Education Regional Accreditation Commission standards and the centrality of engagement. *Journal of Higher Education Outreach and Engagement, 18*(3), 41–69.

Pigza, J. M., & Troppe, M. L. (2003). Developing an infrastructure for service-learning and community engagement. In B. Jacoby (Ed.), *Building partnerships for service-learning* (pp. 106–130). San Francisco, CA: Jossey-Bass.

Pitner, R. O., & Sakamoto, I. (2005). The role of critical consciousness in multicultural practice: Examining how its strength becomes its limitation. *American Journal of Orthopsychiatry, 75*(4), 684–694.

Plater, W. M. (2011). The context for international service learning: An invisible revolution is underway. In R. G. Bringle, J. A. Hatcher, & S. G. Jones (Eds.), *International service learning: Conceptual frameworks and research* (pp. 29–56). Sterling, VA: Stylus.

Post, M. A., Ward, E., Longo, N. V., & Saltmarsh, J. (2016). *Publicly engaged scholars: Next generation and the future of higher education.* Sterling, VA: Stylus.

Prins, E. (2005). Framing a conflict in a community-university partnership. *Journal of Planning Education and Research, 25*(1), 57–74.

Quinn, R., & Meyerson, D. (2008). The positive potential of tempered radicals. In C. Manz, K. Cameron, K. Manz, & R. Marx (Eds.), *The virtuous organization: Insights from some of the world's leading management thinkers* (pp. 247–258). Hackensack, NJ: World Scientific.

Ramaley, J. (2010). Students as scholars: Integrating research, education, and professional practice. In H. E. Fitzgerald, C. Burack, & S. D. Seifter (Eds.), *Handbook of engaged scholarship: Vol. 1: Institutional change* (pp. 355–368). East Lansing, MI: Michigan State University Press.

Ray, D. (2016). *Campus-community partnership: A stubborn commitment to reciprocal relationships.* Retrieved from https://www.aacu.org/diversitydemocracy/2016/spring/ray

Rimmerman, C. A. (2006). *The new citizenship: Unconventional politics, activism, and service* (3rd ed.). Boulder, CO: Westview.

Rogers, E. (2003). *The diffusion of innovations* (5th ed.). New York, NY: The Free Press.

Ross, L. (2010). Notes from the field: Learning cultural humility through critical incidents and central challenges in community-based participatory research. *Journal of Community Practice, 18*, 315–335.

Rychen, D. S., & Salganik, L. H. (2001). *Defining and selecting key competencies.* Cambridge, MA: Hogrefe & Huber.

Saltmarsh, J. (2010). Changing pedagogies. In H. E. Fitzgerald, C. Burack, & S. D. Seifer (Eds.), *Handbook of engaged scholarship: Contemporary landscapes, future directions* (pp. 331–352). East Lansing, MI: Michigan State University Press.

Saltmarsh, J., & Hartley, M. (2011). *To a larger purpose: Engagement for democracy and the transformation of higher education.* Philadelphia, PA: Temple University Press.

Saltmarsh, J., Hartley, M., & Clayton, P. (2009). *Democratic engagement white paper.* Boston, MA: University of Massachusetts–Boston, New England Resource Center for Higher Education.

Sandmann, L. R., Jordan, J. W., Mull, C. D., & Valentine, T. (2014). Measuring boundary spanning behavior in community engagement. *Journal of Higher Education Outreach and Engagement, 18*(3), 83–104.

Sandmann, L. R., & Plater, W. M. (2009). Leading the engaged institution. *New Directions for Higher Education, 147*, 13–24.

Sandy, M., & Holland, B. (2006). Different worlds and common ground: Community partner perspectives on campus-community partnerships. *Michigan Journal of Community Service Learning, 13*(1), 30–44.

Scanlon, L. (2011). *"Becoming" a professional.* New York, NY: Springer.

Schön, D. (1983). *The reflective practitioner: How professionals think in action.* London, UK: Temple Smith.

Schutt, R. (2001). *Inciting democracy: A practical proposal for creating a good society.* Cleveland, OH: SpringForward Press.

Schwartz, I. S., & Baer, D. M. (1991). Social validity assessments: Is current practice state of the art? *Journal of Applied Behavioral Analysis, 24*, 189–204.

Schwartz, S. J., Côté, J. E., & Arnett, J. J. (2005). Identity and agency in emerging adulthood: Two developmental routes in the individualization process. *Youth & Society, 37*, 201–229.

Seider, S. C., & Hillman, A. (2011). Challenging privileged college students' othering language in community service learning. *Journal of College and Character, 12*(3), 1–7.

Shulman, L. (1987). Knowledge and teaching: Foundations of the new reform. *Harvard Educational Review, 57*(1), 1–23.

Siena College Research Institute. (2018). *About NASCE.* Retrieved from https://www.siena.edu/centers-institutes/siena-research-institute/national/about-nasce/

Smith, M. K., Wood, W. B., Adams, W. K., Wieman, C., Knight, J. K., Guild, N., & Su, T. T. (2009). Why peer discussion improves student performance on in-class concept questions. *Science, 323*, 122–124.

Snow, L. K. (2014). Assets, innovation, and academia. In J. Hamerlinck & J. Plaut (Eds.), *Asset-based community engagement in higher education* (pp. 31–52). Minneapolis, MN: Minnesota Campus Compact.

Snyder-Hall, C. (2015). *Civic aspirations: Why some higher education faculty are reconnecting their professional and public lives.* Dayton, OH: Kettering Foundation.

Stanton, T. K., Giles, D. E., & Cruz, N. I. (1999). *Service learning: A movement's pioneers reflect on its origins, practice, and future.* San Francisco, CA: Jossey-Bass.

Sterk-Barrett, M. (2015). *Fostering the spiritual development of undergraduates through service learning.* Unpublished doctoral dissertation, University of Massachusetts, Boston.

Strier, R. (2013). Fields of paradox: University-community partnerships. *Higher Education, 68*(2), 155–165.

Stoecker, R., Beckman, M., & Min, B. H. (2010). Evaluating the community impact of higher education community engagement. In H. E. Fitzgerald, C. Burack, & S. Seifer (Eds.), *Handbook of engaged scholarship: The contemporary landscape: Volume 2: Community-campus partnerships* (pp. 177–198). East Lansing, MI: Michigan State University Press.

Strand, K. J., Cutforth, N., Stoecker, R., Marullo, S., & Donohue, P. (2003). *Community-based research and higher education: Principles and practices.* San Francisco, CA: Jossey-Bass.

Sturm, S., Eatman, T., Saltmarsh, J., & Bush, A. (2011). *Full participation: Building the architecture for diversity and public engagement in higher education.* New York, NY: Columbia University Law School, Center for Institutional and Social Change.

Sullivan, M., Kone, A., Senturia, K., Chrisman, N. J., Ciske, S. J., & Krieger, J. W. (2001). Researcher and researched-community perspectives: Toward bridging the gap. *Health Education and Behavior, 28*, 130–149.

Sullivan, W. M. (2005). Markets vs. professions: Value added? *Daedalus, 134*(3), 19–26.

Sullivan, W. M. (2012). Knowledge and judgment in practice as the twin aims of learning. In D. W. Harward (Ed.), *Transforming undergraduate education: Theory that compels and practices that succeed* (pp. 141–157). Lanham, MD: Rowman & Littlefield.

Suskie, L. (2009). Using assessment results to inform teaching practice and promote lasting learning. In G. Joughin (Ed.), *Assessment, learning and judgement in higher education* (pp. 1–20). Dordrecht, The Netherlands: Springer

Swaner, L. E. (2014). The theories, contexts, and multiple pedagogies of engaged learning: What succeeds and why? In D. W. Harward (Ed.), *Transforming undergraduate education: Theory that compels and practices that succeed* (pp. 73–89). Lanham, MD: Rowman & Littlefield.

Swigonski, M. (1994). The logic of feminist standpoint theory for social work research. *Social Work, 39*, 387–393.

Tajfel, H., & Turner, J. (1986). The social identity theory of intergroup behavior. In S. Worchel & W. Austin (Eds.), *The psychology of intergroup relations* (pp. 7–24). Chicago, IL: Nelson-Hall.

Torres, J., & Schaffer, J. (2000). *Benchmarks for campus community partnerships.* Providence, RI: Campus Compact.

Van Note Chism, N., Palmer, M. M., & Price, M. F. (2013). Investigating faculty development service-learning. In P. H. Clayton, R. G. Bringle, & J. A. Hatcher (Eds.), *Research on service-learning: Conceptual frameworks and assessment: Volume 2A. Students and faculty* (pp. 187–214). Sterling, VA: Stylus.

Van Note Chism, N., & Szabo, B. (1998). How faculty development programs evaluate their services. *Journal of Staff, Program, and Organizational Development, 15*(2), 55–62.

Veloria, C. N. (2015). "Maybe this is because of society?" Disrupting and engaging discourses of race in the context of a service-learning project. *Humanity & Society, 39*, 135–155.

Ventresca, M. L., Waring, A. L., Wahl Halleck, J., Baker, S. M., & Auchard, M. (1986). *Collegiate community service: Status of public and community service at selected colleges and universities*. Boston, MA: Campus Compact.

Verjee, B. (2012). Critical race feminism: A transformative vision for service-learning engagement. *Journal of Community Engagement and Scholarship, 5*(1), 57–69.

Vogel, A. L., Seifer, S. D., & Gelmon, S. B. (2010). What influences the long-term sustainability of service-learning? Lessons from early adopters. *Michigan Journal of Community Service Learning, 17*(1), 59–74.

Vygotsky, L. S. (1980). *Mind in society: The development of higher psychological processes*. Cambridge, MA: Harvard University Press.

Walljasper, J. (2013, April). Urban anchors: Augsburg leads movement to sustain vibrancy, vitality of twin cities. *Augsburg Now*. Minneapolis, MN: Augsburg College.

Weaver, L., & Kellogg, B. T. (2017). Community-campus engagement. In L. D. Dostilio (Ed.), *The community engagement professional in higher education: A competency model for an emerging field* (pp. 118–138). Boston. MA: Campus Compact.

Webster, N., & Coffey, H. (2011). A critical connection between service-learning and urban communities: Using critical pedagogy to frame the context. In T. Stewart & N. Webster (Eds.), *Problematizing service-learning: Critical reflections for development and action* (pp. 245–262). Charlotte, NC: Information Age.

Weerts, D., & Hudson, E. (2009). Engagement and institutional advancement. In L. Sandmann, C. H. Thornton, & A. J. Jaeger (Eds.), *Institutionalizing community engagement in higher education: The first wave of Carnegie Classified institutions* (pp. 65–74). San Francisco, CA: Jossey-Bass.

Weerts, D. J., & Sandmann, L. R. (2010). Community engagement and boundary spanning roles at a research university. *Journal of Higher Education, 81*, 702–727.

Weisbord, M., & Janoff, S. (2010). *Future search: Getting the whole system in the room for vision, commitment, and action*. San Francisco, CA: Berrett-Koehler.

Weiss, C. H. (1995). Nothing as practical as good theory: Exploring theory-based evaluation for comprehensive community initiatives for children and families. In J. P. Connell, A. C. Kubisch, L. B. Schorr, & C. H. Weiss (Eds.), *New approaches to evaluating community initiatives: Concepts and methods* (pp. 65–92). Washington, DC: Aspen Institute.

Welch, M. (2007). Identifying and teaching civic engagement skills through service-learning. In L. McIlrath & I. M. Labhrainn (Eds.), *Higher education and civic engagement: International perspectives* (pp. 103–120). Burlington, VT: Ashgate Press.

Welch, M. (2008). *Be the change: Student leadership manual: Thinking and interaction style inventory.* Moraga, CA: Saint Mary's College of California, Catholic Institute for Lasallian Social Action.

Welch, M. (2010a). OPERA: A first letter mnemonic and rubric for conceptualising and implementing service learning. *Issues in Educational Research, 20*(1), 76-82.

Welch, M. (2010b). A travel guide on the culture, mission, and politics of academia to promote service-learning. In B. Jacoby & P. Mutascio (Eds.), *Looking in reaching out: A reflective guide for community service-learning professionals* (pp. 55–72). Boston, MA: Campus Compact.

Welch, M. (2015). *Academese: An insider look at the in-speak and culture of academia.* Seattle, WA: Create Space.

Welch, M. (2016). *Engaging higher education: Purpose, platforms, and programs for community engagement.* Sterling, VA: Stylus.

Welch, M. (2017). Reframing experiential education: A broader perspective of community engagement. *ELITHE: A Journal for Engaged Educators, 1*(1), 65–86.

Welch, M., & Koth, K. (2013). A meta-theory on the spirituality of service-learning in higher education. *Journal of College Student Development, 54*, 612–627.

Welch, M., Liese, L. H., & Bergerson, A. (2004). A qualitative assessment project comparing and contrasting faculty and administrators' perspectives on service-learning. *Journal of Higher Education Outreach and Engagement, 9*(2), 23–42.

Welch, M., Miller, P., & Davies, K. (2005). Reciprocal validity: Description and outcomes of a hybrid approach of triangulated qualitative analysis in the research of civic engagement. In S. Root, J. Callahan, & S. H. Billig (Eds.), *Improving service-learning practice: Research on models to enhance impacts* (pp. 119–139). Greenwich, CT: Information Age.

Welch, M., & Plaxton-Moore, S. (in press). A holistic framework for educational professional development in community engagement. In P. Green & B. Berkey (Eds.), *Faculty development in the service of community engagement and service-learning: Defining purpose and roles, developing models of practice.* Sterling, VA: Stylus.

Welch, M., & Plaxton-Moore, S. (2017). Faculty development for advancing community engagement in higher education: Current trends and future directions. *Journal of Higher Education Outreach and Engagement, 21*(2), 131–165.

Welch, M., & Saltmarsh, J. (2013). Current practice and infrastructure for campus center of community engagement. *Journal of Higher Education Outreach and Engagement, 17*(4), 25–55.

Welch, M., & Saltmarsh, J. (2017). *The national inventory of institutional infrastructure for community engagement.* Boston, MA: University of Massachusetts–Boston.

Welch, M., & Sheridan, S. M. (1995). *Educational partnerships: Serving students at-risk.* Ft. Worth, TX: Harcourt Brace.

Wenger, E. (2010). Conceptual tools for CEPs as social learning systems: Boundaries, identity, trajectories and participation. In C. Blackmore (Ed.), *Social learning systems and communities of practice* (pp. 125–143). London, UK: Springer.

Whitchurch, C. (2009). The rise of the blended professional in higher education: A comparison between the United Kingdom, Australia and the United States. *Higher Education, 58*, 407–418.

Whitchurch, C. (2012). *Reconstructing identities in higher education: The rise of "third space" professionals.* New York, NY: Routledge.

White, B. P. (2016). Building an organizational structure that fosters blended engagement. In M. A. Post, E. Ward, N. V. Longo, & J. Saltmarsh (Eds.), *Publicly engaged scholars: Next generation engagement and the future of higher education* (pp. 232–245). Sterling, VA: Stylus.

Wiggins, G. P., & McTighe, J. (2011). *The understanding by design guide to creating high-quality units.* Alexandria, VA: Association for Supervision and Curriculum Development.

Williams, P. (2002). The competent boundary spanner. *Public Administration, 80*(1), 103–124.

Winston, R. B., Jr., & Creamer, D. G. (1997). *Improving staffing practices in student affairs.* San Francisco, CA: Jossey-Bass.

Wu, C., & Dahlgren, R. L. (2011). Discourse of advocacy: Student learners' critical reflections on working with Spanish-speaking immigrant students. In T. Stewart & N. Webster (Eds.), *Problematizing service-learning: Critical reflections for development and action* (pp. 263–294). Charlotte, NC: Information Age.

Youniss, J., & Yates, M. (1997). *Community service and social responsibility in youth.* Chicago, IL: University of Chicago Press.

Index

Also available from Campus Compact

The Community Engagement Professional in Higher Education

A Competency Model for an Emerging Field

Edited by Lina D. Dostilio

Foreword by Andrew J. Seligoshn

"This book illuminates important work of thinly acknowledged citizens of academe—community engaged professionals. It advances the movement for publicly engaged scholarship giving voice to their person, place and purpose in academe with myriad inflections beyond campus borders." *Timothy Eatman, Associate Professor, Syracuse University, Director for Research for Imagining America (IA)*

This book, offered by practitioner-scholars, is an exploration and identification of the knowledge, skills, and dispositions that are central to supporting effective community engagement practices between higher education and communities. The discussion and review of these core competencies are framed within a broader context of the changing landscape of institutional community engagement and the emergence of the community engagement professional as a facilitator of engaged teaching, research, and institutional partnerships distinct from other academic professionals.

(Continues on preceding page)